EDUCATIONAL RENAISSANCE

EDUCATIONAL RENAISSANCE

OUR SCHOOLS AT THE TURN OF THE CENTURY

Marvin Cetron
and Margaret Gayle

Introduction by Bill Honig

St. Martin's Press
New York

Design by Richard Oriolo

Library of Congress Cataloging-in-Publication Data
Cetron, Marvin J.
    Educational renaissance : our schools at the turn of the twenty-first century/Marvin Cetron, Margaret Gayle.
        p. cm.
    ISBN 0-312-05422-X
    1. Education—United States. 2. Educational change—United States. 3. Education—United States—Forecasting.   I. Gayle, Margaret. II. Title.
LA217.2.C48   1991
370'.973—dc20   90-48936
                                                          CIP

First Edition: January 1991

10 9 8 7 6 5 4 3 2 1

To my wife Gloria,
who, with her concern and skill has made
a difference as a teacher for twenty-seven
years;

and

To Tanya Gayle,
my oldest daughter, who has brought
her enthusiasm and vitality back to
teaching after ten years;

and

To all teachers
who make their contribution
by touching the future.

CONTENTS

ACKNOWLEDGMENTS

Almost any author of nonfiction must occasionally wonder what it would be like to take credit for a book's merits, and blame any mistakes on external forces. We will never know, for it is in the nature of writing that valuable information and insights arrive from many generous and knowledgeable sources, while only the blame for errors of fact or interpretation can fairly be given to the authors alone. For much of what is valuable here, the credit must go to the following people:

Owen Davies, our friend, colleague, and writer, who took our rough drafts, research materials, and ideas and made from them the book we envisioned.

Marge Crawford, the educational consultant who carried out much of the research on which Appendix B is based and who contributed to this effort in many other ways.

For their many contributions and insights into the leading edge of education: Bill Honig, California Superintendent of Public Instruction; Don Knezek, of the Education Service Center in San Antonio's Region 20; William L. Lepley, director of the Iowa Department of Education; Gary Marx, director of the communications department at the American Association of School Administrators; Toni Patterson, of the Wake County Schools, in Raleigh, North Carolina, who has pioneered in the fields of teacher accreditation and merit pay; John Schultz, superintendent of the Rochester (Michigan) Community Schools; educational consultant Barbara Soriano; Robert R. Spillane, Division Superintendent of the Fairfax County, Virginia, Public Schools; Lajeane G. Thomas, of Louisiana Tech University; and Betty Wallace, formerly of North Carolina Department of Public Instruction, whose analysis of the effects of ability grouping and "grading on the curve" forms one of the most important critiques of American education carried out in this century.

The staff of Forecasting International, including Lorie Patterson and Rebecca Lucken, who contributed both indispensible research and well-developed critical skills, and Charles McFadden, the skilled and indefatigable researcher whose discoveries form the core of Appendix A. Without their efforts, this book could not have been completed.

The dedicated, professional staff at St. Martin's Press, and especially Thomas J. McCormack, Roy Gainsburg, Bill Thomas, Richard Romano, who gave this project crucial support from its earliest days through completion, Andrea Connolly, Josh Marwell, Al Reuben, Claudia Riemer, and Andy Carpenter, for his exceptional cover design.

And finally, above all, Bob Weil, our editor at St. Martin's Press, whose extraordinary skill has contributed almost as much to this book, and to our other works, as his long-standing friendship has added to our lives.

—MARVIN CETRON AND MARGARET GAYLE
September 1990

INTRODUCTION

Our task for the 1980s was to identify the problems of our schools and to develop solutions for them. As will be shown throughout *Educational Renaissance*, we met that challenge far better than we knew.

The early 1980s were a depressing time for educators. As the decade began, many of us sensed that our schools were in trouble. The 1983 report *A Nation at Risk* confirmed our worst fears. Our schools were precariously perched on the brink of disaster. Unless we took drastic measures to reform our entire educational system, our entire American way of life was in jeopardy.

Since then, we have made heroic efforts to improve our schools. In almost every district, schools have upgraded their curriculum and increased standards, and teachers have enhanced both their subject knowledge and their pedagogical skills. Some states, like California, have initiated comprehensive reform strategies that are starting to pay off.

All across the nation, successful efforts in our schools are under way. But these results are too often hidden in a world where the negative story makes a better story than does the good news.

Although we still have a long way to go to make our schools a world-class educational system, many of our schools and districts are on the right track. Their progress is occurring in spite of our nation's incredibly diverse student population and the many social problems that afflict our communities.

Educational Renaissance provides an uplifting view of what *is* working in our schools. Throughout this book, Marvin Cetron and Margaret Gayle have taken a close look not only at the problems facing our schools, but at the solutions now being pioneered by creative educators. They have studied literally hundreds of reform efforts under way throughout the United States. They have discovered what works, and they have learned what mistakes can cause an otherwise promising idea to fail. This book interprets what they have learned. The result is part reportage, part analysis, and part prescription; and it is far more encouraging than most would have dared to hope.

All across the country, in statewide programs and single-classroom projects, parents and teachers, political leaders and school administrators have taken on the difficult challenge of rebuilding our schools. Many of their efforts have been remarkably successful. In the pages to come, you will read of a school superintendent who has cut the dropout rate in his rural district from 35 percent to less than 1 percent, a principal who has used computers to rescue his inner-city students from what seemed to be inevitable failure, and teachers who studied the latest theories in developmental psychology and built a new and radically different elementary school curriculum to fit them. These experiences hold lessons for the entire country.

These educators, and many more like them, have found a solution for virtually every problem that now faces our schools. We need to spend time learning from, encouraging, and supporting these activities. Rather than denigrating the progress resulting from educational reform, we need to build upon the hard work and common focus that has developed in the educational community.

Our task for the 1980s was to identify the problems of our schools and to develop solutions for them. As will be shown throughout *Educational Renaissance,* we—teachers and educators, parents and students—met that challenge far better than many realize.

In the 1990s, our assignment is to take the discoveries of the 1980s and apply them across the board. We must learn from what others have already accomplished.

The United States will spend the next ten years rebuilding its schools. With a lot of hard work, we should enter the new century with one of the best and most renowned educational systems in the world. If we succeed, America will be able to face this historic turn of the century with far greater confidence and strength than it has known in the past forty years.

—BILL HONIG
California Superintendent of Public Instruction

EDUCATIONAL RENAISSANCE

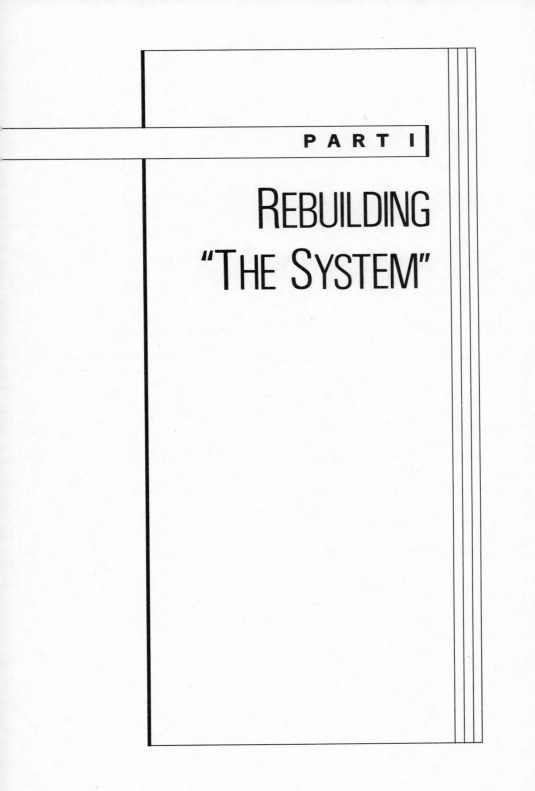

PART I

REBUILDING "THE SYSTEM"

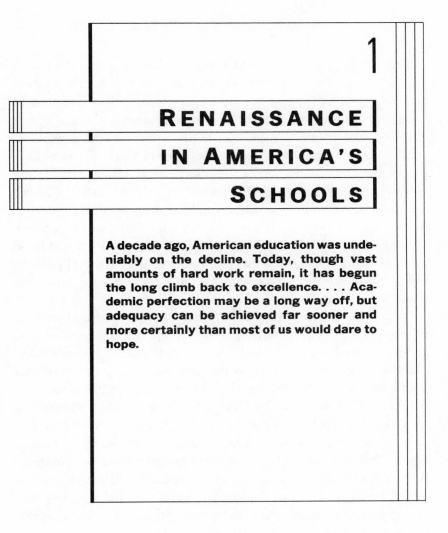

RENAISSANCE IN AMERICA'S SCHOOLS

A decade ago, American education was undeniably on the decline. Today, though vast amounts of hard work remain, it has begun the long climb back to excellence. . . . Academic perfection may be a long way off, but adequacy can be achieved far sooner and more certainly than most of us would dare to hope.

In 1983, the landmark study *A Nation at Risk* taught Americans a lesson they could have learned with a brief visit to almost any classroom in the land: By and large, our schools are no longer doing their job. Not only is it possible to be graduated from high school without being able to read, write, or perform simple arithmetic, but in many parts of the United States, this is indeed the norm. In a nation where 12 percent of all students drop out as soon as the law allows, merely occupying a school desk for a full twelve years is considered achievement enough to warrant a diploma.

This is tragic, both for those whom the vast apparatus of public education has failed and for the nation that must be both supported and governed by them in the future. As the so-called information economy replaces the old skills of manufacturing, the ability not merely to use computers, but to use them to their best advantage, will become indispensable for any but menial work. There will be no place in the job market for the poorly educated, no place in the world economy for a country forced to rely on them. Today's illiteracy is tomorrow's unemployment and national decline.

In the public view, this is a grim time for American education, with grimmer prospects still to come. To find any substantial good news about our schools requires months of digging, and perhaps more than a little luck. Both of us feel, however, that we have done considerable digging.

One of us, Margaret Gayle, has been an educator for more than twenty years, first as a teacher, later as a school administrator, and now as a consultant to school districts throughout the United States. She has spent the last two years studying school improvement programs and, unexpectedly, liked much of what she has seen.

Marvin Cetron took a close look at our schools while researching his recent book *American Renaissance: Our Life at the Turn of the 21st Century* (St. Martin's Press, 1989). In that work, he and coauthor Owen Davies took an unfashionably positive view of America's future. Where others have forecast economic collapse, to be followed by a rapid decline into political and social chaos, they told of a future that offers peace and prosperity to all who can find a place in an increasingly technological world.

Educational Renaissance is not only a direct extension of the research done for *American Renaissance,* but also a fairly radical challenge to the "morass of negativism" that seems to envelop our schools. Of all the problems examined in *American Renaissance,* America's educational problems proved to be by far the most threatening and difficult. AIDS is a terrible tragedy for its victims and their families, but medical research and education in safe sexual practices could yet stop its spread. Drug abuse could be curbed if our leaders were willing to waste less time and money on "tough-on-crime" posturing and spend more on education and treatment programs. But illiteracy is another matter. The nation's school system has been decaying now for at least two generations. It has reached the point where, *in many schools, few teachers could pass the final exam in the courses they are supposed to teach.* Their students, predictably, cannot hope to compete in the world of computers and biotechnology. If America cannot reform its educational system, it is doomed to exactly that economic and social decline which the pessimists foresee. There is not much time left.

It was that recognition from which *Educational Renaissance* grew—that and the extraordinary demand for further information about our schools. In their travels to more than a hundred cities to speak about *American Renaissance,* the book's authors, Marvin Cetron and Owen Davies, were asked about the future of American education more often and with greater urgency than about the drug problem, the economy, the pending reunification of Germany, or any of the dozens of other topics discussed in that book. Most have been surprised at the optimism of the answers.

In preparing *Educational Renaissance,* the staff of Forecasting International made the same discovery that Margaret Gayle had realized: *A Nation at Risk* accomplished its purpose; it jolted people—educators, teachers, parents, students—into taking a hard look at their local schools, and acting on what they saw. Throughout the land, concerned parents and dedicated teachers, public-service organizations and major corporations, are finding ways to revitalize their local schools. Many of them, working mostly in isolation, are already giving young people the education they must have, both to become well-rounded, responsible adults and to prosper in the high-tech, information-rich world of the 1990s and beyond.

These efforts have tipped the balance. A decade ago, American education was undeniably on the decline. Today, though vast amounts of hard work remain, it has begun the long climb back to excellence. If we have not noticed the change, it is because most of the work is being carried out not by some vast program based in Washington, but by hundreds of isolated local efforts involving thousands of people, many of them part-time volunteers. Nonetheless, it is real and supremely important. In wealthy neighborhoods and poor, in cities, suburbs, and farm country, the quality of education in America is on the way up.

The credit for this long-needed renaissance in America's schools goes in part to dedicated, creative educators, in part to a wide variety of new teaching methods, and in part to a new emphasis on the block-and-tackle basics of running a school. In fact, so many different approaches have raised students' achievement levels and cut dropout rates that it almost seems it doesn't matter how teachers and school administrators change their ways, so long as they *do something.* Yet there are some very specific lessons to be learned from America's most successful schools.

Our purpose in writing *Educational Renaissance* is to spread the word, to bring together the many disconnected efforts that are now beginning to heal our schools and the system within which they operate. The lessons in this book, all of them drawn from today's experience, offer an encouraging preview of education as we will soon come to know it. Of the hundreds of local initiatives now restoring quality to their district schools, we have of necessity focused on a relative few. Most are success stories. Some efforts have failed. From their experience, it becomes clear what works and what does not, and what pitfalls await even the best-intentioned parents, teachers, and community leaders when they set out to rebuild a system now more than two generations dying. Their work is the work we will all take on in the next decade.

And all of us will be needed. Any number of authoritative studies have proved all too clearly that educational reform will be a mammoth task. They have shown that only one high-school junior in five can write a comprehensible note to apply for a summer job; that fewer than one-third of seniors know to within fifty years when the Civil War was fought; that a majority of seventeen-year-olds cannot understand an average newspaper article; that barely more than half of high-school juniors know whether 87 percent of ten is more than ten, or less, or equal to it. In one recent study, only a minority of junior-high-school students could find the United States on a world map!

Our situation appears even worse when we compare this sorry record with those of other industrialized nations. Both in classes taken and in the degree to which pupils master the material laid before them, our students lag far behind. One American high-school student in five takes biology or chemistry, fewer still study physics, and only 6 percent take courses in calculus. By contrast, the typical Russian student studies—*and learns*—algebra and physics for five years, biology and chemistry for four, and calculus for two. In Japan, most high-school graduates know more than the average American with a B.A. Japanese companies setting up plants in the United States have found that it takes an American with a master's degree to learn the same statistical quality-control techniques routinely used by Japanese high-school graduates.

And the oft-heard argument that, while our average students are not as well trained as they should be, our best can hold their own with the best of any land simply is not true. Our brightest twelfth-graders, the top 5 percent of those who have taken advanced math courses, when matched against their counterparts from eight other countries in standardized algebra and calculus tests, come in dead last.

The few bright spots in this dismal picture have been the stories of heroes "discovered" by the media. As a nation, we have applauded Jaime Escalante, the calculus teacher at Garfield High School in East Los Angeles, who won fame as the subject of the film *Stand and Deliver.* We have marveled at the generosity of Eugene Lang, the New York philanthropist who volunteered to pay the college expenses of an entire inner-city high-school class, and we have been thrilled when his example inspired more than 125 wealthy people in twenty-five cities to make similar offers.

But these are stories of individuals, and there are narrow limits to what any one person can accomplish when faced with a problem as broad and deep as the decline of education in America. As dramatically as people like Escalante and Lang have improved those few lives they have touched directly, their efforts have made no fundamental change in our national school system.

In the chapters that follow, we will look at many of the less publicized innovations that promise to raise educational performance on a larger scale. From their success, and the occasional failures, we will learn how to give tomorrow's students the education that today's students are missing. It really can be done.

One good cause for optimism about our schools is the very factor most often cited as reason to despair: we face an intimidatingly vast mass of problems, and they have had two generations or more to destroy the foundations of American learning. It makes good sense to look at this from the opposite side: given the enormous array of corrosive forces attacking our educational system, and the long period for which they have been allowed to operate, it seems almost miraculous that our schools are not even worse. There is so much to be done that almost any effort we make to improve the situation is sure to have some benefit. That fabled last straw did not really break the camel's back, but merely drove the poor beast to its knees; find some way to remove even a small part of its burden, and the cargo will again be on its way to market. So it is with our schools. Academic perfection may be a long way off, but adequacy can be achieved far sooner and more certainly than most of us would dare to hope.

There is an even better reason for hope. Almost behind our backs, in the years since *A Nation at Risk* appeared, America's schools have scored impressive gains in student performance. On the Scholastic Aptitude Tests, for example, in just five years the number of students who scored over 450 on the verbal portion of the test grew by nearly 15 percent. So did the number scoring over 500 on the math portion. And the number scoring over 600 in both areas grew by 23 percent.

It is true that average SAT scores remain below their peak of several years ago, but that may not say much about school performance. For every 1-percent increase in the fraction of students taking the SAT, bringing a less elite group into the examining room, test scores decline by two points, a statistic that has remained constant for many years. In 1989, fully 40 percent of high-school seniors took the SAT, a rise sharp enough to explain more than three-fourths of the decline in average scores.

Nationwide, a recent U.S. Department of Education report found that the pool of dropouts has shrunk by one-third since 1979, and that black dropout rates are virtually comparable to whites. Furthermore, nearly one-half of the dropouts eventually graduated or received a graduation equivalent. Advanced Placement courses have nearly doubled since 1982.

The National Association of Educational Progress gathers educational statistics covering the entire student body, not just those going on to college, and they too have found significant improvements in recent years. Virtually all seventeen-year-olds reach the association's two basic reading levels. The number who cannot read at the third, intermediate, level declined by more than one-fourth between 1980 and 1988. And the fraction of students who read at the "adept" level required for high-tech employment grew from 38.5 percent in 1980 to 41.8 percent in 1988.

In mathematics, virtually 100 percent of 17-year-olds reached the first three levels, and the number able to handle moderately complex problems (the fourth level) grew from 48.3 percent in 1982 to 58.7 percent in 1988—a 22-percent increase. In science, from 1982 to 1988, the number of 17-year-old students who did not reach the third ability level shrank from 24 percent to 14 percent, and those who reached the fourth level grew from 37.5 percent to 44.6 percent, or a 19-percent boost. Students who reached top levels in math grew 20 percent and in science grew 14 percent, although only a few students reached these goals (6.5 percent in math and 8.2 percent in science).

There are valuable lessons in each of the state and local programs that have achieved these gains, but for the moment the significant point is clear: America's schools harbor dreadful problems; their dropout rates are far too high, and the academic accomplishments of their students are in many ways far too low. But they can be repaired. In many places, as we shall see, it is already happening.

We will spend the rest of this book looking at the problems of American education and at the solutions we are already beginning to adopt. Let us begin by making a brief survey of the ground to be covered. There is a lot of it.

One reason for the failure of America's schools is that the educational system is designed more for organizational and political convenience than for learning:

- Schools receive accreditation for offering whatever courses the state requires, whether or not students learn anything of value while attending them.

- Schools themselves are governed by local boards of education, which all too often operate as political empires, a throwback to the days of patronage and machine politics; in many cities, education winds up hostage to any number of other goals.
- Courses are often chosen more to appease special interests than to exercise the student's mind or stock it with information. Thus, many schools place sex education, women's studies, black history, and other politically popular or socially desirable subdisciplines on an equal footing with mathematics and American history.

We believe that schools must cover all the subjects mentioned above. There is no denying that history courses long neglected the contributions of black Americans, women, and many others; this is unjust, and it gives students a distorted view of the subject we claim to teach. And the cost of neglecting sex education, AIDS education, and similar matters must be obvious to all.

Yet some topics are more equal than others. These added courses cannot be allowed to cut into the time and resources devoted to reading, writing, arithmetic, and the other core subjects. Sex education should be covered as part of the generalized health course, black history within American and world history, women's studies as a subsection of social studies, and so on. If these subdisciplines cannot be fit within the traditional school year, or paid for within today's school budgets, then children will have to spend more time in school, and society more money on schooling. Unfortunately, this is one segment of school reform where emotions and ideology rule, and the goal of a sound general education often takes second place to other concerns. We see little prospect of quick or easy improvement in this area.

Similarly, textbooks are chosen more to appease special-interest groups than to ensure that students receive a good education. Science texts treat the crucial subject of evolution as briefly as they can, social-studies texts trivialize the differences between American culture and the customs of other lands, and history books subordinate events that reshaped the world to themes of less significance but greater political currency. (In one popular history text, the index entry for Women's Rights is longer than that for the Revolutionary War.) Because a few of the largest states have long followed this policy, even those school districts willing to use more rigorous books are hard-pressed to find them.

And students are marched through the grades in lockstep, rather than being taught according to their needs and promoted according to their achievements. At the end of twelve years, all but the dullest students, and the 29 percent or so who drop out, leave high school with a diploma, whether they can read it or not.

The result of all this is "education" as we have come to know it—short on content and grossly inadequate at passing on to students what little knowledge it does offer.

These systemic failures will be among the most difficult educational problems to cure, because many of them must be approached through the political process rather than directly at the school level, but progress is far from impossible. Almost everywhere, "the system" is already changing. All but five states have reworked their high-school curricula and tightened graduation requirements since *A Nation at Risk* appeared. A few have begun to set up school-accreditation systems based on academic performance. School boards in three of the nation's least successful cities have been stripped of their power and their districts turned over to state or private control. And California, the nation's largest buyer of textbooks, at last has made a start at reforming its selection criteria. All these measures are sure to be copied in school districts across the land.

Another whole class of problems rises from the teaching profession. There are too few teachers to go around, and there is little hope that this will soon change. Teachers are so underpaid when compared with other professions that only 2 percent of college freshmen will be teachers eight years after graduation. Those who do become teachers have, on average, some of the least impressive academic records among college graduates. Worse yet, college education departments are so wedded to their classes in teaching methods that they neglect the core subjects their graduates are supposed to teach.

A wide variety of approaches are being tried, both to find more teachers and to make certain that the ones we now have are capable of helping students to learn. One is to throw money at the problem; predictably enough, school systems that pay well have been finding it easier to attract the teachers they need. Volunteer programs for community members eager to help with their children's education are an obvious and successful way to stretch the supply of teachers, and for more technical subjects, industry offers a huge new supply of potential teachers, most of whom know more about their fields than can any graduate of a teachers' college.

All these programs have been relatively easy to enact. The same cannot be said of programs aimed at ensuring teacher competence or holding teachers responsible for the performance of their students. Such measures as teacher testing, merit pay, and "master teacher" programs have all met stiff resistance from teachers' unions, but well-crafted programs are slowly building a record of educational improvement. They will be a staple of school reform a decade from now.

One of the most effective ideas is not so much to improve the schools as to improve the children in them. With the right encouragement, a child can be an interested, motivated person at five, a competent violinist at six. Without it, he can be headed almost irrevocably toward a life of illiteracy and drugs, reform school and prison.

Unfortunately, that kind of encouragement is the exception rather than the rule. About 25 percent of American children under the age of six now live in poverty. Some 60 percent of mothers hold down jobs, including half of those with babies under one year old. They have little time to give their children the support they need; too many lack the skill and inclination. As many as 7 million children must fend for themselves during business hours. And a growing number of children are recent immigrants, or the offspring of immigrants, arriving with little or no understanding of English in schools where few teachers speak any other language.

Day-care centers and preschool programs fill the void surprisingly well. In one study, a single year of preschool dramatically raised the number of students who completed high school, nearly doubled the number who went on to college, and dramatically reduced the number who had arrest records or were on welfare at age nineteen. Yet many parents are too poor to pay for private day-care and preschool programs, and Head Start was able to provide classroom seats for less than 20 percent of the children poor enough to qualify for them. Building a national network of child-care and preschool facilities will be one of the most pressing demands placed on legislators in the early 1990s. It may do more than any other single measure to improve our youngsters' academic performance.

Another problem: The massive loss of quality in American education comes at a time when we require more of our school systems than ever before. Many observers have suggested that this is more than coincidence. As recently as thirty years ago, a school's goal was to teach its students the basics—English, math, some history, introductory science, and perhaps a foreign language. Such extras as "phys-ed," a year or two of "shop" for the boys and "home-ec" for the girls, and an after-hours driver-training program—subjects no one would have equated with the core disciplines—could be accommodated without straining the system's resources.

Today that focus has been lost. In addition to the many politically motivated courses required in at least some districts, we have asked our schools to combat teen pregnancy, drug abuse, and other societal ills—and many offer a nearly endless list of electives. And the arguments for providing all these courses are difficult to refute. The problems of teenage pregnancy and drug abuse are among our most pressing social ills, and schools are the one place where teens can be brought together for inoculation against them. Familiarity with computers will soon be basic to any well-paid job, and to many entry-level positions as well. No doubt, traditional history courses did tend to neglect the contributions of minorities to our nation's development. And a rich selection of electives does give students a better chance to develop individual talents, to say nothing of making school more attractive to bored youngsters. Serving any of these needs is a laudable goal.

School days have not grown to fit this extra work, the school year has not stretched. Neither has anyone managed to compress the mass of facts, concepts, and skills that go to make up a traditional education. Yet in thirteen states, high-school students can earn at least half of the credits required for graduation from electives. So teachers are forced to give less attention to the learning that Americans once could almost take for granted. Barring some dramatic breakthrough in teaching methods, it is difficult to see how a sharp decline in educational performance could have been avoided.

In response to that growing recognition, some educators have focused on developing a core curriculum. The idea is to identify the knowledge and skills required for modern life, concentrate on those basics, and test regularly to make certain that each child has learned all that is required for each grade before passing on to the next. The goal is to specify not just course titles but the particular facts and skills that students must master before graduation. At least four such efforts are now in the works. In the near future we will build a consensus that covers at least the most essential subjects: English, math, science, history, foreign languages, and computer literacy.

In addition to solving these long-neglected problems, in the 1990s we will finally begin to apply a variety of new teaching methods that for one reason or another have remained limited to experimental classes and pilot programs.

Many schools, for example, already use individualized education programs (EPIs); they suggest which skills in, say, reading or math the student must practice, and they recommend ways of testing to make sure they have been learned. Far more is possible. Nearly two dozen factors affect how well students learn, from the temperature of the classroom and background noise levels to memory and analytical skills. In the future, IEPs will look at students' individual learning styles: whether they learn best in small groups or large classes, alone or with a friend, or from reading, lectures, or computer programs; how much supervision they need; and so on. Teachers will be evaluated in the same way and assigned to large or small classes, good readers or good listeners, as best suits them.

Computerized learning offers even greater payoffs. Unlike human teachers, computers never tire, never forget a key point, never ignore the slow student in the back corner while paying attention to a few bright, compliant favorites. Today's educational software can take a student from letter identification in kindergarten through complex grammar and reading in high school. Testing is constant. When a child makes a mistake, the computer will take him or her back over the lesson, presenting the information in different ways, until the material has been mastered.

In the near future, students will spend an hour or more a day in class sitting at their terminals, working math problems or practicing foreign-language vocabulary and grammar, guided by computer programs that can recognize their weaknesses faster than most human teachers could. The result may not be as good as would come from having highly skilled, caring human beings give each student hours of personal attention, but it is a lot easier to achieve, and it will be a big improvement over today's situation. It may also free time for the teacher to develop more creative interactions with students and their families.

Some of the most basic and productive changes now overtaking our schools result from a new and different understanding of the nature of learning and intelligence which is now emerging from academic psychology. Where the SATs and other standardized exams limit their view of intelligence almost exclusively to our facility with mathematics and language, the new model of intelligence is far broader. Experimental psychologists now believe that there are many different kinds of intelligence—Harvard researcher Howard Gardner puts the number at seven—each operating more or less independently in its own sphere of learning, each reaching its peak at a characteristic age, and each requiring its own specialized teaching methods for efficient learning. The stereotypical "nerd," brilliant with computers but hopelessly clumsy, both physically and socially, translates to someone high in logical-mathematical talent but poor in the special intelligences that deal with spatial awareness, bodily-kinesthetic functions, interpersonal relationships, and probably self-understanding. In chapter 9 we will look closely at how these insights are being applied to the classroom. For now, it is enough to note that radical new movement in education may represent our brightest hope for a dramatic improvement in the performance of our schools.

Finally, there is the subject to which we devoted our last education book, *Schools of the Future: How American Business and Education Can Cooperate to Save Our Schools* (McGraw-Hill, 1985). In that volume, we recommended some partial solutions for the problems of American education, each relying on corporate volunteerism to meet public needs. Many of the measures we suggested have been adopted, or discovered independently, by school districts around the country and put to use with considerable success.

In one sense, business is the ultimate consumer of the education industry's product. When public schools turn out graduates who haven't mastered reading, writing, or finger counting, business suffers. Executives know that through bitter experience; they are eager to help our schools in any way they can. Eugene Lang's dramatic personal contributions are just one example. In cities from New York to Miami to Chicago, corporate philanthropists have been building and staffing schools. Many have achieved dramatic results, graduating up to 95 percent of their students, even in the most downtrodden urban neighborhoods. No single corporate effort can replace the billions of dollars that federal education funding seems unlikely to provide. But dozens of local projects can make a substantial contribution, even on a national scale. Many more will be operating as quickly as they can be set up.

Unfortunately, solving the problems of conventional education is only half of the challenge we face. The other half is to provide career training for all who need it—and not just the traditional auto shop and welding classes, but professional-level training in computer programming, telecommunications, biomedical technology, and a host of other cutting-edge disciplines. Just to meet today's need for skilled workers, vocational programs will have to grow dramatically. And we will ask much more of them in the near future. Today, schools offer adult education as a community service or in hope of earning sorely needed revenue. In future, they will be teaching adults because they haven't any choice. As a society, we will add that chore to drug and sex education and the hundred other things we now expect of our schools beyond the traditional "three R's."

Schools will not find it easy to provide these specialized courses while still improving the core curriculum. They will still be adapting to these increased demands as the new century begins. Yet by the turn of the century, vocational training will be just as crucial as the traditional pre-college program. Most high-school grads a decade from now will be far better equipped for both college and a career than their parents were.

Several pages ago, we promised you a *brief* introduction to problems of American education and to the methods by which they are being solved. Some thousands of words later, we have barely made a start. But we hope at least our major premise is clear: *In the near future, American schools will have changed dramatically, and so will our relationship to them.*

On the outside, most schools will still be the same brick and glass structures—literally the same, half of them nearing seventy-five years old. But on the inside, the changes will be obvious: Classrooms will be full of personal computers and other high-tech teaching aids. Teaching methods will have changed to reflect our growing understanding of the learning process. Teachers will be backed up by volunteers from the community and from local businesses. Most of all, educational standards will be more demanding, and they will be enforced. We will be asking far more of our schools a few short years from now, and giving them more as well. And we will be getting more in return.

In most areas, the first experiments in reconstruction have already begun. From them we have learned more than enough to heal most of the ills that now afflict our national school system. There is nothing to prevent school districts across the country from adopting these and many other reforms—nothing but the inertia of 16,000 school districts. That is rapidly disappearing in the face of political pressure from enraged parents.

The key, of course, is in the hands of parents themselves. If our school systems are to recover their lost quality, if the United States is to survive as an economic leader, parents—and everyone else who reads this book—must accept responsibility for performance of their local school systems. They must offer themselves as part-time teachers and teaching assistants, and they must work with local political leaders to raise school budgets, and with school administrators to see that the money is used to promote effective classes in the core subjects. Above all, they must make certain that their own children understand the importance of a good education and have the support required for the difficult job of learning. In the years to come, more and more people will accept this challenge. The trend has clearly begun.

In the decade to come, a new wave of educational reform will sweep across the land, flowing outward from the growing minority of creative, experimental, and highly successful schools like the ones described in the following chapters. Our children, and our nation, will be the better for it.

2

CUTTING
THROUGH
RED TAPE

Like most large hierarchical structures, the American school system has focused on methods rather than on results. So key academic and management decisions are forced on schools from above, with little regard for their effect on students or learning, or even for their consistency with other policies already in place. This is a prescription for failure.

Many of our worst educational failings grow from the divided structure of our national school system. Funding, hiring of school principals, and related policies are set largely by the community, whose property taxes pay for their children's education, or are supposed to. The curriculum and choice of textbooks are matters for the state boards of education, which also grant schools their accreditation. And for more than thirty years, the federal government has tried to run our schools from the top down, promulgating ever more rules for administrators and teachers to follow, and building ever-larger bureaucracies to see that they do it. At the bottom of this cumbersome hierarchy, with the duty of educating children but little or no say in how the task is to be accomplished, are the teachers themselves.

In theory, if regulations are well conceived and schools adhere to them, students everywhere should receive a sound education. In practice, the system breaks down at almost every opportunity. Parents, school boards, and state and federal authorities have conflicting priorities, which frequently have more to do with politics than with education. And like most large hierarchical structures, the American school system has focused on methods rather than on results. So key academic and management decisions are forced on schools from above, with little regard for their effect on students or learning, or even for their consistency with other policies already in place.

This is a prescription for failure. As American business has found in recent years, the only way to manage a giant enterprise is to set performance goals and give workers the freedom to meet them as best they can. "Micro-management"—telling workers not only what needs to be done but, in excruciating detail, how to accomplish it—simply ensures that nothing gets done efficiently or well. In America's school systems, micro-management can reach ridiculous extremes. In some school districts, teachers are forbidden to throw disruptive students out of the classroom. The resulting educational system simply cannot be made to work.

Healing these ills will be one of the major educational challenges of the 1990s. It will be accomplished not so much by streamlining the multitiered management of our schools—though that is part of the solution—as by a combination of lesser measures. Some reforms now in the works address specific problems, while others are designed to focus the attention of school administrators on educational results rather than on politics, money, and other lesser concerns. Some fall into the category of "school restructuring," defined by education writer Anne Lewis as "changing the dynamics of interactions in the classroom to ensure higher expectations of both teachers and students." (For a definitive look at this critical topic, see *Restructuring America's Schools,* by Anne Lewis, published by the American Association of School Administrators in 1989.) Others focus on the relationship between the schools and the states or communities in which they operate. All these reforms are based on the premise that many of the problems that have undermined American education lie not so much with teachers or with students as with "the system."

One systemic reform that will be as difficult as it is obviously necessary is to link school accreditation with school performance. Most states rely on "process standards" in making accreditation decisions. Schools are accredited, or not, based on administrative practices, graduation requirements, and other secondary matters. One common key to accreditation is a list of course titles. Schools that offer the right courses—that is, courses with the right names, whatever their content—are accredited. Whether children actually learn from those courses has no bearing on the decision.

So far as we know, the only state that has yet enacted a performance-based accreditation system is Mississippi. The state uses three standardized tests to assess student performance: the Basic Skills Assessment Program, the Functional Literacy Exam, and the Stanford Achievement Test. In addition to meeting typical process standards, schools must, to maintain state accreditation, see to it that their students maintain minimum average scores on these tests. Districts that fail are placed on probation and are required to formulate a plan to catch up—and make it work.

A simpler measure needed in most of the nation's school systems is a longer day and year. American children spend an average of 6.5 hours a day, 180 days per year, in school, including recess, "study halls," and electives—one of the shortest school years in the industrialized West. Japanese children, in contrast, work full eight-hour days in school, 240 of them per year. (This does not include homework, of which Japanese students have about two hours per day, while American pupils have perhaps twenty minutes, and Japan's legendary "cram schools," which add at least one more school day per week for students whose parents are set on their success.) In learning as in any field, the more time you put in, the more you can get done. So it is little wonder that Japanese high-school students typically rank two or three years ahead of ours on standardized achievement tests; at graduation, they have spent the equivalent of more than two extra American-style years in school than our students have.

State boards of education could correct this glaring deficiency almost at whim. In Los Angeles, for example, the California board recently replaced the traditional summer vacation with three shorter breaks between "trimesters." Students there now attend school year-round. The change was made to ease the task of providing multilingual classes for the flood of Asian and South American students now inundating the school system; each student spends the same amount of time in class as before. But a similar change could have been made as easily to give students more schooling.

To date, this option has not proved popular among the nation's school districts, for an obvious reason: Running schools for 240 days rather than 180 costs half again as much in salaries for teachers and school administrators and raises such incremental expenses as heat or air-conditioning, lighting, school buses, and building maintenance. In the current atmosphere of unchecked budget deficits, no reform that requires spending money is likely to win many friends in government.

This is one issue we can all use as a test of how serious our leaders are about improving our schools. We need an overwhelming variety of reforms to rebuild learning in America, as we will see in this and succeeding chapters, but we must also keep children in the schools long enough to benefit from the changes. If politicians truly wish to give American students an education equal to the best in the world, they will find the money to extend the school day and year. Our guess—and at this point it can be no more than that—is that by the turn of the century the American school day will have stretched to seven hours, the year to 210 days.

Control over one crucial part of learning lies entirely outside the school itself: the choice of textbooks. This is important, because in many classrooms there is virtually no curriculum other than the material found in the text. For several reasons, which we will examine in a moment, textbooks have less information to offer about any given topic than almost any other resource. Yet they are allowed to absorb virtually all the money available for teaching resources;

computers, videotapes, and other new technologies that might enrich the curriculum must usually be purchased from supplemental
funding that may or may not be included in the year's school
budget. Trade books and works of literature would make excellent
supplements for current textbooks—some might well replace
them—but in most school districts they are unavailable, because
texts must be chosen from a state-approved list. Worse yet, most
teachers refuse to use books that lack a teacher's guide to spare
them the tedious task of actually mastering the material.

There are two separate issues here, decided far from the schools
themselves and for reasons inherently inimical to the cause of education. One, inevitably, is cost. The other is the political debate
over what students should learn.

Textbooks aren't cheap. In 1987 the nation's schools spent more
than $1.6 billion on texts for kindergarten through high school, an
average of $35.65 per student. The Texas book budget, the na-
tion's largest, totaled more than $139 million. Ten states—Texas,
California, New York, Illinois, Pennsylvania, Florida, New Jersey,
Ohio, Michigan, and North Carolina—spent a total of $885 million
among them.

With bills like those to consider, states buy books as sparingly as
possible and use them as long as they can. Almost every state
requires schools to use textbooks for at least five years. Some use
them for seven.

Unfortunately, those texts are obsolete before they reach the
classroom. It takes at least a year to write a textbook; five years is
probably closer to average. Add another year or two to get the
book printed and distributed, and much of what the volume has to
say will be outmoded, while crucial new information will be missing. This is particularly true in areas of rapid progress, such as the
sciences, but events can overtake textbook writers in almost any
field. Social studies and geography texts still in production at the
end of 1989 will be telling students for the next five years that
Hungary, Poland, Czechoslovakia, East Germany, and Rumania
are Communist lands.

Of course, they may omit even that obsolete fact. Vast quantities
of the information that American high-school students once could

have been expected to know appear nowhere in today's texts. Much of it has been replaced by slick graphics intended to capture the attention of television-addicted children. Much of it has been replaced by trivia. And much of it has not been replaced at all. If today's children think that school is "dumb"—just ask one!—their textbooks bear much of the blame.

The problem, again, is systemic. In twenty-two states, the state board of education surveys the offerings of textbook publishers and "adopts" a dozen or so volumes in each field that it believes present the subject adequately. Local school boards may opt for other texts, but in doing so they forfeit any state subsidy for book purchases. Both Texas and California follow this policy, and because these two states each spend about one-tenth of the nation's total elementary- and high-school book budget each year, their choices sway the decisions of editorial boards throughout the textbook industry. Virtually all texts available in the United States have been designed to meet the requirements of Texas and California.

Unfortunately, those requirements have traditionally had more to do with local politics than with education. State book-adoption hearings are open to the public and, like most political processes, are swayed by those members of the public who holler loudest. Until 1983, Texas skewed the process by allowing only testimony attacking books up for adoption. Thus, religious fundamentalists could press to reject science texts that failed to give creationism equal billing with evolutionary theory, while scientists could not defend the volumes. In California, fundamentalists got the board to approve a so-called "antidogmatism statement," which required texts to present evolution as merely one of several hypotheses about the development of life on Earth.

Liberal causes, too, have had their impact on our texts. A touching faith in world brotherhood, an extension of the wishful belief that we could eliminate the causes of war by seeking common ground with our enemies, has almost purged any mention of cultural differences from social-studies texts, while history books sacrifice both accuracy and clarity in order to note the accomplishments of blacks, Hispanics, women, American Indians, homosexuals, and other vocal minorities. A report from the Educational Excellence

Network notes that the pictures in one popular high-school text picture only blacks as Texas cowboys, World War I soldiers, and Civilian Conservation Corps surveyors. The result is a catalog of facts, and occasional fictions, as compellingly readable as the menu at a fast-food restaurant and somewhat less nourishing.

Both Texas and California have made at least preliminary reforms. In 1983, Texas decided to allow people at adoption hearings to speak up in defense of textbooks; since then, most books rejected have been turned down for academic rather than political deficiencies. Two years later, California rejected *all* the texts that publishers offered for junior-high math and science courses. Math books, the board of education complained, were not rigorous enough, while science texts too flagrantly soft-pedaled evolution. In 1989 the state finally repealed its antidogmatism statement.

Just how much change this will bring to the teaching of biology remains uncertain. The California school board began 1989 with a strong endorsement of evolution that relegated creationism to social-science and literature classes. By that November, when guidelines for textbook publishers took their final form, the statement had been watered down and a detailed defense of evolution had been deleted. Members of both camps view the move as at least a partial victory for the fundamentalists, but California school officials say their commitment to evolution remains undiminished. How strong that commitment really is will become clearer when the next round of text selection takes place, roughly when this book appears.

In a democratic society, it is probably inevitable that schools will be swayed by political concerns. In the 1970s and 1980s a variety of partisan interests managed to dominate American society, and the schools lost their focus on education. As the 1990s open, the political current seems to be carrying the schools back to their original purpose, to provide young people with the skills and information required to function in society. We believe that trend will grow stronger throughout the decade. In that case, the systemic reforms begun in Texas and California should soon improve textbooks throughout the country.

Ironically, the one aspect of America's schools that has not been centralized is funding. In effect, we have demanded that communities provide an adequate education for their children without giving them the resources to do so. Reform in this area is desperately needed. And here the trend is toward more centralization, not less.

The problem is not that the United States spends too little on schooling. Some educational activists have pointed out that we spend less of our national income on education than do other nations, and this is true, but it is not very important. What matters is *how much we spend on each student.* For example, Mississippi spent 3.9 percent of its state income on schooling in 1986, while Minnesota spent only 3.7 percent; yet no one would assert that Mississippi's schools were the better funded of the two. Minnesota is a richer state, so its schools received some $4,180 per student in state funds, while those in Mississippi received only $2,350 per student. Measured in this way, and adjusted for relative purchasing power, the United States ranks second in education spending behind Switzerland, with a school budget of $3,310 per student in 1985. This is not to say that devoting more money to the cause of learning would have been a waste of resources, merely that underfunding is not a major handicap to America's schools. Japan achieves its remarkable success with a school budget that totaled only $1,805 per student in 1985.

The problem lies with how America's school budgets are raised and distributed. Where property values are high, money for schooling is plentiful; where they are low, or taxes cannot be collected, it is scarce. The result is that many states suffer enormous disparities in their educational systems.

Texas, with the nation's second-largest school system, has been in many ways typical. The state supplies only 40 percent of education funds; the remainder comes from local property taxes. Thus land values make an enormous difference in the amount that communities can afford to spend on schooling. The Santa Gertrude school district, in southern Texas, has some of the lowest property taxes in the state, only eight cents per hundred dollars of assessed valuation; but because the area is rich in oil and lightly populated, the district spends some $12,000 per student per year on education. By contrast, in the populous, largely Hispanic Edgewood Independent School District in West San Antonio, property tax rates are more than a dozen times higher. Yet property values are low, and the air force base that takes up much of the area cannot be taxed at all, so Edgewood can afford to spend less than $3,600 per student per year. The gap is even greater between Laureles, where the school budget amounted to $13,370 per student for the 1987–88 year, and Red Lick, which could afford only $2,571 per student.

Kentucky faces a similar problem. Here the state pays some three-fourths of the education bill. Yet from the suburbs of Lexington and Louisville to the coalfields of eastern Kentucky, the funding gap could hardly be greater. In suburban Louisville, the Anchorage school district, the state's richest, spends nearly $3,200 per student in local funds on schooling each year. In the Appalachian coal district, Elliot County does well to scrape up $118 per student per year.

In both Texas and Kentucky, the state constitution required the government to provide an "efficient" system of education for its residents, and representatives of the poorest districts sued to have the funding system overturned on the grounds that it was anything but efficient in providing an education. In both, the state supreme court has ruled that property-based school funding is unconstitutional; the Kentucky court went even further, declaring the state school system unconstitutional "in all its parts and parcels." As this is written, legislators in Texas are scratching their heads, trying to figure out how to pay for their schools. Those in Kentucky are trying to rebuild the entire state school system from the ground up.

This story has been repeated often in recent years. Similar suits have been filed in no fewer than forty-two states since the 1960s, and at least three more are expected—in Alabama, Oklahoma, and South Dakota. In ten states the suits were rejected, most of them in the early years of the funding debate. In eleven, the state funding systems have been overturned. Suits are still in progress in Alaska, Minnesota, Montana, New Jersey, North Dakota, Oregon, and Tennessee. And in Illinois, legislators are working to revise the educational funding system, though no suit has reached the state supreme court; some two-thirds of Illinois's school revenues come from property taxes, and yet the richest districts can afford to spend six times as much per student per year as the poorest.

To date, it is far from clear how schools will be funded a decade from now. Texas has neither personal nor corporate income taxes to fall back on, and most legislators have tried to piece together a combination of increases in the sales and tobacco taxes in order to hold off their enactment. In Kentucky, too, funding alternatives remain unsettled as this is written, and no one has any idea where the court's sweeping condemnation of the state educational system will lead. But one thing seems clear: By the year 2000, the vast economic disparities that allow some communities to provide top-flight education while others must struggle just to keep their schools heated in the winter will have been overcome. Whether they are funded by income or sales taxes or by some combination of narrowly focused revenue measures, school budgets will be much more uniform within each state, and most likely throughout the United States.

Yet for some communities facing similar problems, the very local control that Chicago hopes will be its educational salvation has turned school systems into political empires where learning is their least important product. In the most benighted of these communities, administrators are hired and promoted through patronage and nepotism rather than because of their qualifications, city payrolls are padded with "no-show" jobs, and books and janitorial supplies are bought from the company that offers the most profitable kickbacks. The results are easy to predict: decaying schools are understaffed by teachers of dubious competence; administrators are hard-pressed to find toilet paper for the rest rooms, much less textbooks and computers; and students rack up some of the lowest test scores and highest dropout rates in the country.

It is possible to heal most such school systems, but only by radical surgery. No fewer than eight states have enacted "educational bankruptcy laws" allowing the state government to take over local school systems, and perhaps a dozen more have such laws in the works. In Oakland, Jersey City, and Chelsea, Massachusetts, such takeovers have already been carried out. Oakland's schools have been given over to a trustee charged with ridding the 53,000-student system of corruption and mismanagement. New Jersey seized control of Jersey City's 28,000-student school system for similar reasons. Chelsea's schools—plagued by poverty, crumbling buildings, and a dropout rate of more than 50 percent—are now managed by Boston University, the first time a public school authority has been placed in private hands.

If Boston University's plans work out, Chelsea may serve as a model for school-rescue projects throughout the country. Before the takeover, the Boston suburb's five-school, 3,600-student system almost made a fine art of failure. Students' scores on standardized tests have perennially ranked among the lowest in the nation; one year, only a dozen high-school seniors took the SATs. Half of the students in any given grade each year were still in it the next. Absenteeism, dropouts, teen pregnancy, bloated and inefficient bureaucracy—if any school in America had the problem, so did Chelsea.

It will take heroic measures to restore health to Chelsea's sick schools, and Boston University has devised a ten-year plan that involves many of them. Once all of it is in place, it will look after Chelsea children from conception to college. Health and nutrition programs will care for pregnant women and their children up to the age of three. Then preschool and day-care programs will take over. Intensive English courses not only will make certain that children master what for most is a second language, but will carry literacy to their parents on welfare. Children of single-parent families will be paired with mentors to guide their development. And all will receive individualized instruction designed to meet their personal needs.

The Chelsea program took effect with the 1989–90 school year, and it is far too early to tell how well this ambitious undertaking will work out. But it is built on methods that individually have proved successful in other cases. There seems every reason to hope that a comprehensive rescue project will make a dramatic change in the academic performance of Chelsea's children. If so, it is likely to be copied in many other communities trying to cope with educational collapse.

As enacted thus far, takeover laws have limitations that make them less than a panacea for sick schools. For one thing, they apply only to whole school districts; they do nothing for the two or three neglected, run-down, ineffectual schools in a generally middling district. And they take effect only when a district chronically falls beneath state educational standards for minimum academic performance—standards usually so low that no conscientious parent or teacher would voluntarily send children to a school that did not substantially exceed them. Thus it is possible for many school districts to perform far less well than they ought without facing any risk of a takeover. Yet academic bankruptcy laws are one more weapon in a battle where reformers need every weapon they can find. If they allow each state to clean up its single worst school district, they will be more than justified. We will see more such laws passed, and used, throughout this decade.

This change will ease the spread of one controversial brand of school reform, Minnesota's marketplace version of education. Under this plan, pioneered by state governor Rudy Perpich, parents may send their children to any school in the state. Schools must compete for their patronage, and school funds go where parents send their children. This plan is probably the most radical dissolution of centralized power yet seen in America's schools. It also has become the hottest topic in school reform, largely because it has become a key part of the Bush administration's education-reform package. Secretary of Education Lauro Cavazos calls parental choice "the cornerstone to restructuring elementary and secondary education." And in a recent Gallup poll, 60 percent of Americans who were asked favored parental choice.

Under Minnesota's version of this plan, enacted in 1985, parents can send their children to any school in the state, so long as the school has room for them. The state pays travel costs within the student's new district, and throughout the state if the family's income is below the poverty line. And when students move from one school to another, the state "tuition" money that pays for their education—up to $4,000 per year—goes with them. In theory, given the choice, most parents will send their children to schools that provide a good education, and those schools will gain students and flourish, while institutions that do not will lose students and go bankrupt. Thus, all schools will have a strong incentive to improve their programs. In the 1988–89 school year, some four hundred students were attending schools outside their home districts. In most schools, students leaving their home districts have been roughly balanced by students coming in from other areas.

Minnesota's school-reform program was not the first to feature some form of parental choice—nor has it been the last. Boston, Cambridge, and Fall River, Massachusetts; Montclair, New Jersey; and New York City's District 4, in East Harlem, allow parents to send their children to any school within their district, within some locally imposed limits. In all, at least some school systems in forty-three states allow parental choice within the district. Utah has permitted students to attend any school in the state since 1947; relatively few people take advantage of the option, because districts receiving outside students can require parents to pay for their children's schooling. But with Minnesota's locally popular program as an example, parental choice has been attracting attention in other areas. Arkansas, Iowa, Nebraska, and Ohio have all adopted statewide parental-choice plans. Washington State allows underachievers to attend schools outside their home districts. Iowa even allows students to attend school in other states. New Jersey, California, and almost twenty other states are also studying modified parental-choice plans. As school funding is freed from the constraints of local property taxes, communities will find it easier to accept students from other regions, and states will find it easier to pass parental-choice plans.

Not everyone agrees that parental choice is the answer to the problems of American education. Mississippi and Wisconsin have rejected such plans, for a variety of reasons. (Wisconsin has since relented and funded a pilot program for 1,000 inner-city children.) The kindest critics see parental choice as a useless distraction from real school reform. It has, they suggest, found favor with the government only because, by allowing parents to redistribute school funding, it both conforms to conservative political dogma and gives the impression of change without requiring the added spending that would be needed to pay for meaningful reform. The National Education Association, the American Association of School Administrators, and the Minnesota School Boards Association have all voiced that opinion.

Others view free parental choice as a veiled attack on civil rights, because it means an end to mandatory busing plans. And there is evidence that, for some parents at least, an end to busing is one of the idea's appeals. When a Seattle parental-choice program retained involuntary busing to promote integration, parents forced a referendum to strip busing from the plan; the results were discreetly labeled "too close to call." Because of this, most parental-choice plans are modified to prevent the creation of racially imbalanced schools; parents name both the school they would most like their children to attend and one or two alternatives, and school administrators place the students as best they can. In Boston, where school integration has been a contentious problem for decades, administrators report that the vast majority of children wind up in their parents' first- or second-choice schools.

Perhaps the most substantial fear is that good schools will get better, while poor schools will be too strapped for funds to better themselves. But in a sense, that may be the whole point. As the most enthusiastic proponents of parental choice see it, the worst schools have already proved themselves incapable of improvement; it may be better to let such institutions die and start anew.

So far, it is not clear how much Minnesota's parental-choice plan has done for education. Governor Rudy Perpich points out proudly that by 1988, three years after the first pilot project began, the number of foreign-language courses being offered in Minnesota already had doubled, but it is far from clear that parental choice should get the credit for this change. Fewer than 4,000 of the state's 670,000-odd students transferred out of their districts in 1989, in part because the full program is not scheduled to take effect until the 1990 school year.

Yet when it comes to improving educational performance, other parental-choice programs do seem to be working. Since Cambridge, Massachusetts, introduced its plan in 1981, average combined SAT scores in the town have soared by almost ninety points, while the number of students opting for private and parochial school has dropped from some 30 percent of the population to 10 percent; 40 percent of Cambridge students now go to school outside their home districts. In Montclair, New Jersey, students in the fifth through eighth grades have doubled their scores on standardized tests in the ten years since the town's plan took effect. And when East Harlem's District 4 adopted parental choice in 1974, only 40 percent of students made it to school on an average day; today nearly 90 percent graduate. Before the program began, only 15 percent of District 4's students read at grade level; today the figure is 64 percent.

The East Harlem program shows clearly just what it takes to make parental-choice plans work: Failing schools must face real penalties. And there must be enough difference between the area's schools to interest parents in sending their children farther than the nearest institution. District 4 meets both tests. Over the years, three schools in the district have been forced to close for lack of students. Their faculties have done some severe soul-searching, rebuilt their curricula, and reopened. Today those schools, like many of the district's fifty-one other institutions, would be considered magnet schools almost anywhere else. In District 4 they are very much business-as-usual. While giving students a solid background in the core subjects, most of the area's schools have specialized in fields from computer science to the performing arts. Not all such experiments have worked. One of the schools forced to close specialized in sports; skeptical parents quickly put it down for the count, and it has since reopened as New York Prep, with a strong traditional curriculum. Thus, schools competing in the educational marketplace are forced to build a strong reputation for giving more than fair value in a specialty that will interest a significant minority of parents. The result is a better education for all.

There is at least an excuse to hope that parental choice will work out as well for the rest of the country as it has for East Harlem. With an eye on District 4, President Bush has called for enactment of a new magnet-schools program that would set up rigorous, specialized elementary and high schools around the country. According to plan, the program would be backed by $215 million in federal funds, $100 million more than the current budget for magnet schools. As this is written, it is too soon to know whether the program will become reality, or whether it will live up to its promise. Education Secretary Cavazos has claimed that parental choice will soon raise the quality of public education to the standard set by the best private prep schools. If it is supported by a strong enough program of magnet schools, he could turn out to be correct. Whatever the merits of parental choice, this policy will continue to spread and transform the American educational system in the next decade.

As it is practiced in District 4, parental choice does away with some practices that have been part of public education for decades. One is "tracking," the practice of segregating students according to their perceived capacity for learning, with separate classes for the fastest and slowest learners. In theory, tracking is a way to ensure that pupils receive instruction suited to their abilities despite inadequate budgets and other obstacles from on high. In practice, some children in any learning group are still being stretched beyond their capacity, while others are bored to distraction. And once slotted into a remedial class, even gifted children find it almost impossible to escape. They remain academically crippled throughout their school careers. As a corollary, tracking makes it easier to promote children based on time served, rather than on skills acquired. Thus, it often transforms the school from a place of learning into a warehouse where children mark time until they can escape by dropping out. And because minority and low-income children often get tracked into low-achievement groups while wealthier, white students dominate the gifted groups, tracking reinforces the class boundaries that still dominate life in many American cities.

There are probably as many answers to the tracking problem as there are schools where teachers have the freedom and resources to experiment with new instructional methods. Reducing class size, team teaching, cooperative learning plans in which children teach each other, and many more techniques have been substituted for tracking, and all have improved academic performance in some experiments. In many schools, outside management still makes it difficult or impossible to replace the tracking system with more efficient teaching methods, but that is quickly changing. In the last few years, most educators have recognized that tracking is an inefficient and often destructive procedure. Today the practice seems an endangered species of schooling. In the near future it should be little more than a memorable lesson in how not to organize an educational program.

One antidote for systemic problems, and a key feature of most educational reforms now being considered, is what planners call "school-based" or "on-site" management. The idea is that decisions should be made by the people most directly affected by them, because reforms work best when the people carrying them out feel that they "own" the new system and are personally responsible for its results. Thus, state education departments around the country are passing their power down the line to local school boards, school boards are granting broader discretion to principals and to parents, and principals are giving teachers a much larger voice in running the schools. Sometimes the process occurs voluntarily; sometimes it is forced on school systems by voters or legislators or through collective bargaining with teachers' unions.

In its purest form, school-based management allows teachers and the principal to decide within broad limits what to teach, how to teach it, when to schedule classes, how to maintain discipline, and what criteria to use in weighing their students' performance. By law, the school board still has the ultimate say over such matters; and the principal retains both the final authority over the school's daily operation and the ultimate responsibility for its results. But when it comes to teaching, teachers have vastly more control in this system than in centrally managed school systems. This is one brand of school reform that the teachers' unions seldom argue with.

A typical example of school-based management has changed teaching in Brighton High School, in a well-to-do suburb of Rochester, New York. A few years ago, teachers there were delivering the same canned lectures they had given for years, their notes yellowing with age. Then they began to work with the Coalition of Essential Schools, an education-reform organization based at Brown University that specializes in creative teaching methods. Today, Brighton teachers have nearly abandoned lectures, fill-in-the-blank worksheets, and the whole rigid apparatus of more hidebound education. Instead, students are encouraged to learn in a more active way: to write more, talk more, and work harder. Chemistry classes are designed so that students can discover complex scientific principles, much as researchers do. In German class, students sit in discussion groups rather than in rows of desks, act out skits, send letters to German companies—in short, they are *involved.* Students learn faster and understand more, thanks to a curriculum developed within the school by the teachers who have to use it.

In Medford, Oregon, a small logging community in the Rogue River valley, teachers have worked a similar transformation. In 1985, the South Medford High School housed only the ninth and tenth grades; the next year it would expand to include all four years of high school. So four English teachers sat down to develop a new curriculum for the eleventh- and twelfth-grade English classes. One result was the Senior Project, a free-form activity that all students must complete in order to graduate. Seniors have written novels, composed songs, and staged rock concerts to benefit the hungry. One even spent two years building a racing boat. Almost anything goes, so long as it promotes real-world learning and teaches students to synthesize diverse information into a tangible accomplishment. Teachers say the program does exactly that. It is hard to imagine how it would have evolved in a system where schools were managed from the top down.

One of the nation's largest experiments with on-site management is taking place in Jefferson County, Kentucky. Under the plan, which began in 1988, Louisville teachers have evolved a wide variety of programs to meet the needs of students in their schools.

Few students attend Maupin Elementary School for more than three years before moving on to another institution, so they have little chance to build the kind of school identity that promotes learning. The teachers' answer is a new student council that sets standards for classroom behavior, determines punishment for violating them, decides how to use money from school fund drives, and handles many similar chores. The idea reportedly has been a resounding success. According to the teachers, taking responsibility for substantial decisions has given students a sense of "ownership" as no previous effort had. And that, in turn, should result in better grades.

At Lassiter Middle School, with about eight hundred students from a poor neighborhood, teachers focused on improving the instructional process itself. Rather than facing a new class each year, thirty teachers have formed six interdisciplinary teams. Five groups keep the same set of students for their entire three years in the school, while one takes in students from all three grades—a practice used by Montessori schools for several decades. In an even greater departure from traditional methods, the teachers have done away with failing grades. Students who turn in poor work simply repeat the assignment—again and again, if necessary. There is no chance for them just to accept failure; eventually they must take the responsibility to get it right. If need be, teachers continue working with the students through the summer vacation. This project, too, has worked out well. When the first report cards came out after the "no-fail" policy took effect, forty-two out of the program's 150 students had at least one blank spot or "incomplete" where a failing grade once would have appeared. By the end of the year, all but two had passed all their subjects.

Teachers at Fairdale High School added an extra twenty-five-minute period to the school day and devoted it to "teacher-guided assistance." Students can use the time to get help from a teacher, visit the library, make up a missed test, work in the computer room—whatever they choose. They report that the chance to work with the teachers one-on-one has shown them how much the faculty really cares about them. In the long run, that too should yield better academic performance.

No one knows exactly how much benefit Louisville students have gained from on-site management, but it is clear that teachers themselves are satisfied with the results. Plans called for twenty-four schools to participate in the experiment in the first year, forty-eight in the second. But schools could join in only if two-thirds of their employees approved the idea, and the program would grow beyond the first two dozen schools only if two-thirds of the county's teachers voted for the expansion. The experiment easily survived the first year's vote, and by the end of the 1991–92 school year, all 156 Jefferson County schools are expected to adopt on-site management.

One step removed from the classroom is the decentralized control system that took over Chicago's 540 schools in 1989. Several decades ago, Chicago had one of the best big-city school systems in the country. But in 1979, Chicago's educational system had gone broke. Then there were three long, vitriolic teacher strikes in as many years. A vast central bureaucracy has micro-managed the schools with little evident regard for learning. By 1987, then-Secretary of Education William Bennett visited the city to declare that its schools were the nation's worst. Dropout rates were over 50 percent, and those students who stuck out their twelve years received little in the way of an education.

Shortly before his death, Mayor Harold Washington called parents, state legislators, and a variety of school and civic organizations together for an "education summit." By 1988 the group had devised a series of changes that it hoped would eventually restore quality education to Chicago. One key feature of the program was a decision to shift power from the established bureaucracy to local school councils. Each council consists of the school principal and ten elected members: six parents who have children at the school, two community representatives who do not, and two teachers at the school. These councils wield enormous power over school operations. They can make budget decisions, recommend changes in the curriculum, and hire and fire principals, who used to enjoy life tenure. (In this last matter, the principal has no vote.)

As this is written, the first school councils have only just been elected. It remains to be seen whether they can halt the long decline of Chicago's schools. But most onlookers find reason for optimism. After all, the city's educational system has been so bad that nearly any change would be an improvement.

The ultimate test of school-based management may come in the next few years, in New York City, where the newly appointed Chancellor of Schools, Joseph A. Fernandez, has vowed to reform what may be the nation's most change-resistant educational system. Chancellor Fernandez is credited with having turned around the failing schools of Dade County, Florida, carrying out three separate reorganizations during his two-year tenure there. But in New York he faces even greater obstacles.

There may be systemic problems from which New York City's schools do not suffer, but it is difficult to imagine what they could be. Consider a brief list: The school board has made itself accountable to no one. The bureaucracy it controls is as large, unwieldy, and ineffectual as the Soviet farm bureau. The thirty-two community school boards over which it presides, and whose members show little interest in education and less understanding of it, are battlegrounds for local politics. Corruption in the boards is rife; in 1988 alone, seven of their members were indicted on criminal charges. The city's Board of Examiners requires would-be teachers to pass a battery of tests that duplicate the state's exams and can take up to five years to complete. School principals have life tenure; short of an arrest for child molesting, there is no way to get rid of an incompetent principal. State law guarantees them "building tenure" as well: principals cannot even be moved from one school to another against their will. And the unions operating inside the schools can bring the whole system to a halt at a moment's displeasure.

Thus, more than eight out of ten new teachers, unable to fight their way through the duplicate exams, enter the schools as "temporaries," receiving less in wages and benefits than the few beginners who do survive the process. Many of the city's school buildings have too little heat, light, and drinking water; the prestigious Bronx High School of Science began the 1987–88 school year with 150 broken windows; and the city last opened a high school in the early 1980s. And when teachers tried to enter one elementary school before the official 8:00 A.M. opening, custodians locked them out; later they agreed to unlock the doors—for an "opening fee" of $10,000 per year!

All these forces are so entrenched that, after years of trying, neither the mayor nor the state governor has managed to enact any reforms at all. Though a few exceptional schools, and the remarkable District 4, have improved their educational performance dramatically, there has seemed to be little hope of broad reform in New York's schools.

Fernandez has begun his attempt by streamlining the school system's massive central bureaucracy. By combining offices with duplicate functions, shifting 275 people from the department's Division of School Buildings to the newly created New York City School Construction Authority, and similar measures, he hopes to cut some 1,400 people from the 5,200-man staff. How many will actually leave the payroll is unclear, as many of the first few hundred jobs eliminated employ people either tenured as principals and assistant principals, or protected from layoff by union contracts.

The new chancellor may have earned greater prestige in New

York with a few simple acts. Unlike previous occupants of the position, Fernandez has deprived fourteen top school officials of their city cars and accomplished the almost unthinkable task of removing a tenured principal from an out-of-control Brooklyn high school. He will have many more such tasks to perform.

But the centerpiece of Fernandez's Miami reforms, and his stated goal for New York, is the establishment of independent councils that exercise day-to-day control over the schools. Such councils have been established in half of Miami's 267 schools. Though principals and parents participate, teachers from the school itself dominate. They have adopted a variety of innovative teaching methods, from hiring Berlitz instructors to teach language classes under contract, to setting up a curriculum of classical literature chosen to develop skills in critical thinking. The program has significantly improved the morale of both teachers and students in Miami schools, but no one yet knows whether the changes have fostered actual learning. The plan that set up the first councils gave them a free hand for three years before their performance—and that of the schools' students—would be evaluated.

Chancellor Fernandez, in his first few months in office, has yet to establish his first council in New York City, but he predicts that it will not be difficult to find one hundred schools to volunteer for a demonstration program. The city teachers' union has endorsed the plan, so one potential obstacle has already been overcome. Officials from U.S. Secretary of Education Lauro Cavazos on down have hailed the results of Miami's version of site-based management, and virtually everyone in the education community is watching to see how much success Fernandez meets in New York. If his school councils can make a verifiable improvement in the standardized test scores of New York's school children, they are sure to be copied throughout the country.

In our introductory chapter we asserted that America's school system had been designed more for organizational and political convenience than for learning. In fact, no one would deliberately design such a mess. It just happened. And as it did, the goal of education was buried under the deadweight of bureaucratic infighting, misguided programs, and ill-conceived regulations. Thus today we have funding methods that do not provide funds, school boards that pay little attention to the schools, janitors who do not clean up, and, above all, educational programs that do not educate.

The problems discussed above are only a few examples of the pervasive way in which education has taken a backseat to other priorities. The reforms are only some of the changes needed to repair our national school system. There are many others; we will look at them later in this book.

For at least the next ten years, the chief work of educational reform will be to strip away the mass of irrelevancies that have come between schools and education. Thus, most systemic reforms in the 1990s will be designed to meet two goals: they will serve to take school control out of bureaucratic hands and move it closer to the classroom, and they will replace meddlesome state and national regulations with educational performance standards that give local schools a goal and let them figure out how to meet it.

At this point we are still working to define the problems we face. As this book was in preparation, President Bush's education summit recommended six goals for reform, and an additional fifteen sub-goals for our national reform program. It is now up to educators and policymakers in each state to develop strategies to meet them. We hope that some of these efforts will focus on designing schools for the future, not simply trying to improve or reform the ones we have.

Virtually all of us will be involved in this process. Teachers and school administrators, given the opportunities of school-based management, will have to develop classroom methods that foster student achievement and overall school reform. Parents and individual students must be involved in the process and understand the implications and importance of this commitment.

By 1995 we should be ready to measure our progress toward meeting our national goals. It should be clear that we can indeed revolutionize schooling and become a world leader again in the education of our youth. America's future will depend on how well we define our educational goals and meet them.

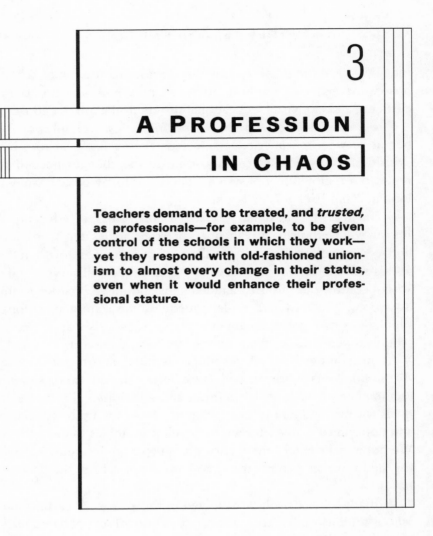

3

A PROFESSION
IN CHAOS

Teachers demand to be treated, and *trusted,* as professionals—for example, to be given control of the schools in which they work— yet they respond with old-fashioned unionism to almost every change in their status, even when it would enhance their professional stature.

The 1970s and 1980s were harsh decades for teachers. The nation changed, often in ways that made teachers' jobs harder. Teachers changed too, in ways they hoped would improve both education and their position within it. Yet in the early 1990s, teaching finds itself under what many teachers perceive as a broad attack from the outside and in turmoil within. It will not soon recover unless both teachers and community leaders change their approach to education.

One big advantage that our most successful schools enjoy over the rest is an ample supply of dedicated, competent teachers. The problem is, there are too few teachers to go around. The shortage is particularly acute in some of the most critical specialties. In science, mathematics, and foreign languages, it is difficult to find qualified teachers at all. And even in less uncommon disciplines, classes in American high schools average nearly eighteen pupils per teacher, when ten would be ideal; in too many schools, they are far larger.

In an orderly classroom, no matter how many pupils share it, disciplined, motivated students should be capable of learning. After all, Japanese classes average more than thirty pupils per teacher, and their achievement records are among the best in the world. But disciplined, motivated students are a rarity in America, and the current shortage of teachers has developed at a time when we are asking more of educators than simple lectures. Japanese children excel in part because Japanese parents know the absolute necessity of a sound education and expect no less than excellence of their offspring. In the United States, in contrast, more and more children come from single-parent homes or two-worker households, where parents have less and less time for their children's education; many seem to have little interest in their children at all. Thus, teachers must provide the individual attention too many children lack. Without it, students quickly lose interest in school, most often permanently. But few teachers can cope with the needs of eighteen students, much less the two dozen or so found in some classrooms. Add to this problem the growing number of students for whom English is a second language, and the shortage of teachers who can meet the needs of today's pupils becomes even more acute. It can only grow in the years to come. After years of decline, class enrollments are growing rapidly, and the generation of teachers who guided the baby boomers through school is beginning to retire. By 1997, an estimated 1.5 million new teachers will be needed.

Unfortunately, there will not be nearly enough new teachers available. Not this year, and not by the turn of the century. One reason is that teachers are still dramatically underpaid when compared with other professions that require a college education. In 1990 the average teacher's salary was $31,278, up 5.6 percent from the previous year at a time when inflation was running at 4.8 percent. Modest as that figure is, it hides remarkable disparities in regional pay scales. Teachers' salaries are relatively high in the Far West ($35,310), in the Middle Atlantic states ($34,689), in New England ($34,698), and in the Great Lakes region ($33,425.) They are far lower in the Plains states ($27,874), the Rocky Mountain states ($27,542), the Southeast ($26,883), and the Southwest ($26,355).

The situation is even worse for those just entering the profession. In 1987 the average starting salary for an accountant was $21,200, new computer specialists received $26,170, and engineers began at $28,500. The average starting salary for teachers was only $17,500, and the pay scale has improved little since then. In forty out of fifty states, a starting garbage collector still earns more than a starting teacher.

As a result, the number of new recruits to the teaching profession has been dropping rapidly. In 1970, one high-school senior in five went on to major in education. By 1987 the figure had fallen to less than one in eight. Only eight percent of college freshmen now say they are interested in a teaching career; on average, only half of them will actually become teachers, and half of that group will abandon the classroom within seven years.

School districts around the country are trying many approaches, both to find more teachers and to make certain that the ones we have are capable of helping students to learn. One is to throw money at the problem. Since 1983, the average teacher's salary nationwide has risen from about $20,700 to $31,278. In Bucks County, Pennsylvania, starting salaries for a nine- or ten-month educational year have risen to as much as $21,600; experienced teachers there earn up to $50,000. In Connecticut, as a result of a $300-million education grant from the state legislature, average starting salaries for new teachers have risen from $15,200 in 1986 to $22,500 this year; salaries for those with a master's degree and years of experience have gone from $30,000 to $42,150. St. John the Baptist Parish, in Louisiana, managed to attract thirty-four new teachers in 1989 by offering them a package of benefits that included $2,000 for living expenses, housing and rental discounts, cut-rate real-estate brokerage commissions, free banking, free appliances, and discounts on new cars!

Predictably, school systems that pay their educators well have been finding it a lot easier to attract the teachers they need than have localities where school employees effectively take a vow of poverty. We can expect average salaries for teachers to rise quickly throughout the decade. But that simply transfers the shortage from wealthy communities that can afford to pay more to poor districts that cannot. Ways must be found either to recruit more teachers or to stretch the abilities of the ones we have.

The most venerable approach is to ask parents and other community members to help out in the schools. From the Hancock Preschool in Hancock, New Hampshire, (population 1,500) to the Hudson Elementary School in New York City's Greenwich Village, schools across the country have established volunteer programs for "civilians" eager to help with their children's education. Parents and other interested adults often act as teachers' aides, freeing professionals to spend more of their time giving individual attention to students who need it. In many schools, the most capable volunteers take on individual tutoring of problem students. Many of them are people who worked as teachers themselves before starting their own families; many are not. This is one obvious and successful way to stretch an inadequate supply of new teachers. By the year 2000, as many as one American adult in five will be volunteering some of their time to help out in local schools.

Yet volunteers cannot solve the teacher shortage. The only real cure is to recruit more full-time educators. Much to the dismay of teachers already accredited, many states and school districts are trying to attract them from other careers. Particularly for technical subjects, industry offers a huge new supply of potential teachers, most of whom know more about their fields than any teachers'-college graduate can. So the idea is to get practicing chemists to teach chemistry, accountants to teach arithmetic, and so on. Give them a few courses in educational techniques if need be, but start by making sure that would-be teachers actually know their subjects.

In one typical program, New Jersey has just begun to experiment with accrediting teachers who possess college degrees and a good knowledge of their subjects, but lack the educational courses that most school systems demand. Recruits are allowed to teach while taking a minimum of educational courses required for permanent certification. The plan not only offers to ease a growing teacher shortage in the state, it also exposes students to the practical work experience their teachers carry over from former careers.

Another promising innovation is "Teach for America," a recruitment campaign devised by 1989 Princeton graduate Wendy Kopp for her senior thesis. A public-policy major, Kopp modeled her plan on the Peace Corps, whose reputation for selecting only the best applicants gives it a prestige that draws top-quality recruits. The idea is to enlist top students from the Ivy League, from prestigious liberal-arts colleges and public universities, and—to provide minority teachers—from leading black colleges. Those who make the grade will complete a summer training institute and go straight to work. School systems that have agreed to accept temporary teachers without formal education credits range from Chicago and Los Angeles to rural districts in Mississippi and North Carolina. A survey at Columbia and Barnard found that 60 percent of the seniors responding said they would be willing to teach in public schools for two or three years before starting their permanent careers. Based on that, Kopp expects 7,500 people to apply in the program's first year. By September 1990, the first 500 teachers will be in the classrooms.

To date, at least twenty states, or individual districts within them, have enacted some form of alternative certification plan similar to the New Jersey program, while others are either pending or under discussion in at least eleven more states. Most of the existing programs remain in their formative stages and thus far have produced relatively few new teachers.

All these programs have been contested by teachers' unions, which seem to view alternative certification as a threat to the image of professionalism with which they would like to endow their members. In the case of New Jersey, the battle stretched on for more than a year. But in the 1990s, these experiments with alternative certification will grow dramatically, while new ones modeled on them will spread throughout the United States. By the turn of the century they will begin to relieve the crippling shortage of teachers in science, mathematics, and other fields where industry now out-competes our schools for capable personnel.

Yet finding new teachers for our schools is only half the job. We must also ensure that they teach effectively. And there is reason to wonder just how good the next generation of teachers will be at their jobs. Because teaching has become such an ill-paid, low-prestige field, teachers' colleges simply can't recruit the best students. SAT scores of high-school students who plan a teaching career average as much as forty points lower than those of students headed toward other professions.

And political and social leaders have begun to wonder whether the teacher-training programs that cater to these students are really capable of turning out competent educators. The painful fact is that after receiving their education degrees, few new teachers actually know anything worth passing on to students. Too many college education departments are so wedded to their classes in teaching methods and applied child psychology that they neglect or ignore the core subjects their graduates are supposed to teach. Thus, in Massachusetts only one elementary-school teacher in five has taken any college-level math or science. This is one more area in which teachers feel themselves under attack.

The National Education Association and other ranking members of the "education establishment" fiercely defend the need for the pedagogical training in which they have invested much of their own careers. They point, in particular, to research (emanating from college education departments) that purports to show that trained teachers handle their students differently from, and presumably better than, well-meaning outsiders who know their subjects but not classroom management and teaching theory. For example, Dr. Pamela Grossman of the University of Washington reports that English teachers with pedagogical training stress expository writing—an active exercise and a useful skill—in their classes, while English majors who lack education classes tend to focus on literary criticism, a passive and relatively useless activity. Dr. David C. Berliner of Arizona State University suggests that teachers without the standard credentials tend to be confused, even overwhelmed, by the busy classroom environment.

So far, it is not clear that these isolated, and perhaps less than objective, studies are valid, but let us give them the benefit of the doubt. Even if their conclusions prove true, proponents of teaching courses will still have some explaining to do. If what the college education departments are selling is so valuable, for example, why is it that private schools tend, on average, to do a far better job of educating their students than do public schools, though few require their teachers to have degrees in education? And how is it that education courses are supposed to enable a teacher to impart knowledge of, say, high-school physics without first learning that subject himself?

With such questions in mind, several states have dramatically revised their teacher-training requirements, not just for second-career educators, but for college-age trainees. As explained below, three states have set narrow limits on the amount of time that prospective teachers must spend in education courses, while one has both eased entry-level standards for teachers and toughened them later in the educator's career.

California now limits undergraduate teacher training to no more than one year, including one semester of student teaching. The law also forbids teachers' schools to require more than nine semester hours of education courses before students begin their on-the-job training. Three to four of the twelve to sixteen credits required must be devoted to the skills required in teaching reading.

Virginia now requires prospective teachers to major in one of the liberal arts or sciences. The state also has limited teacher-training courses to eighteen semester hours of classroom work, not counting student teaching.

Beginning in 1991, Texas will also require applicants for teaching certificates to have college degrees in academic subjects (reading is considered an acceptable "interdisciplinary" academic subject) and will effectively abolish the education major altogether. Texas also will limit teacher training to no more than eighteen semester hours of education courses, including at least six hours of student teaching.

Connecticut, in contrast, has eased certification standards for new teachers, but has made them far more stringent for those with experience. (The rules apply, of course, only to teachers now entering the system.) Education degrees are no longer acceptable in Connecticut; would-be teachers must now major in the subjects they hope to teach. Students are granted only a one-year teaching certificate at first, and to get that they must pass both a state competency exam and a test of their subject knowledge. During their first year, an experienced teacher guides their professional development; at the end, a team of six assessors decides whether to grant them an eight-year provisional certificate. Those who pass the cut must take thirty hours of college-level study and teach successfully for three years in order to receive a professional teaching certificate. And even that is not permanent; to maintain their certification, teachers must complete another ninety hours of professional training.

Whether any of these regulations, all enacted since *A Nation at Risk* called for major reforms in teacher training, will set the pattern for other states, it is too soon to tell. One critic has claimed that under the new limits, California teacher-training programs often must eliminate courses in the teaching of science, art, physical education, and other special subjects so as to have enough time for reading, math, and language arts. And the National Council for Accreditation of Teacher Education has threatened to strip education departments at Texas colleges of their accreditation on the grounds that their abbreviated programs no longer meet national standards; it probably will have done so by the time this appears. But in the end, these may be mere delaying tactics by an establishment fighting to hold back the tide. If California, Virginia, and Texas find that their new standards ease their shortage of educators without harming the academic performance of their students, other states are sure to follow their lead.

There is one other approach to ensuring that teachers can handle their jobs: evaluate their performance, reward the best workers, and weed out the worst. In any other "business" it would be a matter of course. In the field of education, such proposals have touched off some of the worst battles yet seen.

Unfortunately, the idea that teachers should be held accountable for the results of their efforts has not won much favor among "educators" themselves. When famed businessman H. Ross Perot pushed an education-reform program through the Texas legislature in 1984, it included both a master-teacher program and subject-by-subject competence testing for teachers. The proposals drew such bitter opposition from state teachers' unions that Perot described the battle to enact them as "the worst dogfight of my career."

One part of the Texas plan was a simple literacy test for teachers. At least it *should* have been simple. Yet even after two attempts, 11 percent of the teachers taking the test failed it. The state teachers' union eventually took the state to court, charging that, no matter what the intent, requiring teachers to have mastered English discriminated against minorities and those in certain age groups and specialties. The court agreed, and the literacy tests have been deleted from the Texas program. In one of the nation's largest school systems, it is now officially acceptable for teachers to be unable to read the textbooks they use in class.

One reform effort that fared somewhat better was pioneered by former governor Lamar Alexander, of Tennessee. His $1-billion, three-year improvement program, enacted in 1984, began with a 20 percent pay raise for all teachers over three years. It also set up kindergartens in each school district, limited class sizes, mandated a state competency test for graduation from high school, toughened math and science requirements, added a computer literacy requirement, and set up a summer program for gifted students.

A key, and controversial, feature was one of the nation's first "master teacher" plans, funded by a one-cent increase in the state sales tax. Under the program, the state's outstanding educators receive the title of "master teacher" and are paid to take on extra duties. The program took effect over the objections of the state teachers' union, which still complains that classroom evaluations for master-teacher status do not measure actual teaching performance and that being passed over for the honor has a demoralizing effect on competent educators. Yet more than 6,000 of the state's 46,000 teachers now receive from $2,000 to $7,000 in merit pay each year.

Further, the program as a whole has proved remarkably successful in improving reading scores in the state's poor rural districts. In Clay County, for example, failure seems foreordained; the average adult income there is only $6,600 per year, and 38 percent of the population is illiterate. Yet remedial reading programs for first- and second-graders, paid for out of the new sales-tax revenues, have raised students from fourteenth place to third among nearby counties on standardized achievement tests. SAT scores have risen and dropout rates have fallen since the program began. Whatever the flaws of Tennessee's merit-pay system, they clearly have not harmed the state's schools, and proponents credit the program with having stimulated better performance by a majority of teachers.

A similar merit-pay program in Fairfax County, Virginia—a wealthy suburb of Washington, D.C. where success should have been far easier to accomplish—appears to have survived a troubled infancy. It got its start in 1986, when the Fairfax Education Association agreed to accept teacher testing and merit pay in return for a 30-percent across-the-board raise for teachers over three years. Teachers who volunteer for the program undergo six classroom evaluations and then are rated by their school principals. Those who receive the top rating qualify for a merit-pay raise of up to 10 percent. Those receiving the lowest rating could be fired. In the first year, 339 teachers were evaluated; 138—40 percent—qualified for merit pay, and only nine teachers were rated less than competent. None received the bottom rating. By spring of 1989, the number of teachers evaluated had leaped to 3,623. Fully 2,198 teachers—26 percent of the teachers in the school system—received excellent ratings and qualified for pay raises of about $4,000. Two percent, or 175, fared so poorly that three-member intervention teams were assigned to help them boost their performance, and twenty-three were recommended for firing.

For years now, the National Education Association, union for three-fourths of the teachers in America, has steadfastly opposed such measures as merit pay and teacher testing. Instead, the organization has maintained, all teachers should be better paid, not just those who receive top ratings; NEA leaders have argued that evaluations conducted by principals—the usual technique—could be subjective and unfair. That changed unexpectedly early in 1989, when the organization's president at that time, Mary Hatwood Futrell, praised the Fairfax County program as a model for similar plans all over the country. The features that won her favor were the heavy involvement of teachers in the program and the fact that teachers all got a substantial raise before the merit-pay plan took effect.

Since then, the program has passed through a difficult shakedown period. Fairfax teachers voted to continue the merit-pay plan, but they complain that evaluations are too subjective, even arbitrary. Teachers who received poor ratings in the 1988 observation period filed more than 120 grievances with the school board. Morale has sunk to an all-time low, they say, in part because there are now two classes of teacher—those who qualify for merit pay and those who do not—and in part because rather than sharing teaching tips with their colleagues, teachers now hoard them, the better to compete for a raise. Worse yet, the school board has reneged on the 10-percent merit-pay raises, substituting merit *bonuses* of 9 percent. Pay raises would have been added in when calculating future raises and retirement pay. Bonuses are not. In the long run, the difference will cost teachers several thousand dollars per year. And worst of all, local civil-rights groups have pointed out that teachers receiving merit pay are disproportionately white, while those fired for incompetence are nearly all black. The Fairfax Education Association vowed to kill merit pay in their district and then ignored the issue altogether for some months, focusing on their own proposal to turn control of the district's schools over to "school councils" dominated by the teachers who work in them. The plan remains in place, however, and at this point it appears that it will survive as an example of how a good idea can overcome flawed execution.

To be fair about it, there are problems with any reform plan that relies on teacher testing. Morale does suffer, at least temporarily, when testing begins. According to one study, it takes about four years for teachers to recover their spirit after they find that someone with the authority to promote or sack them will be looking over their shoulders. And it may be, as teachers' unions often suggest, that students suffer during this "down" period, though there is no evidence to show that educators teach less well or students learn less quickly when teachers are feeling glum.

More critical is the question of just what should be tested, and how. The obvious way to evaluate teachers is to test their students: those whose pupils learn the most from a given course are the best teachers, and those whose students learn the least are the worst. It is an objective standard, and with some adjustments for local economic and sociological factors, it sounds both to-the-point and fairly workable.

Instead, most teacher-testing efforts are limited to multiple-choice tests of general knowledge and familiarity with pedagogical techniques. The best, such as Fairfax County's moribund program, examine not how the students turn out, but how well the teacher demonstrates education-course skills, such as classroom management and lecture style. Teachers rightly complain that such classroom observations are subjective, too often arbitrary, and always influenced by the observer's agenda and relationship with the teacher under scrutiny.

A third approach, still under development, is the "teacher portfolio." The portfolio attempts to be a comprehensive profile of the teacher's experience and abilities. A typical sample might include biographical information, a series of lesson plans, samples of students' work, a log of how the teacher assessed the students' progress, and even videotapes of classroom work or laboratory experiments. Once the portfolio is complete, teachers go before an examining board to explain their teaching and testing methods. The technique's Stanford University developers have yet to develop a system for rating portfolio quality. Nonetheless, the National Board for Professional Teaching Standards (NBPTS) is relying on their work in developing a voluntary program for certifying teacher competency, slated to begin in 1992.

To date, none of these techniques seems really adequate to the task. Teacher portfolios offer improvement over previous evaluation methods, but they still center on the evaluators' subjective reactions to the teacher. The NEA and other teachers' organizations seem willing to accept it, largely because the NBPTS, which proposes to apply it, is made up of fellow teachers. Thus the process seems akin to medical certification and bar exams, in which professionals are rated by their colleagues rather than being evaluated by outsiders. At this point, it seems likely that portfolios, or something like them, will form the basis of teacher-evaluation programs in many school districts before the 1990s are out. Yet for society, portfolios—and indeed any method of evaluation acceptable to teachers—may be inadequate. Like previous testing techniques, they remain distant from the single most important criterion measure of a teacher's performance: how well the students learn. The controversy over teacher testing is one that will not soon be resolved.

Old Miss Grundy, with her chalk and blackboard and blue-gray bun, is no longer with us. She has been replaced by men and women trained in the latest teaching methods, classroom management practices, and developmental psychology. Yet this apparent flowering of professionalism has not paid off as well as teachers might have hoped. As a society we respected the teachers of an earlier generation, even as we winced at the thought of their rote drills and sometimes arbitrary discipline. On average, we grant far less esteem to the products of college education departments today. It shows in the plummeting number of young people who enter the field. It shows at meetings of the National Education Association and other teachers' organizations, where discussions often revolve around such cosmetic questions as how to improve the teacher's image in the public eye. There is a very simple solution, but it requires a change of attitude that teachers clearly find difficult to accept.

To a large extent, teachers have brought their image problem on themselves. In this chapter and the preceding one, we have seen the contradictions in several positions they hold dear.

Teachers demand to be treated, and *trusted,* as professionals—for example, to be given control of the schools in which they work— yet they respond with old-fashioned unionism to almost every change in their status, even when it would enhance their professional stature.

They complain, accurately, that they are too few to handle the job required of them, yet resist any attempt to increase their numbers, save the numbers that appear soon after the phrase, "Pay to the order of . . ."

They claim the right to police their own members, as doctors and lawyers do, yet reject the accountability that true professionalism carries with it. That the Texas union could sue to overturn a literacy test that found its members wanting, rather than correcting the problem, stains the reputation of teachers far beyond that state's borders. And when did you last hear a teacher volunteer to risk being sued for malpractice if his charges left school illiterate?

The public sees these contradictions, too. Little wonder that many Americans consider teachers part of the problem of education, not part of the solution. To change that image, teachers will have to resolve the conflicting values that inspire it.

One of us (MG) dropped out of the National Education Association more than fifteen years ago, in despair because the NEA could not decide whether to act as a professional association or as a labor union. It has yet to make such a decision. If it is to be a professional association, it must learn to evaluate its members by the educational "health" of their student patients—and weed out those members whose students regularly fail. If it is to be a union, then teachers must let the NEA tend to salaries and benefits and, in professional matters, submit themselves to organizations whose sole purpose is to ensure the quality of education in America's schools, as measured by the success of the students graduated from them.

The 1990s will perpetuate many trends that teachers deplore. School systems across the land will continue to recruit new teachers from other careers; in the end, it will matter little whether college-trained educators help these newcomers to hone their skills or try to obstruct their progress, and thereby damage their own professional reputations. School systems will continue to adopt merit pay and teacher testing, whether educators welcome the chance to polish both their professional skills and image, or fight it as a threat to organized labor. More than twenty states fund some such program already, and at least seven more are working on incentive plans. All of this amounts to a dramatic change, both within the teaching community and in its relationship to society. It is a change that will serve our students well.

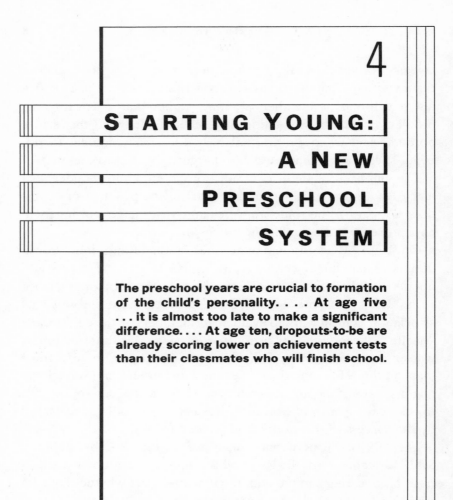

4

STARTING YOUNG: A NEW PRESCHOOL SYSTEM

The preschool years are crucial to formation of the child's personality. . . . At age five . . . it is almost too late to make a significant difference. . . . At age ten, dropouts-to-be are already scoring lower on achievement tests than their classmates who will finish school.

Ten years from now, the average elementary school will be a far different place from today's eight-hour institutions. They will still provide formal schooling for the kindergarten-through-sixth-grade age group (though, as we will see in later chapters, the teaching methods used will have changed substantially), but a whole new set of duties, staff, and even students will have been added. By the late 1990s, most schools will be open from seven o'clock in the morning to six at night. They will be home to both a preschool program for three-to-five-year-olds and a day-care program for school-age children whose parents are unavailable in the early morning or after school. During school vacation, they will offer day care for all.

The change has already begun. More than thirty states now offer prekindergarten classes for four-year-olds, four times as many as in 1980. And about 15 percent of the nation's 16,000-odd school districts either provide some form of child care or allow community groups to use their buildings for the purpose. Similar programs are on the drawing boards in many other regions. In 1988, no fewer than 130 bills proposing one form or another of child care were introduced in Congress. Though not one of those competing proposals passed—election-year bills are, after all, meant less for enactment than for display on the campaign trail—it seems clear that this is one brand of school improvement that has support from virtually everyone involved in education—the Bush administration, its rivals in Congress, the National Governors' Conference, teachers, and parents.

There are several reasons for this sudden burst of interest in preschool and day-care programs. One is that there are more children who have no one to look after them during the day. Fully 65 percent of mothers with school-age children now work outside the home. So do half of all mothers with children below the age of five. In fact, the fastest-growing segment of working mothers consists of those with children under one year old; more than half of them now work outside the home, up from about 23 percent as recently as 1982. For many of these mothers, private day care is either unavailable or unaffordable. So their children must fend for themselves during working hours when they are not in school. Obviously no mother is going to go off to work and leave a one-year-old at home alone, but as many as 7 million school-age children—estimates vary widely—do return to an empty home after school. According to the Department of Education, some 220,000 do not even have a home to go home to—and the National Coalition for the Homeless puts the figure at 500,000 to 750,000.

The number of children left unattended is growing rapidly, not only because more women are taking jobs, but because there are more children to be left alone. In 1978 there were only 9.1 million children between the ages of three and five, down from a peak of

10.9 million in 1970. By 1986 the number had soared to 11 million; it is rising still, and will not stabilize until the middle of this decade.

And there is a growing shortage of affordable preschools and child care in the United States. The key word is *affordable*. According to a survey carried out in 1985, two-thirds of four-year-olds and more than half of three-year-olds in families with annual incomes of $35,000 or more attended preschool programs. Among families with incomes under $10,000, fewer than one-third of four-year-olds and only 17 percent of three-year-olds enjoyed the same benefit. Full-time day care costs at least $150 per week for babies and $50 to $100 per week for preschoolers—as much as most moderate-income families can bear. Just hiring a babysitter at the minimum wage runs $750 per month. And full-fledged commercial preschools can cost up to $6,500 a year. Bills like those price most American working families out of the market. Most struggle to find some other way to meet their children's needs during working hours. A growing number fail.

No one is quite sure how much damage it does a child to be left alone during the day. Some studies have shown that "latchkey children" are more likely to do poorly in school, and eventually to drop out. Others have found no difference between children whose parents are available during the day and those who go home to an empty house. A few researchers have even found that children who care for themselves during the day learn a sense of responsibility and independence earlier than others. The most likely interpretation is that children who would have grown up competent and confident under any circumstances are not harmed by being left alone, while those at risk for other reasons are further handicapped by the experience.

What is certain is that no one *likes* the situation, not adults and not the children themselves. Most parents who leave their children alone during the day report feelings of guilt and worry about how their absence will affect their children. In a recent Harris poll, more than half of American teachers reported that they believed being left alone after school hours is the most important factor undermining the performance of their students. And in a surprise discovery, the editors of the children's magazine *Sprint* found that 70 percent of children asked to think of a scary situation said that they were most afraid of being left home alone.

Further, in the last twenty years, psychologists have gathered conclusive evidence that the preschool years are crucial to the formation of the child's personality. By the age of two or three, the process is well under way. At age five, when children reach kindergarten, it is almost too late to make a significant difference with anything short of intensive therapy. And in the fifth grade, at age ten, dropouts-to-be are already scoring lower on standardized achievement tests than their classmates who will finish school—the result of problems unnoticed in earlier years. Though it is still possible to intervene at this point and salvage failing students, it is clearly better to make sure they never reach the point of failure. This is one more role for tomorrow's preschool programs.

It is a role they play surprisingly well. Some of the most credible proof comes from the Perry Preschool Program, in a blighted section of Ypsilanti, Michigan. Researchers have been following 100 area residents continuously since 1962. Half attended the Perry Preschool for a single year, while half did not. The difference is clearly visible in the adults they became. More than two decades later, fully two-thirds of the preschool alumni had finished high school, compared with fewer than half of those who missed out on the program. Some 38 percent of the Perry graduates had gone on to college or job training; only one in five of those who had not attended preschool had any post-high-school education. Fully 45 percent of the preschool students were self-supporting by the age of nineteen; only one-fourth of those who went straight to grammar school could say the same. At age nineteen, the non-preschool group had produced 117 babies per 100 people; the former preschool students had borne only 64 per 100. By 1988, more than half of the non-preschool group had criminal arrest records, and nearly one-third were on welfare. Some 31 percent of the preschool students had been arrested, and 18 percent were on welfare—still too many, but a dramatic improvement.

The nation's largest preschool program is beginning to gather similar data. Educational researchers once pronounced Head Start a disappointing failure, because while its students left the program with higher average IQ levels than their peers, that early advantage invariably disappeared in the early years of grammar school. But in the mid-1980s they took a broader view of the program—and found results similar to those of the Perry Preschool study. Some 65 percent of Head Start students graduate from high school, compared with only 52 percent of those in their neighborhoods who miss out on the program. Head Start graduates are also less likely to require special-education classes, to be held back, to be arrested, or to become pregnant in their teens. They are more likely than others to attend college or hold down a job.

Head Start has been called the most successful government program of the last thirty years, so it comes as no surprise that it serves as a model for many of today's preschool and child-care programs, and of those proposed for the future. In a Head Start class, children play, paint pictures, practice counting and motor skills, and in general get used to the idea of spending the day away from home and finding a place in a society of their peers. Moreover, it both involves parents in their child's preschool program and helps them to solve their own personal and economic problems. Four out of five parents with children in Head Start programs volunteer to act as teacher's aides or provide other needed services. In return, Head Start programs offer them a variety of help, which ranges from nutrition education to free medical and dental checkups, family counseling, and references to local social service agencies. As a side effect, they may even get parents off the unemployment rolls. Those who volunteer as teacher's aides go through a well-respected training program, and many find paid jobs in private child-care programs.

Head Start began as a half-day program for three- and four-year-olds, and more than four out of five children in the program still attend for only four hours per day. However, the program has begun to adjust to the growing need for comprehensive care. Sixteen pilot projects around the country have set up day-care services for Head Start students. Children from the programs are "farmed out" to homes where carefully screened providers watch over up to five preschoolers each. Providers are trained by the school system's early-childhood specialists. The Head Start office provides books, musical instruments, and other such resources, to make sure that children continue their early education, rather than simply being warehoused until their parents come home from work. School monitors visit each home weekly to make sure that the providers are living up to the program's standards. For parents who cannot afford the cost of private day care, it offers a way to avoid abandoning their children each working day.

There are several answers to the needs of preschoolers in addition to the Head Start model. One successful program is HIPPY, the Home Instruction Program for Preschool Youngsters. Developed in Israel some twenty years ago to prepare immigrant children for that country's high-pressure school system, the statewide program now offers 1,400 low-income families in Arkansas a way to prepare their children for school. HIPPY is a two-year preschool program in which mothers teach their own children the skills they will need when they reach school age. HIPPY supplies mothers of three- and four-year-olds with books and worksheets for the curriculum, and mothers spend fifteen minutes per day with their children, five days per week, thirty days a year. Each week, paraprofessionals from the local school system visit the home to give parents training and advice.

Though mothers and children spend little time on the program, it has proved remarkably successful. After sixteen months in the program, children in one school improved their educational levels by an average of thirty-three months. As a side benefit, half of the mothers in two Arkansas counties, all on welfare, either returned to school, applied for job training, or found a job. At almost any price, such results would seem a bargain. At an actual cost of $500 to $600 per year—less than one-seventh the average cost per student of Head Start—they seem nearly miraculous.

In the Robert Taylor Homes on Chicago's decaying South Side, the nation's largest public housing project, the Center for Successful Child Development is taking child-care and preschool services all the way back to conception. Philanthropist Irving Harris came up with both the idea and half of the $1.2 million required to fund it. (The remainder was authorized by Congress and delivered by the federal Department of Health and Human Services.) Harris recruited 145 children who will enter kindergarten at Beethoven Elementary School in 1993, and thirty pregnant women whose children will also join the class. The Beethoven Project, as it is known, gives both children and mothers social, medical, and educational services for the first five years of the children's lives. Mothers receive prenatal care, counseling, and classes in child care. Children will get whatever medical care they need, and when the time comes, they will be enrolled in the project's preschool. A staff of trained social workers, teachers, and visiting doctors mans the center itself, which is housed on one floor of a Taylor tenement formerly used by vagrants and drug addicts. In addition, eight residents of the Taylor Homes have signed on as "family advocates," whose job it is to make sure that mothers and pregnant women keep their appointments at the center.

It is too soon to tell whether the center will make any difference in the school careers and later lives of its beneficiaries, but the program has already attracted strong support. Senator Edward Kennedy's Comprehensive Child Care Development Centers Act, signed into law in April 1988, authorized funding for Beethoven-style pilot projects in up to twenty-five cities. And the plan, starting early with an all-out effort to save the children of the poorest of the poor, makes an intuitive kind of sense. "If we don't do something with these five million people, they will grow to ten million," Harris points out. "Can we afford not to do it?"

Private enterprise, too, is moving to fill the gap in existing services, for obvious reasons. Two-thirds of the jobs created between now and 1995 will be taken by women—and four out of five will become pregnant at some time during their careers. Companies have found that it is a lot easier to attract and keep employees, both men and women, if they help them figure out what to do with the kids during the working day. It is also a lot cheaper to subsidize a worker's child-care bill, or even to provide an on-the-job nursery, than it is to find and train a new employee every time someone quits to care for their children.

One pioneer in the field is Nyloncraft, Inc., an auto-parts company in Mishawaka, Indiana. Ten years or so ago, the company had to hire and train 900 employees per year—at a cost of $2,000 each—just to maintain a work force of 250. Then the company set up a full-time nursery and preschool for children of its employees. It is an exciting life for children, whose daily activities can range from reading to horseback riding, and it costs parents just $33 per week. The company picks up another $28 in expenses, but at that it is a bargain. In 1987, when the nation's average job-turnover rate was 14 percent and the company employed 450 people, only twenty-five employees quit.

Grieco Brothers, a Lawrence, Massachusetts, clothing manufacturer, had a slightly different problem in 1984. The region's job market was booming in those days, and it was hard to attract employees to factory jobs that paid $8.75 an hour. The problem was so bad that the firm actually considered closing its doors. Instead, it set up an on-site child-care center. Unable to fund the operation on its own, the company got a neighboring clothier to join the project, then sought contributions from the city council, private foundations, and the state government. The employees' union agreed to a contribution of one cent per hour by each factory worker, and the state government added nearly $300,000 to subsidize fees for low-income parents. When the center opened after nearly two years of groundwork, it quickly solved the company's personnel problem.

More than 200 companies, 500 hospitals, and fifty government agencies have set up child-care centers on or near the job, but there are some less ambitious alternatives that have proved almost equally effective. Something over 1,500 companies offer child-care subsidies as an optional benefit, deducting the cost from an employee's gross income. Others operate referral services that help employees to find outside programs. And in several cases, neighboring companies have joined forces to recruit and train people willing to take employees' children into their homes during the day. In Minneapolis, a center called Chicken Soup offers day care for children with colds and more serious ills. Its operations are underwritten by a dozen local corporations, which also pay three-fourths of the $40 daily fee for the service. We will see many more innovative approaches to private child care in the years to come.

But probably the most influential program in the next decade will be the "Schools of the 21st Century," developed by Dr. Edward Ziglar, the Yale psychology professor generally regarded as the father of the Head Start program. We described Dr. Ziglar's basic concept at the beginning of this chapter: he would keep our public schools open throughout the working day, and long enough before and after so that parents could drop their children off on the way to work and pick them up on the way home. During that period, a separate faculty would provide competent, reliable care for children aged three through twelve whose parents were unavailable. Three- and four-year-olds would attend preschool programs, while five-year-olds would spend half a day in the regular kindergarten classes, then move to the child-care facility.

A comprehensive plan would offer even more services. First-time parents would be able to come to the school-based centers for prenatal advice and classes in parenting. Family day-care homes in the neighborhood could look to the centers for training and continuing guidance. And the child-care faculty would provide an information and referral service for those with special needs, such as night care or social services. Pilot programs for the Schools of the 21st Century are already operating. The experiment began a decade ago in Independence and Platte counties, in Missouri. Its first stage was an outreach program called Parents As First Teachers, designed to train new parents in the skills of parenting. In 1986, the first infant and toddler day-care center began operating within local elementary schools. And in 1987, before- and after-school care programs went into operation. Parents pay $18 to $24 per week for the before- and after-school program and $45 to $55 per week for full day care. Parents who cannot afford the service receive private subsidies. Perhaps unexpectedly, the program is actually self-supporting. The schools must keep the building clean and heated, so parents pay only for staff salaries.

Since then, thirteen local programs have been phased into operation in the Kansas City area. Connecticut has allocated $500,000 to set up at least three demonstration programs in 1990. And in 1988, Connecticut Senator Christopher Dodd and Michigan Representative Dale Kildee introduced a bill into Congress that would have anted up $120 million to establish at least one demonstration school in each state, sixty Schools of the 21st Century in all.

There are problems to be overcome with Ziglar's concept. Adding day-care services to a suburban or rural school building that may not be operating at capacity is relatively easy; doing the same in an urban school where classes overflow into the halls will not be. And maintaining a livable staff-to-student ratio—ideally not over one-to-ten—may require more trained early-childhood specialists than are available.

We believe these problems will be met and conquered. Not all child-care and preschool programs will share space in our existing elementary schools. Some will operate in other public buildings, others in private facilities donated or rented for the purpose, and still others in buildings constructed specifically for the purpose. But the services Ziglar envisions will be available throughout the country before the twenty-first century is a decade old.

In the long run, we envision an American child-care system that resembles those already available in virtually every nation of Western Europe. In Belgium and France, 95 percent of the nation's three-to-five-year-olds go off each morning to a nursery school or play group; they remain there for up to nine hours per day. In Italy, Germany, and Denmark, something over three-fourths of the children in this age group attend a preschool program. In Sweden and Finland, the figure is about two-thirds. And even in Britain and Ireland, which lag behind the rest of western Europe, half attend preschool and child-care programs.

France's *école maternelle* program, founded in the last century, sets the standard for European preschools. All children are eligible to attend, beginning three months after their second birthday; children of working mothers are favored only when space runs short. The preschool program is far more than simple day care. The curriculum is geared to the children's developmental level and is designed to promote their cognitive development. Like all European preschools, *école maternelle* is government-funded. Parents pay only for their children's lunch and for after-school child care; preschool is free.

Clearly, the American preschools and day-care centers of the early twenty-first century will differ form those of Europe in some crucial ways. Our tradition of local control ensures that they will not be monolithic programs operated by the central government. Most will be funded largely by state and local governments, with programs established as close to the grassroots level as possible. Both private schools and corporations will continue to offer their services. And given the budgetary problems of the state and federal governments, most parents will continue to pay for the programs their children attend.

But ten years from now, the shortage of preschools and day-care facilities in this country will be a thing of the past. And ten years after that, our national dropout rate will fall, test scores will climb, and we will know that the difficult task of building a whole new educational infrastructure was well worth the cost and effort it required.

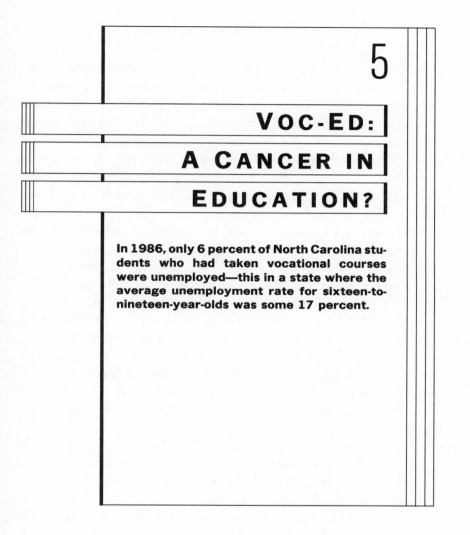

5

VOC-ED: A CANCER IN EDUCATION?

In 1986, only 6 percent of North Carolina students who had taken vocational courses were unemployed—this in a state where the average unemployment rate for sixteen-to-nineteen-year-olds was some 17 percent.

Among all the changes that will sweep our schools in the 1990s, probably none is more inevitable than the coming renaissance of job training as an alternative to the standard high-school curriculum. Ten years from now, any state that has not built a modern vocational-education program will be scrambling to catch up with its more foresighted neighbors.

The coming renaissance will be a dramatic change for voc-ed, which throughout much of the country has been struggling just to survive. In Illinois, for example, the high-school student population has shrunk by 17 percent since 1980; enrollment in the state's vocational-education programs has fallen 28 percent, and two of thirty-two voc-ed centers have been closed. Connecticut's vocational enrollment peaked at 12,408 students in 1983; by 1989 it had fallen to 10,484, one of the state's seventeen vocational-technical schools was running at 61 percent capacity, and another was at only 34 percent. And Maine's twenty-eight voc-tech schools were running at only half capacity in 1989. This pattern is repeated throughout much of the country.

Ironically, school reform itself is to blame for this decline. In their eagerness to tighten standards in traditional high-school programs, no fewer than forty-five states have raised the academic credit required for graduation. The change has often come at the cost of reduced vocational offerings. In California, for example, between 1982 (before *A Nation at Risk*) and 1985 (two years after), schools raised the number of sections of mathematics offered to their students by 19 percent. Science sections were up by 22 percent, foreign languages by 12 percent. In sharp contrast, they provided 21 percent fewer sections of home economics, 16 percent fewer of industrial arts, and 11 percent fewer business-education sections.

Thus, students who opt for a full job-training program, and can find the classes they need, have little chance to meet college entrance requirements. That is important, because about two-thirds of vocational-program graduates have traditionally gone on to two- or four-year colleges before entering the job market. Parental pressure to get a college degree has not fallen, so vocational enrollments have.

The reforms of the 1980s may also have diluted the value of a vocational-school education. Spending more time on academic studies inevitably means spending less on job-related courses. During the 1950s, the heyday of vocational education, voc-ed programs called for three years of job-specific training, a total of 1,620 classroom hours. By the mid-1980s, the average had dropped to just over 1,330 hours. Students today have less opportunity to master vocational skills than they would have had a decade ago.

Unfortunately, this has occurred at a time when good vocational programs are needed as never before. This need grows from two fundamental changes that are now transforming both the job market and American society as a whole.

One is the massive growth of technology, an economic and social force whose impact we have only begun to feel. Technology is now creating hundreds of new jobs; at the same time, it is rendering many existing careers obsolete and raising the educational level required for many traditional forms of employment; already, an estimated 73 percent of jobs require at least some information-processing skills. Thus the technical work force has become the fastest-growing job sector by far. In the 1990s, the demand for technical workers is expected to grow at least twice as fast as that for others.

Perhaps because many of us are intimidated by technology, we tend to imagine that it takes a college degree to master computers and other such wonders. In fact, fully three out of four people who hold down technical jobs are either technicians or blue-collar workers. Few of them require a college degree. For would-be data-processing specialists, medical technicians, and similarly skilled workers, a good vocational education can be a surer route to a career than the traditional academic skills. This is true even in fields that require further training in a two-year college program. In the future, some 75 percent of new jobs will not require a college degree, but will require specialized training of the kind in which vocational schools once excelled.

Treated in the 1980s as a poor relative of college-preparatory courses, our national voc-ed system has been unable to attract and train the students who need its help. As a result, the demand for skilled entry-level workers has considerably outgrown the supply. Thus the youth unemployment rate is three times the national average, while well-paid jobs go begging because there are too few trained workers to fill them. And as salaries in technical jobs rise quickly, the real mean income for males aged twenty to twenty-four has declined by almost one-third since the early 1970s.

In the near future, the shortage of trained technical workers will grow even worse, because of the second fundamental change in society: the "baby boomers" have produced fewer offspring per person than any generation in history, so the entry-age labor pool is shrinking in a way not seen since World War II drained the world of its young men. In 1985, some 30 percent of the workers in the United States were sixteen to twenty-four years old. By 2000, the figure will be barely 16 percent. Twenty years ago, employers could take their pick of motivated entry-level workers, many of them with good vocational skills. Ten years from now, there will be too few new job-hunters with any level of training.

In an effort to cope with the scarcity of skilled workers, companies like IBM, Ford, and Xerox now spend $210 billion per year to train their employees. Some of that corporate educational budget goes to remedial classes in the "three R's," offering skills that forty years ago would have been required for a high-school diploma. Much more corporate money funds the kind of job training that only the best public vocational schools now provide.

Unfortunately, corporate education in the Fortune 500 mold reaches only a minority of workers. Perhaps one-third ever receive any form of on-the-job training, and relatively few of them are the entry-level employees who by rights should have received basic vocational training in high school. Most first-time job-hunters find employment in very small firms; in 1984, more than 40 percent of people in their twenties worked for companies with fewer than nineteen employees. Such employers have neither the time nor the money to provide training in basic vocational skills. As entry-level workers already prepared to hold down a job become harder and harder to find, the small companies that depend on them will find it ever more difficult to survive.

Well before the 1990s are over, this worker shortage will begin to slow the growth of many high-tech industries on which the United States must depend for its survival in the international marketplace. We will feel the impact of this development throughout our economy.

If we permit it to occur. The best way to prevent economic disaster is to begin now to rebuild our vocational-technical programs so that they can meet the demands soon to be placed on them. At a minimum, this means replacing the old-fashioned auto shop/industrial arts/home-ec focus to provide courses suited to the modern, high-tech economy; the workers of the 1990s require classes in robot technology and repair, hazardous-waste control, medical technologies of all kinds, and many similar specialties. Some other changes would help as well. A few school systems have already shown the way.

One dramatically successful vocational program operates in Council Bluffs, Iowa. It suffers the same problems that plague other voc-ed systems: a declining school-age population, tight budgets, and rising academic graduation requirements. Yet vocational enrollments leaped by 32 percent in the 1988 school year alone, and Council Bluffs has added six new vocational programs in only three years. There are now eighteen vocational programs in a district of only 9,800 students.

Local school leaders cite a number of factors that they believe are crucial to this success. One is a curriculum plan that makes it easy for students to find a niche in the local job market. In grades nine and ten, Council Bluffs voc-ed pupils take short "exploratory programs" designed to introduce them to possible careers. In grades eleven and twelve, they take preparatory or cooperative education programs. Preparatory programs give students in-depth training in such fields as auto maintenance, child care, office work, and health technologies. Cooperative education actually places students with local businesses to gain practical work experience related to their school courses.

So far, there is not much about the Council Bluffs system that could not be found in dozens of other voc-ed programs. Four factors help to make it work, and each will play a major role in the success of future vocational programs:

- A tight focus on the real-world job market. New courses are designed, and old courses updated, to meet the needs revealed by surveys of the job market in Iowa and Nebraska conducted periodically by the U.S. Department of Labor and Iowa and Nebraska Job Services.
- An emphasis on the traditional academic skills. Math, science, and communication are stressed continuously by weaving them into each practical course. So are higher-level thinking

skills. This integrated approach may give students a firmer grounding in the "three R's" than do book-and-blackboard classes.

- Iowa Western Community College. IWCC conducts all preparatory classes under contract to the Council Bluffs Community School District. Students gain more than access to the college staff. Where vocational classes correspond to those given by IWCC, they may receive up to one semester of college credit per course. In a two-year vocational program, they can complete up to half of their college requirements while still in high school.

- Money. Vocational classes cost, on average, two to three times as much as academic courses, so voc-ed programs are invariably strapped for funds. The state of Iowa contributes up to $1,200 per pupil sent to a regional vocational program—this in addition to the usual budget. The state also pays up to half of the money required for equipment to start a new program. Council Bluffs administrators add to this by scraping for every possible source of added funding. As a result, vocational courses cost the school district only $96 per credit in local tax dollars, compared with $200 for academic courses.

All these efforts have given Council Bluffs a vocational program that thrives while others struggle just to survive. Other communities could easily duplicate them. In the years to come, many will do so.

One current trend in voc-ed is to prepare students not to find jobs but to build their own businesses. North Carolina is pioneering in this field as well. Their approach can be seen in action at the Way Off Broadway Deli, just off I-95 in St. Paul's. It is one of four businesses owned and operated by the state's secondary-school students. REAL Enterprises, the sponsoring agency, and its founder, Jonathan Sher, have hit on a model that works in rural areas. Entrepreneurship, another practical project, got its start when the North Carolina Small Business and Technology Development Center asked vocational teachers how their coverage of entrepreneurism could be improved. About a third of the responding teachers had owned their own businesses, and virtually all of them endorsed the idea of a course in how to evaluate a business idea and turn it into a successful company. As an outgrowth of these projects, local executives helped prepare teachers to develop "trainer" businesses, and fifty-five of the state's best voc-ed students took a five-day workshop in finance, marketing, and other basics at the University of North Carolina. After that, it took more than a year of hard work to ready the first business to open its doors. Today the deli and its companion endeavors teach the basics of entrepreneurism through hands-on experience.

Alaska's Mount Edgecumbe High School, a 200-student boarding school in the state's southeastern panhandle, offers another example of student business-building. Students there operate Edgecumbe Enterprises, a four-year-old export business that sells smoked salmon to Japan. Mount Edgecumbe has organized its program around the economic and social relationship between Alaska and the Pacific Rim nations. This theme runs through all the school's courses, and students must take at least one year of Japanese or Mandarin Chinese, and one year of studies in Pacific Rim cultures in order to graduate. When the idea of a hands-on business came up, trading with the East was the obvious field to enter. Students helped write the business plan, design packaging and promotional literature, and analyze markets and expenses. They have even made three marketing trips, two to Japan and one to China. In spring of 1989 the firm made its first shipments to Japanese customers, who paid $24 per pound for the students' product.

In tapping this market, Mount Edgecumbe's students have learned firsthand a lesson that everyone in business is being forced to master: the world has shrunk so rapidly that there are no purely local industries left. Anyone who hopes to make a career in business must think globally. Thus, the global viewpoint should be introduced into the curriculum wherever possible, and particularly in the vocational and technical subjects. Student-run companies provide a level of global business understanding that no classroom lectures could hope to achieve. This is another approach that we believe many schools will adopt during the next decade.

One more model worth following is Oklahoma's Self-Employment Training Program, a six-month course for fledgling entrepreneurs. The course is built around the development of a business plan, in which each student details the process of turning an idea into a profitable company. The students attend seminars on business topics and weekly one-on-one meetings with their instructors. Then they examine their chosen industry, analyze local economic trends, and actually write a business plan. By the summer of 1988, 146 students had completed the program. Fully sixty-one had opened their own businesses, which a year later employed 102 people.

Though Oklahoma is the only state thus far to adopt this method of entrepreneurial training, that kind of success should help it to spread rapidly. The Self-Employment Training Program is now being marketed for use elsewhere by Control Data Corporation, in Minneapolis. So far, more than a dozen schools in other parts of the country have taken up the idea.

In many communities, vocational education is rapidly providing answers to educational problems and economic decline. Throughout the 1980s, Pittsburgh has suffered both. Though several surveys have ranked it as the nation's "most livable city," its traditional mainstay industries, steel and heavy manufacturing, have been failing for many years. As a result, Pittsburgh has lost more than 100,000 jobs since the early 1980s. In addition, more than half of the city's 40,000 students are from minority groups, and seven out of eight are poor enough to qualify for government-subsidized lunch programs. The dropout rate is 27 percent, and one teenaged girl in ten becomes pregnant. More than half of young black men are unemployed.

In response to all these problems, Pittsburgh has made a determined effort to strengthen its vocational programs, with a good deal of success. The city's high schools now offer close to forty courses in vocational and technical fields such as computerized auto mechanics, accounting, business computing, and dental assistance; more than half of all high-school students are enrolled in at least one of them. A program called Occupational and Academic Skills for the Employment of Students (OASES) teaches construction theory and tool technology to more than 100 middle-school students who seem likely to drop out of traditional courses. The Select

Employment Training Program provides tutors and mentors for about 2,000 poor high-school students each year. Schenley High School serves as a high-tech magnet school; courses range from basic electricity to digital electronics and robotics, and the theme permeates the traditional academic courses as well.

One of the city's most successful programs is the Business and Finance Academy, a school-within-a-school housed by the Westinghouse High School. The academy is one of three set up by the Edna McConnel Clark Foundation and the National Urban League. (The others are Houston's Microprocessor-Based Equipment Technology Academy and the Financial Service Technology Academy, in Portland, Oregon.) Each year the academy takes in fifty freshmen with problems such as chronic truancy and sleeping in class. Students spend their next three years in a special finance program designed with the help of five area banks. Local businesses provide mentors, summer jobs, and entry-level employment after graduation.

The results show just how much can be accomplished, even with students who are clearly in trouble. The academy's graduation rate is fully 100 percent. Seven out of eight students have graduated with a grade-point average of 2.5 or better. Half go on to college, and another 40 percent are in the military or a full-time job a year after graduation.

In fact, though Pittsburgh's program is one of the nation's most dramatic success stories, there is nothing new about using vocational education to keep potential dropouts in school. Philadelphia has had problems like those of its neighboring city, and it has been using voc-ed to fight them for more than twenty years. In 1969 the city set up the first of four high-school academies: the Academy of Applied Electrical Science, the Academy of Automotive and Mechanical Science, the Philadelphia Business Academy, and the Philadelphia Health Academy. Local businesses provide technical assistance, special equipment, money, and jobs for students, both during the summer and after graduation. All the schools have strong academic programs as well as vocational classes, but curricula are tied to the school's specialty. At the Academy of Automotive and Mechanical Science, for example, algebra problems are related to car repair, while at the Academy of Applied Electrical Science, math examples relate to electricity and electronics.

The academies are not traditional magnet schools. They target students whose skills or motivation are so poor that they would not qualify for standard vocational training. Some 95 percent are minority students. When they enter one of the academies, nearly all rank in the bottom third of the nation's students on standardized achievement tests. Yet their dropout rate approaches zero, and fully 85 percent of academy graduates are employed a year after graduation.

One of the nation's most successful voc-ed systems belongs to North Carolina. The state's secondary-level program serves upwards of 300,000 students, nearly 65 percent of the state's seventh-through-twelfth-graders. In addition to taking the updated consumer home economics and industrial-arts programs, students can specialize in agribusiness, business and office skills, health occupations, occupational home economics, marketing, and trade and industry. By the time students graduate from one of these programs, they are ready to begin careers in child-care services, manufacturing, marketing, communications, or a variety of other fields. The most popular program is business and office skills, with more than 130,000 students. Second, with 84,000 students, is "career exploration," a general orientation program designed for students who have yet to map out their future.

The state has worked hard to ensure that these courses equip students with the skills they need to make it in the real world. In the 1986–87 school year alone, North Carolina schools added 625 new voc-ed courses, expanded or modernized 1,103 more, and dropped fully 1,206 courses that had become obsolete. And this attention to market needs is paying off. In 1986, only 6 percent of North Carolina students who had taken vocational courses were unemployed—this in a state where the average unemployment rate for sixteen-to-nineteen-year-olds was some 17 percent. Fully two-thirds of the state's voc-ed graduates report that their work is closely related to the classroom experience. In all, this is probably the best in vocational education as we traditionally have known it.

But North Carolina also provides an advance look at the voc-ed programs of the early twenty-first century. It can be found at the Lincoln County School of Technology (LCST), in Lincolnton. Built with a grant of just over $1 million provided by the Timken Foundation, LCST opened in 1987 with 450 students. Unlike most vocational schools, Lincoln is more of a magnet program or an extension of the regular high-school program. During the day, it is open to all juniors and seniors from the East Lincoln, Lincolnton, and West Lincoln Senior High Schools. From mid-afternoon until ten P.M., adults attend the same courses for community-college credit, provided by nearby Gaston College. The same building also houses the Economic Development Office for Lincoln County, forming a close link between vocational programs and the local business leaders who provide jobs for their graduates. This new community education and training facility is a model for school financing: state funds, local school funds, local businesses, and a national foundation all contribute to its support.

LCST offers the traditional 1950s courses in auto mechanics, carpentry, and office administration, but the curriculum is aimed squarely at the job market of the late 1990s. Courses fall into three broad categories: health and human services, business and marketing, and industrial technologies. Within these groups are such major subject areas as geriatric care, child care, paralegal services, management and entrepreneurship, and computer-aided design. Specific courses include computerized accounting, CNC (computerized numeric control) machining, and desktop publishing. Students in any specialty area may dabble in the other fields whenever their schedules allow. There are no generalized "computer literacy" courses; computers are so much a part of every program that it is hardly possible to attend LCST without mastering their use in your chosen field. Graduates are eligible to attend Gaston College, which offers two-year associate degrees in health and human services, business/marketing, and industrial technologies.

A critical part of the LCST program is work experience. Local employers have cooperative education programs to give the school's students practical, paid, on-the-job training. The goal is not so much "vocationalism"--providing specific job skills—as employability, giving students the complex of generalized skills, attitudes, and discipline required to get and hold any job. This is one feature that virtually all vocational schools will adopt in the years to come.

LCST has not been operating long enough yet to quote statistics about the workplace success of graduates, but it seems clear that the school has found a major part of the formula for vocational education at the turn of the twenty-first century, and has the total support of the community's businesses and industries. Its students should have little trouble finding a home in the modern workplace.

Lincoln is not alone in this. At least three other vocational centers around the country offer similar programs; in fact, Lincoln County's curriculum and methods were in part modeled on them.

Oklahoma's Francis Tuttle Vo Tech Center, in Oklahoma City, offers twenty-eight outstanding career programs, most of them in fast-growing high-tech fields. Among them are aviation, banking, finance, computer-aided design, robot technology, and process and pneumatic control. In addition, there are some unusual programs designed to meet local needs. One specializes in the care and training of horses. Another, designed for small business, deals with bidding for contracts with the government and larger industries. In six years of Tuttle's operation, more than 240,000 high-school students have taken at least one course at the facility, as well as 10,000 adults.

The nearly new Great Oaks Joint Vocational School, in Cincinnati, has graduated only 3,000 high-school students since its opening, and has given single courses to more than 65,000 adults. Its courses in aviation and other growing careers is supported by a strong focus on academic subjects and by a variety of programs for students with special needs. One unique program trains would-be Ford dealers, while another specializes in harness racing, a major industry in the region.

In the Tidewater Basin of Virginia, the New Horizons Center has built itself a unique support network within the community. In addition to offering high-tech subjects, advanced-placement programs, and special courses for the gifted and talented, New Horizons draws on the Governor's School of Science for academic and technical support. Its 1,400 students per year also receive practical guidance from mentors provided by local business and by the National Aeronautics and Space Administration.

All these schools have some common elements, which we believe are critical to the success of vocational training in the 1990s. One is a rigorous focus on the job market: courses for Linotype operators and old-fashioned welders have been replaced by desktop publishing and robotic welding, and each school provides unique courses keyed to local industries.

All three do their best to be accessible to any student who needs their programs. They operate from 7:00 A.M. to 10:00 P.M. five days a week throughout the year. They even provide computerized training vans that carry business education to local factories and offices. And students need not sign up for an entire four years; they can study what they need, from one course through an entire program, and then return to their home schools or to work.

Finally, all three schools stress academic as well as vocational subjects. This attention to their students' continuing education is a growing trend among vocational schools, and one that we believe is a key to their long-term success. Students in traditional vocational programs take nearly as many academic courses, on average, as those in standard academic high schools, but the courses have tended to be somewhat watered down, and many of them have been one-shot courses that did not allow students to build a useful level of competence in any subject. So-called "tech-prep" programs seek to remedy this defect by encouraging voc-ed students to take more advanced courses, especially in English, science, math, and computer science. Most schools adopting them have coordinated their efforts with those of local colleges to make certain their courses will be accepted for college credit.

One leader of the tech-prep movement is the Center for Occupational Research and Development. CORD has devised a variety of two-year technical curricula that many institutions accept for college credit. Among these are Applied Mathematics, Applied Biology/Chemistry, and the Principles of Technology program chosen by former Education Secretary William Bennett as part of his James Madison High School curriculum. In their first year, these programs concentrate on basic concepts; in the second, they move on to applications. For example, Principles of Technology spends its first year examining such ideas as force, work, energy, and power; in its second year it deals with the complexities of waves and vibrations, transducers, radiation, and optical systems. Nearly two dozen four-year colleges have agreed to recognize Principles of Technology as satisfying a laboratory-science entrance requirement. Similar programs will be a common feature of advanced voc-ed programs in the coming decade.

The next step up from tech-prep are the "2+2" and "2+2+2" programs, in which eleventh- and twelfth-grade vocational programs are coordinated with courses in local junior colleges (2+2) or four-year colleges (2+2+2). The idea is to provide an integrated educational system that gives students a solid background in both academic and vocational subjects. Though 2+2+2 programs are too new to provide solid statistics on the success of their students, it seems clear that they are one wave of the future. Lincoln, Tuttle, Great Oaks, and New Horizons all offer such programs, and many vocational schools with more traditional programs are hurrying to follow their lead. For students who find it difficult to learn in more formal, less "relevant" high-school programs, 2+2+2 may offer the best route to both a rewarding career and higher education.

We could go on telling voc-ed success stories for the rest of this book. Oklahoma's program has more to offer than Tuttle's courses and the program in entrepreneurship we singled out. Florida's vocational program is so good, especially at the community-college level, that its graduates have become a major attraction for high-tech industry, which has flowered along the hundred-odd miles of Interstate 4 from Orlando to Tampa–St. Petersburg. And local programs worthy of attention are dotted all over the American map. But we think the point has been made: Vocational education more than justifies its place in the national school system. For all the reasons we cited at the beginning of this chapter, it will experience its own educational renaissance throughout the rest of this decade.

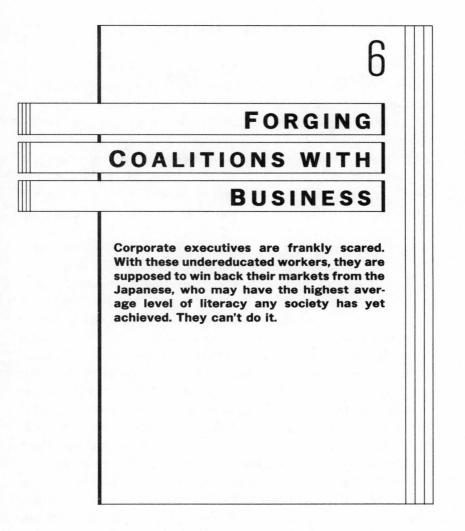

6

FORGING
COALITIONS WITH
BUSINESS

Corporate executives are frankly scared. With these undereducated workers, they are supposed to win back their markets from the Japanese, who may have the highest average level of literacy any society has yet achieved. They can't do it.

Here is the easiest forecast in this book: In the 1990s, American business will become ever more deeply involved in our schools. Large corporations and small ones all over the country will send their executives to work as mentors with students at risk of dropping out. They will sponsor classes designed to teach the skills students will need for success in later life. They will pay to send teachers to training seminars. They will even pay their own employees to drop out of the corporate life and become teachers themselves. We know all that for a fact, because this trend has been building for more than ten years.

Business leaders have taken a long, hard look at America's schools, and they do not like what they see. As things stand, the next generation of workers will not just be too small to fill all the job openings that industry could create for them, it will be too ignorant. According to federal estimates, about three-fourths of all jobs created in the 1980s were for white-collar workers—nearly 20 percent were professional and technical openings—and the proportion is growing. In 1989 the average job called for 12.8 years of education; by 2000, 13.5 years will be needed, thanks largely to the growing role of technology in almost all industries. Yet nearly one million children drop out of school every year, and find that they are all but unemployable. To hold down most jobs these days, workers must read at least as well as the average high-school student once did—well enough, say, to cope with *The New York Times;* about 70 percent of the reading required in a cross-section of typical jobs is at the ninth- to twelfth-grade level. Yet an estimated 27 million Americans have trouble reading the *National Enquirer,* and their writing and math skills are no better. Another 46 million function at what used to be the level of fifth-to-eighth-graders—and as things stand the number will be larger ten years from now. According to the *Business Roundtable,* "as many as sixty percent of high school graduates are not prepared for entry-level jobs."

Already, companies are finding it next to impossible to locate people to fill job openings. When four New York City banks went looking for 250 people qualified to take entry-level jobs, they could find only 100. A Chicago bank found that three-fourths of the people who applied for its entry-level jobs could not even fill in the application forms. When the New York City telephone company tested 3,000 job applicants, only 25 percent were found employable. And when Motorola tested 3,000 job applicants at its Arlington Heights, Illinois, facility in 1988, half failed; the company requires new employees to demonstrate fifth-grade math and seventh-grade reading skills. In this decade, American industry will be forced to hire one million new workers each year who cannot read, write, or count well enough to do their jobs.

As a result, companies are now doing much of the schooling that public institutions once did. They now spend $210 billion per year to train their employees—about $30 billion more than the national budget for primary and secondary schools. Much of that goes for remedial programs to teach the skills any high-school graduate once would have possessed. More than 30 percent of companies that employ 10,000 people now offer remedial instruction for their employees, and the number grows larger every year. By 1993, Motorola alone will have spent $35 million to teach basic reading skills to employees; the firm's total training budget amounts to $50 million per year. The Aetna Institute for Corporate Education, operated by Aetna Life & Casualty, in Hartford, Connecticut, serves no fewer than 28,000 students per year; Aetna spends $40 million a year on employee education. David Kearns, chairman and chief executive officer of Xerox Corporation, estimates that teaching workers basic literacy and math skills, and absorbing the lost productivity while they are learning, will cost industry $25 billion per year until our schools can again handle the task themselves.

Corporate executives are frankly scared. With these undereducated workers, they are supposed to win back their markets from the Japanese, who may have the highest average level of literacy any society has yet achieved. They can't do it. Because of this, according to a recent poll by the Conference Board, two-thirds of American companies now say that education is their number-one community-relations concern.

They are showing that concern in a wide variety of ways. According to a report by the National Center for Education Statistics, there were more than 140,000 "education partnerships" sponsored by industry and private foundations—up from 42,000 only four years earlier. More than 40 percent of the nation's grammar and high schools participate in at least one such cooperative program, and the number is growing so rapidly that it will reach virtually 100 percent well before the turn of the century. Over 9 million students were involved in such partnerships. Many company-based programs were limited to providing guest speakers, hosting tours, and similarly modest efforts, but many were far more ambitious. According to the Council for Aid to Education, corporate donations to precollege education totaled some $200 million in 1987. They are rising rapidly.

The best known collaboration between business and our schools almost has to be the I Have A Dream Foundation, started by industrialist Eugene Lang, who returned to his New York City school to deliver a speech and stayed to offer college scholarships to any students who made it through to graduation. Lang backed up his offer by hiring a guidance counselor/social worker to help students cope with their personal obstacles, and volunteered his own time to act as a mentor for the children whose lives he was trying to change.

Lang's spur-of-the-moment idea has proved remarkably successful. There were sixty-one students in that first eighth-grade class; seven years after Lang made his offer, fifty of them had graduated from high school, and thirty-six were in college. Other philanthropists inspired by this one example have given the same chance to upwards of 8,000 inner-city students.

Some other corporate education efforts have been aimed a lot more closely at meeting the company's own needs. In the mid-1980s, Toyota USA looked a few years into the future and found itself staring at a problem: By the early 1990s, its dealers were going to need up to 4,000 new technicians. The company had no idea where to find them. It solved its problem by setting up the Toyota Technical Education Network, a consortium of fifty-six vocational schools and community colleges, to develop a special curriculum for would-be auto repairmen. From their first day on the job, Network graduates are ready to work on Toyota cars. More than 1,000 students are now enrolled in the program. To date, something over four out of five who have completed their training have taken jobs with the company.

Most corporate education programs fall somewhere between Eugene Lang's selfless generosity and Toyota's enlightened approach to its own bottom line. Companies have tried a rich variety of ideas to aid our schools.

Since 1982, Ashland Oil, a Kentucky-based refiner, has put its entire regional advertising budget into education. A key part of their effort is a campaign to lower the dropout rate. Its major weapon is a series of commercials aimed at dropout-prone children and their parents. One shows a young girl holding her baby. "Jobs are pretty scarce around here," she warns. " 'Specially since neither my husband or me finished school. Things are gonna be different for this one. He's gonna stay in high school if I have to tie him to his chair. Sometimes I wish someone had done me that way." The commercials were so effective that the National Advertising Council and the Council of State Governments adopted them—stripped of the Ashland logo—for a nationwide public-service campaign.

In 1987, General Electric opened a new plastics factory in poor, predominantly black Lowndes County, Alabama, then discovered that its new neighbors were too poorly educated to fill the 350 jobs created by the plant. In response, the company has poured $1 million into a five-year program that aims to triple the number of children the county sends to college. Part of the money will go for scholarships to Alabama colleges. The rest is funding supplemental teacher training, SAT-preparation courses, and Saturday classes in math and science.

General Electric is also a guiding force behind the Manhattan Center for Science and Mathematics, in New York City's impoverished Spanish Harlem. In their off-hours, company executives tutor students and teach special classes to prepare the mostly-minority children for engineering and science courses at such prestigious institutions as MIT and Stanford. The results are impressive. Where the school once graduated only thirty students from a class of 1,000—it was then known as Benjamin Franklin High School, and was closed down because of its dismal performance—in the first two years of its reincarnation, 95 percent of the seniors won their diplomas.

In Massachusetts, Polaroid Corporation decided to help solve a desperate shortage of science and math teachers. The firm's "Project Bridge" pays up to ten company employees each year to attend a year-long teacher-certification program at Harvard University or Lesley College, in Boston. Teachers-to-be receive their full salary, tuition, books, and other expenses.

Nearly ten years ago, American Express and Shearson Lehman Hutton joined forces with the New York City public schools to create the Academy of Finance, a two-year program that trains high-school students for careers in the financial services industry.

Students take their full course loads plus classes in economics and finance and seminars designed to inculcate good work habits. The program has grown dramatically since its early years. In New York, some fifty major financial companies now contribute to the program. American Express now sponsors finance programs in thirty high schools in fourteen cities, and has launched an Academy of Tourism and Travel, with branches in New York, Miami, and London. The academies are not rescue programs for potential dropouts; juniors and seniors must have a 75 average to get in. But for those who are already motivated, they have proved uncommonly beneficial. About 90 percent of academy graduates go on to college.

We will close out this brief survey with a look at two of the nation's most ambitious and comprehensive coalitions between the business and education communities. We believe that many of the educational programs of the 1990s will follow these models.

In a Chicago ghetto called North Lawndale, local corporations have set up the tuition-free Corporate Community School for two-to-eight-year-olds. Like Eugene Lang's I Have A Dream Foundation, the school is the creation of a local boy made good. Joe Kellman grew up in Lawndale until the age of fourteen; today he heads a glass business with sales of $100 million a year. He has managed to recruit many other wealthy Chicago executives to his cause. Among the school's sixty or so sponsors are Sears, Baxter International, United Airlines, McDonald's, and Quaker Oats. Unquestionably, any educational program in North Lawndale needs all the help it can get.

Being born in this part of Chicago is a difficult way to begin life in modern America, a guarantee that you will be poor and bereft of successful role models. Four children out of five in the neighborhood are born to single women. It is impossible to grow up without being exposed to drugs and violence. And until the Corporate Community School came along, it was impossible to find a good education, if by some miracle you understood the need for one. In 1986, Chicago students did so badly in one standardized test that fully half of the city's high schools ranked in the bottom 1 percent of U.S. schools.

Joe Kellman's school does its best to compensate for its sorry environment by providing social services that the government has not. Parents are invited in for adult education classes that can eventually get them a high-school diploma—or at least keep them from falling too far behind their children's reading skill—and incidentally maintain the crucial parental involvement in their children's education. When teachers discovered that one child was living in an abandoned building without heat or utilities, they arranged for public assistance. And the school teaches basic hygiene to children who have little experience of it.

There is nothing revolutionary about teaching at the Corporate Community School—just the best conventional education that a $1-million-a-year budget can buy. Teachers receive about 10 percent more than those in the city's public schools, and they are spared the bureaucratic suffocation endemic in big-city institutions. Classes are limited to twenty-five students, and teaching methods are carefully tailored to the individual student's needs. There is no hint of tracking, because there are no set grades; students learn at their own pace and move on only when their current subject has been mastered.

It is a decade too soon to tell how much effect the Corporate Community School will have on the lives of its graduates; the first class entered the program in 1988. But it is clear that local parents are betting an education at the business-backed school will mean more than one at local public schools. In 1988, the first 150 students had to be chosen by lottery from more than 1,000 applicants. A year later, with only fifty openings, over 1,400 applied.

Another exemplary coalition between the school and business communities is the Cincinnati Youth Collaborative, a citizen-action group that offers a broad range of educational and social services. Supported by such firms as Procter & Gamble, Cincinnati Bell, General Electric, and Cincinnati Milacron, the CYC program begins with preschool and follows the city's students through entry into college or their first jobs.

There are two preschool pilot projects so far, one at the McKinley Elementary School and one at Taft High School, and four classes for three-year-olds in all. Students in the programs make a beginning at learning to read, write, solve problems, and get along with others, but less-specific benefits may be even more important. Children in the school district come primarily from poor inner-city families. Many suffer from low self-esteem, belligerence, and other behavioral disorders that, left unattended, could easily condemn them to educational failure. Aided by a consultant from the Cincinnati Center for Development Disorders, the preschool program offers them their first chance to get help.

The Taft District Project, based at Taft High School and at the Porter and Bloom middle schools, offers a variety of programs aimed at helping at-risk students to improve their academic performance and remain in school. These include Earn & Learn, which provides both summer jobs and remedial classes; EdVenture, which gives many students their first exposure to local cultural centers and to the campuses of nearby universities; and Jobs for Cincinnati Graduates, a part-time employment program designed to help high-school juniors remain in school after they have decided to drop out. Other programs have found mentors and tutors for students in need of individual attention, helped to introduce team teaching to local middle schools, and offered supplementary training classes for Cincinnati public-school teachers.

For those nearing graduation, CYC offers two kinds of program: Some efforts are designed to route students into college, while others help to fit those destined for the workplace into jobs available in the area. CYC's College Information Center provides seniors and their parents with catalogs and supplementary information from every college and university in the country and helps them to fill out college applications and financial aid forms. A program known as Scholarships for Our Kids provided grants totaling $200,000 to 127 local graduates attending college in the 1988–89 school year. A year later, some 220 students received a total of $300,000. For those not attending college, the Jobs Network helps to place high-school graduates with local companies. In 1989, Employer Forums helped Cincinnati businesses and social-service agencies to find both summer and permanent jobs for more than 250 graduates. Other agencies associated with the Cincinnati Youth Collaborative help to place more than 1,000 young residents in permanent jobs each year, and found more than 4,000 summer jobs for young people in 1989.

Though CYC has not been in operation long, the group is already gathering precise, businesslike data on its successes and failures in meeting its goals. The organization had hoped to increase by 2.5 percentage points per year the number of students scoring at or above the national norm in reading, language, and mathematics; in the 1988–89 school year, it hit its target in reading and language, but scored a miss in math. It hoped to increase student promotion rates by 1 percent per year in the first grade and by 2 percent in grades seven through nine; promotions shot up by 2.6 percent in the first grade, but fell short of the target in the upper levels. A third goal was to increase the percentage of high-school students enrolled in one or more academic courses; in this it succeeded handily.

By now it should be clear that business not only has a vital interest in the American school system, but is putting its time and money where its needs are. Coalitions similar to the ones described above have been springing up throughout the United States. At this point, there is hardly a Fortune 500 company that is not involved in the schools of every community where it has a major presence. Many mid-sized concerns have followed their lead. In the 1990s this trend will gain such momentum that no school system in need of help will have to go without. This enormous and growing corporate support represents a source of funding and personnel that the federal and state governments combined could never hope to equal. For America's students, this is one of the most hopeful developments we have to offer.

PART II

CLASSROOM REFORMS

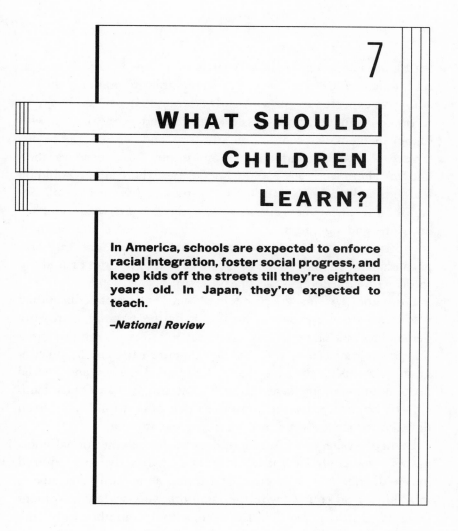

7

WHAT SHOULD CHILDREN LEARN?

In America, schools are expected to enforce racial integration, foster social progress, and keep kids off the streets till they're eighteen years old. In Japan, they're expected to teach.

–National Review

In part, the dismal performance of schools today reflects a simple dilution of standards. Faced with tight budgets, overcrowded class-rooms, teacher shortages, and endless social problems, educators have simply given up. It seems that if society is not willing to pay for well-educated high-school graduates, then it will have to settle for ignoramuses.

But in part, poor academic achievement also reflects a growing uncertainty about what constitutes a good education in a modern society. A century ago, though illiteracy was common, there was at least a broad consensus about what students needed to learn. The traditional "three R's" were the irreducible minimum a literate adult was expected to know. A truly educated man would be fluent in other languages, both classical and modern, comfortable with higher mathematics, familiar with history, and—in this age of discovery—conversant with "natural philosophy," as science was then known. There were one-room schoolhouses where all this could be learned, and routinely was. Today, Greek and Latin have all but vanished from our nation's schools, while English, math, and science are endangered species of learning. Students and teachers spend valuable class time on sex education, phys-ed, antidrug propaganda, and an endless list of electives that have little or nothing to do with education as we once knew it.

For school systems, the problem of where to devote educational resources is made even more difficult by the large and growing demand for special programs. Handicapped students require attention to their special needs. Toddlers require early-childhood programs. "At-risk" students demand remedial classes and special dropout-prevention efforts. All such programs, no matter how laudable or necessary, take up resources that once would have been devoted to basic education for mainstream students.

Perhaps worse, there is little uniformity in the educational smorgasbord that confronts today's students. Courses that are required in one district may be electives in another and wholly unavailable in a third. And courses with the same title vary widely in content from one district to another, from one school to another within the same district, and often from one classroom to another within the same school. Introductory algebra in a Chicago magnet school has little in common with the same course as taught elsewhere in the city, much less in a poor rural district in the Deep South. In the best schools, students are still exposed to the information they need in science, math, and history, if not in Latin. But in much of our national school system, we have allowed course contents to become so diluted that students often could learn as much by taking the day off as by attending class.

Is this one reason that students today lack what once were basic skills, that both teachers and students spend so much of their attention on other matters that key information is lost, even in courses nominally devoted to the fundamentals? Some educators have begun to think so. And in response to that growing suspicion, they have focused on developing a core curriculum. The idea is to identify the knowledge and skills required for modern life, concentrate on those basics, and test regularly to make certain that each child has learned all that is required for each grade before passing on to the next.

In some cases, at least, this attention to basics has already paid off. The Anoka-Hennepin school district, in a blue-collar suburb of Grand Rapids, Michigan, has achieved one of the best overall reputations for effective teaching in the Midwest. Superintendent Lewis Finch gives the credit to the development of a core curriculum followed by teachers throughout the district. Students are tested often, both district-wide and in each of the thirty-six schools. In each school, the teachers and principal look at the test scores and decide which subjects require greater emphasis. As a result, the district's 33,000 students consistently turn in some of the state's best scores on standardized tests.

Similar success stories are even easier to find overseas. One reason that Japanese students know so much about mathematics, science, Japanese and foreign languages, social sciences—in short, the basic knowledge that has become so rare among American high-school graduates—is that educators there have little doubt about the information that makes up a basic education. "In America, schools are expected to enforce racial integration, foster social progress, and keep kids off the streets till they're eighteen years old," the *National Review* summarized the situation. "In Japan, they're expected to teach." The Japanese national Department of Education sets a curriculum that guides schools throughout the country. Principals receive a detailed syllabus for courses in Japanese language and literature, science, math, social science, moral education, music, and physical education. Inspectors visit each institution at frequent intervals to make sure that teachers conform to the program. Standards are far higher than those in most American public schools, and Japanese children are held to them until the age of fifteen.

National curricula govern education throughout most of Europe as well, though few specify the material to be covered in as much detail as does the Japanese plan. Great Britain, the last European nation without a standard syllabus, has finally enacted a curriculum that includes English, science and technology, mathematics, history, geography, music, art and design, and a few foreign languages. Students will spend about 70 percent of their time in learning these core subjects, devoting the rest to another foreign language, extra science courses, or other options.

That leaves the United States as the only major nation in which virtually all educational planning remains in the hands of local authorities. Since *A Nation at Risk* startled educational leaders into action, many states have adopted at least the outlines of a standard core curriculum, but few have significantly changed what goes on in the classroom. Though curricula specify which courses students must pass, the course content is up to the school district, or even the individual teacher. In too many cases, the good intentions embodied in the curriculum amount to very little, as the tests quoted earlier in this book demonstrate all too clearly.

In the next ten years this situation should improve dramatically, because American educators will spend much of the coming decade working to formulate a core curriculum for our grammar and high schools. At least four major academic organizations are sponsoring projects that aim to produce a standardized national curriculum. Several dozen local teachers' organizations are making similar efforts; among them are Chalkdust, in New York City; Rethinking Schools, in Milwaukee; and Substance, in Chicago. Community activist organizations are contributing their efforts; these include Chicago Schoolwatch; the Citizens Education Center, in Seattle; Parents United for Full Public School Funding, in Washington, D.C.; People United for Better Schools, in Newark; and the Southern Coalition for Educational Equity. In addition, there have been uncounted attempts to specify the core "competencies" in subjects such as the sciences, where educational performance is low and the consequences of failure are high. The goal is to define not just course titles but the specific facts and skills that students must master before graduation. Once that is accomplished, the task of funneling the necessary information to students, and making sure that they absorb it, should be a good deal easier.

Probably the most famous mainstream attempt to define educational norms for American schools is the "James Madison High School" curriculum proposed in 1987 by former Education Secretary William J. Bennett. As reforms go, it is a fairly modest proposal. Bennett would set requirements for only thirty-six courses out of the forty-eight to fifty-six that most students take over four years. They would include four years of English, concentrating on literature and writing; three years each of science and mathematics; three years of social studies, emphasizing Western civilization and American history; two years each of physical education and a single foreign language, chosen as a local option; and one semester each of art and music history. The most radical idea in the package is that the Madison concept applies to all students; there are no allowances for vocational programs or for other concessions to students who will not go on to college. For teachers who find something incongruous, or at least impractical, in the idea that all students both need and deserve a sound basic education, whether or not they plan to go on to college, the Bennett curriculum has been difficult to accept.

Ironically, one of the most radical curriculum proposals is best known for a feature that many see as a return to the educational past—a rigorous focus on the classics. This is the "Paideia program," developed by the famed philosopher Mortimer J. Adler, founder and director of the Institute for Philosophical Research, in Chicago.

We will look more closely at this proposal in chapter 9, for Paideia is more than just a proposed curriculum; it reorders virtually all of teaching as it is practiced in our public schools. Dr. Adler wants students, and teachers, to *think*.

On the surface, this emphasis seems applicable to almost any course content. In practice, Adler argues that only the most enduring works have enough substance to "carry" a curriculum that requires students to think as well as to memorize. Thus pupils study not textbooks but original texts, and not just any writings but those that have done the most to advance Western thought—books usually considered "too difficult" for primary- or secondary-school students and often neglected even in college. One typical Paideian seminar grafted as an elective onto a standard high-school curriculum carried students through no fewer than thirty of the classics in a year. Included were such works (or excerpts from them) as Plato's *Republic,* Aristotle's *Ethics, The Canterbury Tales,* the Declaration of Independence, and Einstein's *Geometry and Experience.* A full weekly school schedule based on the Paideia program would include three classes each of English, social studies, math, science, art, and phys-ed, as well as five classes in a foreign language and, at some point, typing. These relatively standard courses would be supplemented by "coaching labs" in writing, science, math, and reading/language; a problem-solving lab; and a free-form seminar in which students would debate the great questions of philosophy.

Unlike the James Madison High School curriculum, the Paideia program is actually being carried into practice. Supported by the National Center for the Paideia Program at the University of North Carolina in Chapel Hill, more than 125 schools are in the process of adopting some form of Paideia-style instruction. Most common is the "Wednesday Revolution," a series of seminars for the whole school added to a more traditional curriculum. However, at least a few institutions are reorganizing their entire programs around the classics-based coaching-and-seminar format.

Like the Bennett program, Paideia makes no distinction between students who will go on to college and those who will not. It allows no time off for vocational classes and little for electives. On those grounds, some educators have rejected it as elitist and excessively visionary. "The ills of education are the ills of society and cannot be cured until society itself is healed," is one frequent response. Yet, according to early reports, students participating in Paideia classes show a dramatic growth in thinking and communications skills and much greater interest in school. There is even some evidence that Paideia-based schooling may cut dropout rates, presumably because its active, participatory style both keeps students interested in their classes and gives them a sense of accomplishment. If these preliminary findings hold up, the arguments against Paideia may be beside the point.

Proposals such as the James Madison High School and Paideia represent only one side of the current wave of curriculum reform. Almost every subject area is undergoing its own reformulation. Many of these efforts are being carried out by teachers' specialty associations, and others by state education departments dissatisfied with the results of their present programs.

The California education department, for example, recently announced a plan to revamp the teaching of history and social studies throughout the state's public school system, from kindergarten through the senior year of high school. To see what is wrong with history and social-studies courses today, one need only look at history as it was taught a century ago. In the works of Edward Gibbon and Thomas Babbington Macaulay, stories of the past come alive with the passions of their times, told with a force and beauty that still enthralls anyone capable of appreciating English prose. No student not already emotionally brain-dead could sleep through an hour of reading Gibbon, any more than most can stay awake through five minutes of reading the shopping lists of names and dates that now pass for history texts. If California has its way, history texts five years from now will have returned to the people-and-stories format so long lost. In addition, the new program will select key moments in history for detailed analysis, rather than presenting it all as an undifferentiated mass. Religious and ethical traditions will also receive new emphasis.

Mathematics is in for curricular revision under a proposal developed by the National Council of Teachers of Mathematics (NCTM) and supported by no fewer than forty math organizations. The plan deliberately avoids the "national curriculum" format, which thoroughly embarrassed the organization in the days of the ill-fated "new math" movement, offering instead fifty-four guidelines intended to help local districts develop their own programs. Teachers, it advises, should spend less time on rote learning and more on problem-solving and the use of math in the real world. Students would even be allowed to use calculators to permit them to solve problems that they understand conceptually but cannot yet handle on their own. For example, third-graders could not calculate the average weight of students in their class on their own, because they

have not yet learned to divide by double-digit numbers. With a
calculator, the mechanics become easy and the focus remains on
problem-solving. In the long run, this emphasis on manipulation
and concepts could replace the traditional courses of algebra, trigo-
nometry, geometry, and calculus by an approach that integrates the
individual subjects around unifying themes. NCTM leaders estimate that it will take ten years or more to put the proposed changes
into effect.

By far the most ambitious of the specialized curriculum-reform
plans now under way is "Project 2061," named after the year in
which Halley's Comet will next return and sponsored by the American Association for the Advancement of Science, the National Science Foundation, IBM, and the Carnegie Corporation. This effort,
which began in 1985 and will not be ready for broad practical
application before 1993, seeks to replace traditional science teaching in the middle schools with four general categories of understanding. Students leaving school, the project leaders hold, should
understand what science is and how it relates to our culture, how
science views the structure and evolution of the universe, how
science fits into its historical context, and the scientific habits of
mind that help one comprehend both the world and the technical
issues that often shape contemporary politics.

All the standard concepts found in today's science curriculum
will survive in the new one—evolution, the structure of the atom,
and so on—but it is not at all certain that the traditional courses in
biology, chemistry, and physics will remain. Instead, the idea is to
organize these subjects as series of projects that carry students
through both science and math, and even delve into related literature, history, and economics. A dozen or so broad themes would
be visited and revisited throughout the student's school career. For
example, the study of evolution would examine not only the evolution of living organisms, but also of the physical universe, and even
cultures and political systems. Atmosphere and the weather would
be interpreted to include geophysics, the transfer of energy
through the earth's environment, and perhaps the economic and
social impact of the climate. In this way, the science educators hope,
students will build a far broader understanding of science and the

scientific perspective than is possible in the traditional lecture-and-test-tube classes.

By comparison, reform in the crucial area of English and reading remains at a relatively early stage of development. The first major critique of the English curriculum, the English Coalition Report, *Democracy Through Language,* appeared in the summer of 1987. It recommended eliminating the traditional basal readers and allowing even the youngest students to read more demanding literary works. In the coalition's view, the goal of English and "language arts" teachers should be to integrate oral skills with those of writing and an appreciation of literature. The National Council of Teachers of English echoed the recommendation six months later, and teachers in the field seem to be reaching a consensus that will eventually replace the Dick-and-Jane approach with more sophisticated reading. Many details of the what-should-be-studied-when variety remain to be worked out, however. It seems likely that English and reading curricula will remain far less uniform than the study of science. As the school-restructuring movement gains momentum, teachers will formulate their own literature-based programs in each school district.

Limiting the discussion to a few examples of curriculum reform makes this aspect of education seem far less chaotic than it truly is. In fact, the debate over what children should learn and how it should be taught is energetic and sometimes acrimonious. In *Conflicting Conceptions of Curriculum* (McCutchan, 1974), Elliot Eisner and Elizabeth Vallance identified no fewer than five separate and often conflicting philosophies of curriculum design, each with proponents who have little use for the others. What Eisner and Vallance call the "structure of knowledge" school upholds the traditional subject-matter divisions, concerning itself with both teaching methods and course contents, while the "development of cognitive processes" camp prefers the exercise of cognitive skills to the compilations of facts typical of today's courses. The "curriculum as technology" crowd concerns itself with the mechanics of presenting information, while proponents of "self-actualization" insist that students should be led to discover concepts and information for themselves. Finally, the "social reconstruction-relevance" school believes that students should be trained to rebuild society to fit the proponent's view of a viable or just future. From social studies to mathematics and foreign languages to art, representatives of all these academic movements are slugging it out for control of the curriculum, and the outcome is yet in doubt.

So American educators will spend much of the next decade working to formulate a core curriculum for elementary and secondary schools. The goal is to specify not just course titles but the specific performance standards or competencies that students must master before graduation. Exactly how that knowledge is delivered to each student will remain in the teacher's hands. In the end, schools most likely will have as many model curricula to choose from as there are prestigious educational theorists. But most will be variations on a common theme: giving students the competence to function as independent adults in the world after graduation.

Education in America will never be as uniform as it is in Japan, either in subjects covered or in quality of teaching. Each school system will adapt whatever model curricula gain the greatest credibility to fit their own views of local needs. Yet it seems clear that the period of ferment is quickly coming to a close. In the near future, we will build a consensus that covers at least the most essential subjects: English, math, science, and computer literacy. Throughout the country, parents soon will be able to send their children to public schools, confident that their offspring are actually getting the education they need.

8

DESKTOP LEARNING

Computers are more than automated drill-masters, or substitutes for human teachers. ... They free students to develop analytical and creative abilities ... which are all but ignored by traditional teaching methods.

We have been hearing about computers in the classroom ever since the late 1970s, when PCs first began to spread through the land. So far, they have had relatively little impact in most school districts. There are something over 3 million personal computers in America's schools today, about one for every twenty students. Far more are needed. If it turns out that, after raising pay scales and recruiting people from outside the profession, we still face a teacher shortage, as seems likely, then computerized instruction will be our only hope of making up the deficit.

As the 1990s open, a variety of new and newly useful technologies are also promising to transform our nation's classrooms. Among these are computer networks, interactive CD-ROM, "distance learning"—courses presented at a central location and delivered to schools by satellite transmission, microwave relay, or fiber-optic link—and the old-fashioned television.

In a school system short of help, it is easy to see the benefits of computerized learning and related technologies. But it turns out that computers have unique powers that even the best teachers would find difficult to duplicate. Unlike human teachers, computers never tire, never forget a key point, never ignore the slow student in the back corner while paying attention to a few bright, compliant favorites. Even the earliest computer-aided learning programs could take the place of drill books; as software has improved, they have begun to replace some kinds of textbooks as well. The best such programs already incorporate the "reasoning power" needed to diagnose the student's learning deficiencies and tailor instruction to compensate for them. Today's educational software can take a student from letter identification in kindergarten through complex grammar and reading in high school. Testing is constant. When a child makes a mistake, the computer will take him back over the lesson, presenting the information in different ways, until the material has been mastered.

"We can put thirty computers in a room, and they will go as fast or slow as each child needs; the child controls it," observes Congressman James Scheuer (D.-N.Y.) "He has an equal and comfortable relationship, building his morale and self-esteem, which can only enhance the learning process."

A growing number of classroom computers are linked to another innovation: interactive videodiscs or CD-ROMs. Derived respectively from the videodisc that competed rather unsuccessfully with videotape for consumer acceptance and from compact audio discs, these technologies can store vast quantities of information in convenient, almost indestructible form. One commercial product stores "Compton's MultiMedia Encyclopedia," created by Encyclopedia Britannica—some 31,000 articles, 10,000 maps and photographs, and 5,800 maps, charts, and tables—with room enough left over for the entire *Merriam-Webster Intermediate Dictionary* and a variety of software to manipulate the information. Another packs a 160-hour course in physical science—both physics and chemistry—for junior-high-school students onto fifteen videodisc sides. Students can run back and forth through the material at will, taking charge of a nuclear power plant, watching explosive chemical reactions, manipulating radioactive materials, and carrying out many other realistic experiments that would never be permitted into a real-life high-school laboratory. Even *The Oxford English Dictionary* can now be had on CD-ROM.

There is already ample proof that computerized learning works, both in middle-class schools with motivated students, and in poor districts where a tradition of learning has yet to be established. It can enrich successful educational programs and salvage failing school systems.

In well-to-do Walnut Creek, California, a research team from the Lawrence Hall of Science has been working with teachers to improve science courses. They have found that computers can sometimes make difficult concepts clear, even where hands-on experiments fail.

For example, Douglas Kirkpatrick discovered that his eighth-grade physical science students had trouble understanding the difference between heat and temperature. As one student put it, "*temperature* is all the degrees, but *heat* only refers to temperatures that are above warm." Kirkpatrick had tried using laboratory experiments to demonstrate the basic concepts of heat, but students seemed to spend their time recording temperatures and making pretty graphs of their data without ever really understanding what they had seen.

Enter the researchers from Lawrence Hall, bringing with them sixteen computers donated by Apple, some laboratory equipment, and curriculum materials developed by Boston's Technical Education Research Centers. Using the computers to collect data and graph the results freed the students to think. Kirkpatrick became a coach rather than a conduit for information, helping students to understand when poorly calibrated probes and other artifacts had distorted their data, and guiding them in figuring out for themselves the scientific principles of heat. When something was not clear, the computers made it easy to repeat an experiment to clarify the point. And the students learned. Kirkpatrick now comments that "I can't imagine a physical science laboratory without computers anymore."

Principal Harry Donahoo, at Chicago's Zenos Colman School, had to play academic catch-up to give his neighborhood's children any chance at learning; computers came to the rescue. Faced with a desperately poor achievement record among his students, Donahoo has equipped his K–8 facility with four advanced computer laboratories made by WICAT Systems, of Marina Del Rey, California. After seeing what the computers can do, he plans to add at least one more.

When the program started, Colman's academic performance ranked a grim ninth from the bottom out of Chicago's 400-plus elementary schools. Today, it ranks sixty-fourth from the bottom. If that sounds less than outstanding, consider: Colman sits in the heart of the Robert Taylor Homes, the largest public-housing project in the United States. Nearly all of the school's 800 or so students live in poverty, many in homes with a single semiliterate parent. Before the first computer system came in, students averaged only 4.2 months of reading improvement and 5.5 months' worth of gain in math in a ten-month school year. By 1988 they were averaging 8.4 months of gain in reading and for the first time won a full ten months of improvement in math. Superintendent Donahoo gives almost all the credit to the computer-learning labs.

"I can put a child on the machine in kindergarten," he says. "It starts off with letter identification and progresses to very complex questioning of children at the eighth-, ninth-, and tenth-grade level. When the child answers incorrectly, it will take him to various levels to make him think back his answers. The same is true in math, English, spelling.

"The results have been fantastic. Five years ago, if 10 or 15 percent of our children were at grade level in reading and 20 percent were at grade level in math, that was great. Last year, for the second time, we graduated one-fourth of our students at the national norm level or better in reading and nearly 40 percent in math."

The key to the system's success, Donahoo believes, is the way it involves teachers in the process. In most schools, the computer labs are "pull-out" programs; some of the students go to the lab, while the remainder stay in class with the teacher, able to do little more than work on their homework. Teachers understandably resent that kind of interference with their class programs.

But because the Colman School's labs are built around large, sophisticated computer systems capable of handling an entire class at once, no one is left behind. The computer lab becomes a normal part of the teacher's day, and the teachers also gain from the experience.

"One of our older teachers was very reluctant to participate in the program," Donahoo chuckles. "Three weeks later, she was running from terminal to terminal, telling the children, 'Don't hit that return button until I copy that sentence down! Don't hit that return button!' It was changing her whole way of teaching reading, and I've seen the same thing happen with teachers in math and the other subjects. I can't think of anything else that would have given us the kind of results we've seen with computerized instruction."

District 5, in Orangeburg, South Carolina, has also learned from experience what a difference computers can make. It is a poor, largely rural school system, 80 percent black, and 70 percent of the students qualify for free or reduced-price lunches. Few of the pupils' parents have more than a high-school diploma, and many lack that. In the mid-1970s, District 5 racked up the kind of educational performance that gives middle-class parents nightmares. Only 14 percent of students scored above the national average on standardized achievement tests, and the dropout rate ran a dismal 35 percent. Today, fully 57 percent score above the national average. Only eighteen of the 2,000 high-school students are missing from class—a potential dropout rate of less than 1 percent!—and superintendent James Wilsford vows that they will be found and returned to the fold.

One major part of the Orangeburg program has been a move to computerized teaching methods. "We start kids on computers in kindergarten and continue from that point," Mr. Wilsford reports. "They have computers in all their classes. The remedial program is built around computers; they do a lot of the work. Any child who is below state standards in reading or math is assigned to 108 hours of computer-aided instruction in that area, a whole hour a day of extra study for a year."

Computers have several advantages over human teachers, he points out. The machines never tire and never forget a key point in an explanation. More important, a child working at a terminal never has a chance to daydream during a lecture. "It puts them in response mode," Wilsford says. "With the computer, we're getting 100 percent out of them at all times."

The Orangeburg superintendent does not give computers sole credit for transforming his school. A strict testing program makes sure all that instruction has "taken;" students who do not measure up are assigned to summer school or repeat the grade the following year. But, he adds, "Kids drop out when they become so poor at going to school that it's a daily frustration to them. They're not going to put up with that. So the first thing is to get their instructional programs squared away, so they are learning and being productive." Clearly, that is one place where computers excel.

One of the fastest-growing and most widely accepted of the new classroom technologies is the one many of us blame for turning our children's minds to mush in the first place: television. Virtually every school in the country has at least one TV. Many have one in every classroom. This has made it easy, and relatively inexpensive, to adopt televised educational services as new offerings have come along. Aided by the spread of videocassette recorders and by the development of satellite-based educational TV networks, schools are now integrating the former "boob tube" into their regular courses. In Oregon, for example, half of all teachers use instructional television in their classes. And students in Wisconsin spend an average of forty-five minutes of their class time watching television every school day. This trend can only grow as we progress farther into the 1990s and more televised educational services become available.

In late 1989 the Congressional Office of Technology Assessment reported that "distance learning" projects are planned in all fifty states; many are operating already. Most of these are video courses, given for credit, that link teachers and students with a two-way hookup. Teachers lecture, just as in most classrooms, and students can ask questions when they need a point clarified.

One of the largest services—there are four major players in this field so far—is run by the Midlands Consortium, a satellite network with studios at Oklahoma State University, in Stillwater. Its broadcasts reach some 60,000 students from kindergarten through high school in twenty-eight states. Nearly 5,000 high schools offer credit for Midlands courses, taught over television by professors at Oklahoma State and Kansas State University, and the number is growing rapidly.

A typical Midlands client is Dexter Regional High School, in central Maine. Dexter Regional has been with the Midlands program since 1988. In its first year the high school enrolled only seven students in video courses; they took classes in government and calculus. Since then, the school's video curriculum has broadened to include chemistry and other courses. An advanced-placement chemistry class with a single student cost the school just $300—a bargain, given that Dexter could never have afforded to supply a teacher for the course.

One television service that has not been so eagerly received is Whittle Communications' Channel One, a daily news program that supports itself by selling advertising time to companies with products aimed at the grammar- and high-school audience. Schools subscribing to Channel One get free video equipment, but are forbidden by their contract to use it to edit out the commercials. Yet many school districts, including the entire state of New York, have refused the service. As this is written, it seems that Whittle has signed up enough viewers to make a go of its novel program.

Even if Channel One never makes it to the air, it has spurred a minor revolution among cable TV operators. Ted Turner's Cable News Network was first to leap into the field with CNN Newsroom, a series of daily fifteen-minute news programs covering world events, science, business, and other topics. Turner has essentially given up his copyright to the programs, so teachers are free to do with them as they please. Cable operators all over the country have hurried to provide schools with free hookups, and some are packaging the service with related material supplied by other channels. In New York and New England, Continental Cablevision is bundling CNN Newsroom with Assignment Discovery, a documentary series from the Discovery Channel; C-Span Short Subjects, educational vignettes about the workings of Congress and government agencies; the Weather Education and Awareness Project, from the Weather Channel; and a variety of programs from the Arts & Entertainment channel. Schools have welcomed these services eagerly. By the end of 1989, a few months after Cable News Network announced CNN Newsroom, nearly 5,000 schools had signed up for the program.

Some of the nation's most innovative school systems have found their own uses for cable television. High schools in Pleasantville and Ossining, New York, share a Latin teacher through a cable-TV link; the program has been running successfully since 1983. Ossining Middle School and nearby Mamaroneck High School both start their day with a news program broadcast from their own cable studios to most homerooms. Many similar projects can be found in other communities. Many more are sure to come.

Some other forecasts that seem obvious are more difficult to make. Given all the success stories in which computers and other gadgetry have promoted learning, saved students from dropping out, and even saved whole schools from academic collapse, it seems likely that the average classroom a decade hence will be outfitted with all the high-tech conveniences that ten more years of development will offer. We certainly would like to make that forecast, for little seems more certain than that computers and telecommunications, in the hands of teachers who know how to use them effectively, could go a long way toward solving many of the problems that now beset our schools. Yet the reality is that while educational television and videodiscs will proliferate as quickly as schools can adapt to them, we cannot guarantee that computers will do the same. Barbara Soriano, a Washington-based educational consultant, points convincingly to a number of obstacles that could slow, or even prevent, the adoption of computerized instruction.

One problem is that teaching styles are changing, and it is not certain that computers are as well suited for the new environment as they were for the old one. In fact, it has never been easy to fit computers into the classroom. Computers are meant for single users. Even where many terminals are linked to a huge mainframe, only one person at a time can work at the terminal. Yet classrooms are group-oriented and are fast becoming more so. The most innovative and successful schools today are adopting team learning. Students work together, stimulating each other's ideas and passing information back and forth. In that environment, a computer on every desk could turn out to be as useful as the sand from which its chips were made.

For a while, the champions of educational computing will try to adapt to the new style of learning by designing their programs as "groupware," i.e., software meant for cooperative use by many students, all linked by computer network. The concept has worked well for business, where people working on the same project can be in different offices or even different countries. But when everyone is in the same classroom, it is a lot easier and more satisfying just to talk. In the early 1990s, perhaps a third of our school computer laboratories will be equipped with networking systems. How much use they will receive is far less certain.

Add to this a changing curriculum. In the 1990s, corporate America will deliver a message that the public will believe—because, in fact, it is substantially true. To help their students make it in the modern world, high schools must provide advanced courses in science, technology, and math. Textbook publishers will meet the demand by simply adding chapters to their existing books, and cramming a few more facts into each chapter. Software publishers will have no such opportunity. It just is not as easy to alter a computer program as it is to rewrite a book. Software firms will be forced to develop their courses anew, repeating the process every few years, and prices are likely to remain high.

And that brings us to the real problem: money. It should be easy to sell computers to taxpayers; in a survey of parents at one typical school in Fairfax, Virginia, fully two-thirds cited computers as one of the most important topics their kindergartners should learn about in school. Yet in today's tight-budget environment, it may not happen. Computers seem cheap if you look at them from the right angle: the estimated $2 billion spent on instructional hardware over the last decade amounts to only five dollars per student, less than 0.2 percent of the total yearly budget for primary and secondary schools. But it was still $2 billion—enough to put 50,000 students through almost any state college in the country, or to put effective antidrug education programs in our schools. According to the Office of Technology Assessment, it would cost another $14 billion to buy the hardware for a major expansion of computers in our schools, and that omits the price of software or networking accessories. Suddenly the chances of computerizing our schools appear less promising.

Yet, with all that said, it remains almost impossible to imagine the classrooms of the year 2000 and not picture arrays of advanced personal computers that hackers now can only wish for. The reason is that computers offer far greater opportunities for learning than merely automating math or vocabulary drill. One of the most important goals of education in the high-tech, information-rich world is to teach students the survival skills they will need long after they leave school: how to analyze a problem, find information, make decisions even when complete information cannot be found, plan a job, and get it done. According to most business leaders, the young people who graduate from high school, and even college, today lack these abilities to a degree that renders many of them almost unemployable. We are only just beginning to figure out how schools can correct that deficit.

Some of the most promising work is being carried out with the aid of the Christa McAuliffe Institute for Educational Pioneering. Each year the institute selects outstanding educators to examine an important theme in education. In 1988 the theme was "Preparing All Students for the Twenty-first Century: Creative Uses of Technology in Education." Three of the Christa McAuliffe Educators that year were Gail Morse of J. M. Alexander Junior High School, in Huntersville, North Carolina; Alan November of the Wellesley Middle School, in Wellesley, Massachusetts; and Ron Fortunato, head of the NORSTAR Project at the Norfolk (Virginia) Technical Vocational Center. In computers, each has found a way to teach skills that no lecture or textbook can.

Gail Morse's science class at Alexander Junior High is a multimedia laboratory stocked with Macintosh computers, modems, videodiscs, and CD-ROMs capable of manipulating vast quantities of information. When her students have, say, a report to prepare for class, they can sort through thousands of slides, pages of text, audio recordings, and even movies, all stored on disc. The computers search for and organize the information in moments, so students can find in minutes information that in a traditional library would take hours or days. Because of that, they are free to spend their time considering the subject, deciding what information they need, and figuring out how to present it to the class. All their effort goes into learning the "high-payoff" skills, rather than into the mechanics of information searching.

Alan November's elective class in "Creative Problem Solving with Technology" not only gives students practice in thinking, but solves problems for community leaders as well. November's students act as computer consultants for local business leaders and service organizations with problems to solve. In one typical project, a student who had seemed at risk of dropping out volunteered her time to develop a 200-page directory of recreation services for the disabled in metropolitan Boston; she wound up demanding access to the computer lab during her summer vacation so that she could continue her work. Others have devised an automated mailing system for personalized sales letters, inventory programs for small business, and budgeting systems that work with personal computer spreadsheet programs. The process requires them to understand enough of the "client's" business to understand the problem, figure out how to solve it, write reports, develop a proposal, and put the idea into practice. They handle all these activities without much in the way of help from their teacher. There are no lectures in the course, and few other reminders of the way students had to learn in the pre-computer days. November's role has become to help his students clarify their ideas and put them into practice.

Ron Fortunato's NORSTAR course offers students an experience few adults will ever have: they design science experiments that one day will fly on the NASA space shuttle. Students spend upwards of fifteen hours per week on the process, and even more time during the summer months. NASA scientists and managers act as mentors for the students, and computer spreadsheets and computer-aided design programs take care of the drudgery. When a project calls for a skill beyond the normal curriculum—calculus, for example—computer software handles the calculations, while students get to watch the results. Students quickly gain a conceptual understanding of a difficult subject, yet most of their thinking time goes toward the more important and universal challenges of applying the abstract concept to a real problem.

In all these classes, computers are more than automated drillmasters, or substitutes for human teachers. They are a source of information and feedback that helps students to create and evaluate their own ways to solve practical problems, and even to model the results of putting them to use. In this, they free students to develop analytical and creative abilities that are required for any productive role in the modern world, but which are all but ignored by traditional teaching methods. Computers free educators as well by sparing them the drudgery of teaching basic knowledge and allowing them to concentrate on these high-order skills. This is the real promise of computerized education. The new wave of interactive multimedia formats in which computers select the appropriate educational resources for each student will be the automated tools for the classrooms of the nineties.

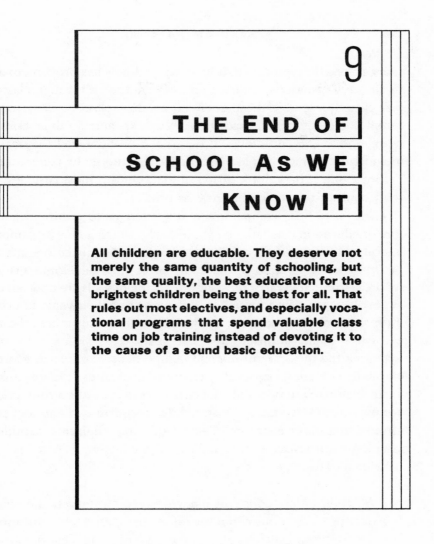

9

THE END OF SCHOOL AS WE KNOW IT

All children are educable. They deserve not merely the same quantity of schooling, but the same quality, the best education for the brightest children being the best for all. That rules out most electives, and especially vocational programs that spend valuable class time on job training instead of devoting it to the cause of a sound basic education.

So far, most of the school-reform efforts we have discussed have grown from one or two basic concepts and sought to cure the ills of education while leaving the fundamental premises of our schools more or less intact. Some school districts have raised their pay scales to attract more and better teachers, who will work in an educational system that remains fundamentally unchanged. Parental choice may put great pressure for change on the schools that are subject to it, but it leaves open the question of what those changes should be. Even computerized learning methods seek primarily to supercharge a teaching process that in today's schools has broken down. In all these proposals, students are expected to sit through classes that closely resemble those attended by their parents. They must listen to their teachers, read their textbooks, and do their homework, and in the end they will be graded on how well they have memorized the facts and learned the skills mastered by generations before them. If they don't drop out first. On this most basic level, it all seems pretty much business as usual.

There have been comparatively few attempts to rethink the nature of education itself and the processes by which it may be gained. Yet a few leading educators have undertaken that difficult task, and their work stands among the most promising developments in school reform. Several of these new teaching models are now building enough practical experience to demonstrate their value to even the most committed skeptics, and we expect that many more schools will adopt them within the next five years.

One of the most promising and comprehensive efforts is Mortimer Adler's Paideia proposal, introduced in chapter 7. In its purest form, Paideia would rebuild schools almost from the ground up, not only discarding today's watered-down course contents and returning to a more hearty intellectual diet, but replacing standard teaching methods with more difficult and effective techniques.

Paideia's basic tenets are these:

- All children are educable. They deserve not merely the same quantity of schooling, but the same quality, the best education for the brightest children being the best for all. That rules out most electives, and especially vocational programs that spend valuable class time on job training instead of devoting it to the cause of a sound basic education.
- Each student's achievement must be weighed against his or her own capacity to learn, not compared with the performance of others. Thus, letter or number grades are replaced by extensive written critiques of the student's performance.
- American schools should prepare their students to earn a decent living, to be good citizens of the Republic, and to make themselves a good life. In part because of this, schooling must

give them a good start on the lifelong process of becoming generally educated, and schools must be judged on how well they accomplish this task.

There are three modes of learning, which Dr. Adler defines as "(1) the acquisition of organized *knowledge* in three fields of subject matter—language, literature, and the fine arts; mathematics and natural science; history, geography, and the study of social institutions; (2) the development of intellectual *skills,* all of which are skills of learning and of thinking; and (3) the enhancement of *understanding* of basic ideas and values."

Therefore, Adler believes, there are three modes of teaching, which every teacher must master and use: the didactic, which is teaching by lecture, supplemented by textbooks, demonstration, tests, and other traditional aids; coaching, in which students practice their skills with the supervision of a teacher; and Socratic or "maieutic" teaching, in which educators use leading questions to help students develop their own insights into the material. (Clearly, this places an unaccustomed burden on teachers to be very good themselves at the skills of learning and thinking.)

Socratic teaching is the real key to Paideia. To join the movement, a school need implement only the "Wednesday Revolution," a series of weekly seminars in which the whole student body joins in to discuss, say, Plato's *Apology,* Euclid's treatise on algebra, or Martin Luther King's "I have a dream" speech—any topic that offers practice in critical thinking about a difficult and important subject.

The full Paideia program sets aside specific times for all three kinds of learning, with lectures, coaching, and seminars in all subjects. A typical high-school schedule devotes three periods per week to English, social studies, math, science, art, and physical education, five periods to a foreign language, and five periods to computer literacy, typing, or a similarly practical subject. In addition, there are eighty-minute "coaching labs" in writing, reading, science, and math; a problem-solving lab; and the two-period weekly seminar.

Most of the 125 or so schools that have adopted Paideia have simply shoehorned a seminar into their weekly schedule, but a few have reorganized their entire program around Adler's ideas. One such participant is Suitland High School, in Suitland, Maryland. The change began in 1986, when Suitland established the Paideia-based University High School, a magnet college-preparatory program set up as part of a court-ordered desegregation plan. Since then, it has spread to the other components of the "Suitland Complex," a general-admission high school, a Center for Visual and Performing Arts, and a Vocational-Technical Center.

In Suitland, Paideia has been dramatically successful. In 1986 the high school was one of the least successful in Prince George's County, plagued by low test scores and chronic racial tension. Only two years later it was one of the top five schools in the county, racial tension had eased dramatically, and President Ronald Reagan had chosen it as the site of a major speech on education prior to the 1988 State of the Union address. "The transformation in Suitland's organizational climate, staff morale, and management structure combined with its concentration upon Paideia have led to students' outstanding performance on a battery of state-mandated competency tests," reports program supervisor John L. Brown. "Test data, however, only begin to reflect the increasing ability of students to handle open inquiry and critical thinking with self-assurance and maturity." Similar reports can be found almost everywhere that Paideia has been adopted.

If Mortimer Adler's radical reforms have been well received, albeit within the limited universe of schools that have adopted them, the same cannot be said of Theodore Sizer's Coalition of Essential Schools. Dr. Sizer, a well-respected Brown University professor whose credentials include terms as dean of education at Harvard and headmaster at the prestigious Andover Academy, has attempted to distill the best of 1960s-style progressive education into a complete program of reform for both course contents and teaching methods. The result is again a radical change from the schools in which baby boomers and their parents struggled for passing grades.

A Sizer-style classroom closely resembles one of Adler's seminars: students debate, say, the rise of labor movements at the turn of the century, while teachers try to guide the discussion and maintain order. That is a task for which many of today's teachers are unprepared, and this free-form approach to education has cost the program support in some of the schools where it has been tried. Even when didactic teaching is required, students are expected to take an active part in class discussions, while teachers act more as coaches than as lecturers.

Like Dr. Adler, Dr. Sizer believes that students do best when challenged by rigorous academic courses. Accordingly, he too would do away with electives and vocational programs and concentrate on thinking skills and core concepts. And rather than trying to race through a sweeping syllabus, Sizer wants teachers to cover fewer topics, but more deeply. And when testing time arrives, students must prove their mastery with essays and individual projects rather than by answering the traditional multiple-choice exams.

In some ways, this "less is more" approach is even more radical than the classics-based Paideia program. The Coalition of Essential Schools does away with such standard subjects as social studies and algebra. Instead, knowledge is grouped into two-hour interdisciplinary courses with titles like "humanities" and "math/science," and organized around abstract themes like "justice." Information from all the traditional subjects is then related to the theme.

When it works, Sizer's brand of education works well. In New York City's celebrated East Harlem school district, one of the brightest of the bright spots is Central Park East Secondary School, a 400-pupil junior/senior high school that opened in 1985. The school program is built almost wholly on Coalition principles, and three-fourths of its sophomores score above the city average on standardized reading tests. At Hope Essential High School, a school-within-a-school magnet program in Providence, Rhode Island, 90 percent of the 1989 graduating class went on to college, compared with 6 percent of those in the traditional program. And in Baltimore's Walbrook High School, where the overall dropout rate is 23 percent, a Coalition program reports that only 2 percent of its students drop out.

But the Coalition of Essential Schools has a checkered history at best. Teachers at Brighton High School, outside Rochester, New

York, voted to leave the program, in part because teachers with peripheral specialties—physical education, business skills, and the like—viewed Sizer's rigid focus on academics as a threat to their jobs. One-fourth of the 100 Coalition students at Hope Essential High School transferred back to less demanding courses in the 1988–89 school year, and discord is rife between Coalition teachers and those in the regular program. And when McCullough High School, in the Houston suburbs, considered joining the Coalition, angry parents forced the school board to back down when it was learned that *the school football team would be unable to practice during class time.* Nonetheless, the Coalition has grown steadily since its founding in the mid-1980s. As this is written, roughly a hundred schools have adopted its program in one form or another, and Sizer's ideas appear certain to play a major role in rebuilding American education.

Clearly, reforms such as the Paideia program and the Coalition of Essential Schools could go a long way toward improving our national educational system. Just as clearly, it will not be easy to turn their promise into reality.

Far more fundamental than any of the changes discussed so far, a revolution in our understanding of learning itself is well under way. It has to do with the nature of intelligence: there is a lot more to it than how well we deal with mathematics and language, the skills tested by the SATs and other standardized exams. According to Harvard psychologist Howard Gardner, we all have at least seven different kinds of intelligence in varying degrees. In addition to the linguistic and logical-mathematical talents measured by most standardized tests, there are special intelligences that deal with spatial awareness, bodily-kinesthetic functions, music, interpersonal relationships, and self-understanding. Students learn a lot faster when their courses are designed to appeal to all of these faculties than in lecture-and-workbook classes.

The best of our traditional schools seem to have understood all this intuitively and have designed their curricula to engage all facets of a child's ability. For just one example, look to Fairfax, Virginia, a community of about 350,000. Mantua Elementary School seems quite ordinary on the outside. But enter its tiled halls, and you will find yourself surrounded by multicolored posters depicting cultural highlights of Kuwait—all written in Arabic. Others appear in languages ranging from German to Vietnamese—and all are readily understood by children who are eight or nine years old. Mantua's children "speak" American Sign Language as well. Third-grade classes are well stocked with desktop computers, and there is a separate room for video equipment. Parents are in the school constantly, working as teachers' aides and special tutors.

While many schools can barely cope with the core curriculum, Mantua offers specialized classes for almost any need. There are classrooms filled with high-technology devices to aid disabled students. Gifted students attend programs for the uncommonly talented. At one end of the building, a care center for school-age children continues the educational process long after traditional school hours have ended.

Mantua's educational system works. The school's average students rank far higher than the national average on standardized tests, and all the specialized programs manage to extract top grades from students who in many cases might be expected to fail. Similar programs are available—and successful—in places from Manhattan to Ventura, California.

Yet even more dramatic successes are possible when teachers consciously take their lead from the work of pioneering educational theorists. At the Key School, a two-year-old K–6 facility in Indianapolis, teachers have designed a whole new curriculum based on the theories of Harvard's Dr. Gardner and of University of Chicago behavioral scientist Mihaly Csikszentmihalyi.

The program includes many of the features that help to make any school a success. Parents are required to attend parent-teacher meetings and encouraged to act as advisers, not only to their own children, but to others. Members of the community are recruited both to give classroom presentations and to work on the committee that organizes them. The school offers day care from 7:00 A.M. to 6:00 P.M. for students whose parents cannot be home during working hours. And the "extended day program" offers extra classes from computers to tap dancing. But the school's essence is far more radical.

The Key School is the first in the country designed to give equal attention to all seven of the intelligences delineated by Howard Gardner. Interdisciplinary classes cover all the standard academic subjects, but in addition each student receives almost daily instruction in art, computers, music, Spanish, and physical education.

None of the intelligences is ever slighted. "We're very rigid about that," says principal Patricia Bolaños, who led the team that designed the program. Children who need extra help with one of their classes do not cut music or phys-ed to get it; instead, they are tutored after hours.

In each subject, the approach is decidedly nontraditional. Phys-ed does away with team sports. Instead, activities such as tumbling and croquet develop flexibility, coordination, and stamina. Music classes are an even greater departure. At Key School, children start learning the violin in kindergarten and move on to other instruments as they grow older.

More novel yet is the twice-a-week "flow activity"; children use most of this time to play board games. According to Howard Gardner, one of the best ways to identify a child's talents is to watch him or her playing at games and puzzles designed to exercise the seven intelligences. Key School teachers combine that idea with the theories of Mihaly Csikszentmihalyi. High achievement, he says, is motivated not by competition but by the pleasure of a mental state he calls "flow," the easy, open productivity that people achieve when they take on a challenge that forces them to learn, yet is not quite beyond their reach. Flow activity is designed to keep children in this happy condition.

All these courses are tied together by a schoolwide theme that changes every nine weeks. The first theme was "connections." In each class, in each grade, teachers organized their material to integrate Gardner's theory of intelligences into the children's lives, link individuals with groups, and so on. Another theme was "changes in time and space." For this, they looked at the history of their city since the 1930s, when their school building was erected, a social-studies focus that recruited people from the community to talk about the changes they had witnessed over the years.

At the end of the nine-week period, each child must produce a project to illustrate the theme. Anything goes. For "connections," one girl built a diorama showing how turtles interact with people. For a theme called "working in harmony," a boy profiled the local Wonder Bread factory, then organized fellow students into a production line making peanut butter and jelly sandwiches.

Four times a week, children meet in "pods," in-depth study groups that mix up to a dozen children of all ages and specialize in a particular cognitive area. There are pods for math, physical science, architecture, choir, instrumental music, and a variety of other topics. Students choose their own pods, with their parents' help. Again, the idea is to build on those intelligences in which children show the most promise.

Critics complain that the Key School has some advantages others do not, and some weaknesses as well. They point out that its low student-teacher ratio would benefit any conventional grammar school that could afford to hire more staff. And the Key School puts so much effort into its ambitious curriculum that teachers may not have enough time to help those with learning difficulties. Mrs. Bolaños points out that although several of their students would have qualified for special-education classes elsewhere, none of their parents have chosen to take them out of Key School.

In all, Key School's performance speaks for itself. Its 150 or so students are not chosen for high intelligence or creativity; they are picked by a computerized lottery. About 40 percent are black, slightly more live in single-parent families, and more than one-third are from low-income families. In short, they form a very average cross-section of the Indianapolis student population. Yet when they leave the Key School, nearly all apply to one of seven magnet junior high schools meant to train the brightest children in math and science, visual arts, performing arts, and so on. Their acceptance rate is the highest in the city.

Already, at least two other schools are being built on the methods pioneered at Key School. More are sure to follow. It will take decades to rebuild the nation's educational system around this new understanding of the developing mind, but elements of the Key School techniques can and will be incorporated into traditional classes in short order.

In the long run, the radical reforms discussed above may be the brightest hope for America's schools. An ideal educational system would probably combine elements of all these proposals. Throughout the country, children at all levels would learn with the natural ease of the lucky few at the Key School. They would hone their thinking and learning skills on the classics and be graded by how well they live up to their own native ability, as the Paideia program urges. They might well find that the traditional subject divisions have been combined into interdisciplinary courses that stress thinking ability and depth of understanding, rather than rote memory, as pioneered by the Coalition for Essential Schools. And they would surely spend more of their time in relatively free-form activities such as discussion and group study, rather than in lectures, individual worksheets, and the other solitary pursuits found in the traditional classroom. Already, many school districts have strong back-to-basics movements, and many teachers are experimenting with limited doses of group learning.

There are many obstacles to be overcome before the majority of American students will benefit from these reforms. In many states, where standardized testing and the traditional letter grades are mandated by law, Paideia schools must still hand out failing grades, even when the student who lags behind the class is doing the best he can. Scarcely a school district in the land is ready to abandon its vocational programs—much less its football team!—in favor of Socrates and Galileo for all. And there are still some problems to be worked out in adapting these new ideas to special-needs students.

Yet the highest hurdle for radical reformers may be the attitudes and limited abilities of teachers themselves. As Theodore Sizer has demonstrated, the nation's phys-ed and home economics teachers have little sympathy for any plan that would do away with their specialties, even when the change is clearly in the students' best interests. In fact, though many teachers claim to want a more rigorous, effective educational system, we wonder how many would give up traditional classroom discipline and take on the challenge of keeping students productive in the unstructured debates of a Coalition school. And in a nation where many educators would flunk the final exams required of their own students, how many possess the knowledge and thinking skills needed for the Paideia program's intellectually demanding Socratic style? The most serious obstacle slowing the spread of these new teaching methods is the dearth of teachers capable of adopting them.

Despite such problems, there seems no doubt that in the next decade or so, Paideia, the Coalition of Essential Schools, and the Key School will have an enormous influence on educators. Though comparatively few schools will adopt these programs whole, elements of each concept will filter into classrooms throughout the nation. As a result, academic performance should rise quickly, and dropout rates fall, in the years to come.

PART III

PROFILES OF
PROGRESS

10

FAIRFAX COUNTY, VIRGINIA: A NATIONAL ROLE MODEL

Fairfax County is clearly at the forefront of the school-reform movement in the United States, and residents just as clearly like that idea.

In a time when schools across the United States are struggling with low attendance and poor academic performance, Fairfax County's schools work, and area residents know it.

If any region in the land can give its children a good education, it should be Fairfax County, Virginia, a suburb of Washington, D.C. Wealthier than the vast majority of American communities, and with a much higher average level of education, Fairfax has all the advantages that many other districts can only envy. Most of all, its people truly care about their children's education. In fact, Fairfax does a good job of teaching its students. Thomas Jefferson High School, in Fairfax County, has the highest number of National Merit Scholars of any school in the United States. By almost any measure—dropout rates, SAT scores, the number of children who go on to college, and so on—this county has one of the best public school systems to be found.

Success has not made Fairfax residents complacent, however. Since the early 1980s, the county has been a national leader in the school-reform movement. As we have already seen, it has raised teachers' salaries, established one of the first working merit-pay systems, and lengthened the school day—and the list grows longer every year.

The three reports that follow use the experience of Fairfax County to illustrate some valuable lessons about several aspects of school reform. The first looks at the nuts and bolts of school restructuring. This first section was written by the man who has championed school reform in Fairfax County, Superintendent of Public Schools Robert R. Spillane.

RESTRUCTURING THE SCHOOL DAY IN FAIRFAX COUNTY

The politicians, pundits, and professors who have been calling for reform of our schools for the past six to eight years have often acted as though what needed to be done was obvious and that doing it would be easy. Bureaucratic inertia has been typically seen as the major barrier to change. Those advocating reform have often spoken and written as though parents and teachers, businesspeople and government leaders were hungry for reform, but that what some referred to as "the blob" (meaning the educational administrators) has stood in the way of the tidal wave of reform. Those of us who work in school systems and who have been working to improve education in real schools with real students and real teachers in real communities know better. Educational reform is neither obvious nor easy, and "the blob" has no corner on the blockage market.

The school system of which I am superintendent is the tenth-largest and one of the most affluent in the United States. Ninety percent of our students go on to college, and the community strongly supports its schools, as evidenced by 70-percent support for bond issues in recent years. At the same time, the community is looking for ways to improve its schools even more. Another section of this chapter describes a major reform that we have been able to implement successfully: performance evaluation and merit pay for teachers.

One of the changes most frequently called for by those advocating educational reform is an increase in the amount of time students are in school. The National Committee on Excellence in Education's 1983 booklet, *A Nation at Risk,* which some see as the opening salvo of the current reform movement, recommended that "significantly more time be devoted to learning." It asked school districts and state legislatures to "strongly consider seven-hour school days, as well as a 200-to-220-day school year." Before 1983, much educational research had already indicated that more student "time-on-task" improved student learning (not exactly a counterintuitive finding). After 1983, the calls to provide more time for instruction increased in number and intensity. Many states, including Virginia, were also increasing high-school graduation requirements, further pushing at the limits of existing school schedules. At the same time, the "day-care crisis" added a noneducational force to the momentum for a longer school day.

The reform movement's call for more instructional time simply reinforced what had long been recognized and discussed in Fairfax County public schools: more and more was being added to school, nothing was being taken away, and something had to give. For many years, our high- and intermediate-school students have had a six-period, six-and-a-half-hour school day. Our elementary students have had a six-and-a-half-hour school day on Tuesday through Friday and a four-hour day on Monday. The two-and-a-half-hour early release on Mondays was to give teachers a block of time for parent conferences, planning, and staff development activities. For as long as I had been superintendent, the school board, the staff, and the community had talked about the need to increase instructional time for students, to respond to increased graduation requirements, to protect elective programs, to strengthen the fine arts at all levels, and to deal with fragmentation and the crowded curriculum. Given these circumstances, it seemed a good bet that restructuring the school day to provide slightly more instructional time would be a "motherhood and apple pie" issue—and a shoo-in with the community, the teachers, and the school board. Right? Wrong.

In the autumn of 1989, after years of studies, pilots, and surveys, a staff committee presented an exhaustive report with five different options for restructuring the school day, K–12. The report was presented throughout the school community, using every available forum to obtain input on an educationally preferred and affordable option. We even produced and circulated a videotape explaining the pros and cons of the various options. When, after substantial input and discussion, I made my recommendations to the school board, I laid out a total package—grades K through 12—that took into consideration all the many concerns and issues raised over the years.

I recommended the following:

- that the elementary school day be restructured to a six-and-a-half-hour uniform day with the additional 150 minutes of weekly instructional time equally allocated between the core curriculum and art, music, and physical education;
- that the intermediate- and high-school day be restructured to seven forty-seven-minute periods by adding thirty minutes to the student day (and no time to the teacher day).

The plan had many educational advantages. At the elementary level, it would

- provide flexibility with the addition of seventy-five minutes in the core curriculum for the local school to address the special needs of its population;
- provide students with additional art, music, and physical-education instruction;
- create greater flexibility in scheduling itinerant-teacher and student pull-out programs;
- create larger blocks of planning time during the instructional day—five forty-five-minute blocks and one sixty-minute block per week.

The major costs at the elementary level would be to hire 220 additional teachers: fifty-eight art teachers and 162 music and physical-education teachers.

At the secondary level, the recommended plan would create a seventh period to allow students to satisfy graduation requirements as well as pursue core academic subjects and courses that meet individual needs, talents, and interests. It would also provide an additional nonteaching period in which teachers could be assigned such instructionally related responsibilities as tutoring for students at risk, curriculum coordination, study skills programs, and school team or department chair planning. The major costs at the secondary level would be for 275 additional teachers.

To ensure the widest possible discussion of my proposal, we developed another extensive schedule of public forums, including meetings of school faculties and PTAs, a community teleconference during which I answered call-in questions, and two lengthy, countywide public hearings. The entire process was a case study in school/community dynamics and the realities of reform.

The testimony presented during six hours of public hearings provides some interesting insights into the grassroots difficulties of education reforms—even the relatively uncontested reform of adding instructional time to the school day. The teachers' unions opposed my final recommendation for predictable reasons: at the secondary level, the added nonteaching period meant that "teachers will receive no additional compensation, but more work"; at the elementary level, "teachers teach for seventy-five more minutes while losing approximately fifteen minutes of the very limited planning time they have now" (per week). Union representatives also objected to increasing average class size to twenty-seven students in intermediate and high school, citing the academic stress on students and the pressure on teachers.

Individual teachers, especially teachers of music and other electives, favored the extended school day, which "could provide our students with a wealth of opportunities never before open to them while capitalizing on the expertise and special interests of one of the finest teaching corps in the country." A similar view was expressed by some community organizations, which called the proposal "a highly desirable initiative" that "should be of significant benefit to students." Many high-school students cheer the greater flexibility and the opportunity to take additional subjects, especially elective courses.

Other groups, especially parent groups, were opposed primarily because of greater stress on students: "Our children are already overburdened with a high-pressure core curriculum and a stressful day that does not allow ample time for recess. . . ." Parents cautioned about the high suicide rate in Japan and asked, "What is it we want from our children?" Why are we "pushing our children from the time they hit kindergarten or before?" This concern about student stress pervaded the testimony of those who opposed the proposal.

Practically all groups recognized the significant budgetary implications of the proposal in a virtual no-growth budget: "If you decide that the restructured school day is an educational priority, please fight for the additional funds with which to implement it." Another approach was to use the reality of limited new resources to argue against implementation. The school board's final action was, in fact, a compromise. They voted to approve the extended day at the secondary level and to defer action at the elementary level until the next fiscal year. They did, however, approve the restructured elementary day "in concept"; those who oppose it have been heard to say that they will mobilize their forces for next year.

This year, however, we have won a significant reform for the 60,000 Fairfax County Public Schools students in grades seven through twelve. They will have the expanded educational opportunities of a seven-period day and more time devoted to learning. The real reform, of course, is not the additional time itself; it is improving the quality of the instruction students receive during that time. We are confident that we are doing that with our teacher performance evaluation program; in this case, at least, more really is better.

Admittedly, change is incredibly more complex in a very large system like Fairfax than in a smaller school system, but school administrators everywhere encounter similar barriers and behaviors when they begin to implement reforms. Public process is usually prolonged by predictable attitudes, and action is seldom swift. Those who think that educators are moving too slowly in reforming schools ought to try it. We *are* making progress. We are moving toward the renaissance of American education. And we will get there faster when we have reached a national consensus on our expectations for students, when teacher unions understand professionalism, when funding for long-term reforms is dependable, when parents place greater value on the intellectual development of their children, and when the entire community supports the academic mission of schools.

The next report, also written by Superintendent Spillane, makes a powerful argument for one of the most useful—and maligned—brands of school reform yet developed.

DISPELLING THE MYTHS ABOUT MERIT PAY

Merit pay has, for years, been a small but powerfully symbolic obstacle to reforming the teaching profession. Small because, in and of itself, merit pay doesn't improve teaching; powerfully symbolic because it shatters fundamental myths about the teaching profession.

Professional Myth No. 1

A teacher is a teacher is a teacher. There are no distinguishable differences among teachers. All teachers are basically alike and, therefore, should be treated alike—same evaluation, same salary, same stagnant career. This indefensible logic reduces teaching to the least common denominator and assumes that imposing a uniform curriculum assures uniform teaching. It places on textbook publishers the responsibility to produce "teacher-proof" textbooks with excessively complex, detailed, cookbook directions for presenting instructional material. The verbatim scripts in some teacher editions are an insult to any intelligent teacher and a sad commentary on our lack of confidence in classroom teachers.

Professional Myth No. 2

There are differences among teachers, but they cannot be publicly acknowledged even though everyone (especially teachers themselves) privately recognizes them—because that would explode the myth of sameness and cause divisiveness among teachers. This logic leads us to today's most common (and hypocritical) approach: Pretend they are the same and treat them that way.

Professional Myth No. 3

There are differences among teachers, but it is impossible to identify them because the teaching act is too obscure, complex, mysterious, and unfathomable to be described. It is, therefore, impossible to distinguish and evaluate the components of quality teaching. This logic disregards the substantial research findings of the decade, and underlies the common fear that observation forms will reduce teaching to shallow, simplistic checklists of classroom behaviors.

Actually, however, some groups attempting to compensate for this fear have fallen into the opposite trap of developing voluminous observation forms that are far too comprehensive to be functional. The fear of either extreme is understandable; what is not logical is the conclusion that we are incapable of finding a reasonable middle ground.

Professional Myth No. 4

A slight variation of the same argument is that the teaching act is too obscure, complex, mysterious, and unfathomable to be understood by anyone other than teachers. It is especially unfathomable to those who evaluate teachers, namely principals. This "logic" ignores the fact that principals are also educators who have had classroom teaching experience—in addition to training in the supervision of instruction. If today's principals are better building managers than instructional leaders, the fault lies more with organizational priorities than with inherent abilities. Changing principals' priorities is simply a matter of changing the organization's priorities and expectations. If we want strong instructional leaders who are credible evaluators of teacher performance, then we must select, train, and evaluate principals on the basis of those characteristics.

Implicit in this argument is the false assumption that teachers themselves have no role in evaluating other teachers or determining who gets merit pay. Administratively imposed merit pay plans, which are susceptible to the common criticism of patronage, are educational dinosaurs. In this day and age, it is inconceivable to me that any merit-pay plan would be proposed without the active involvement of teachers at every stage of development—from design to implementation.

Professional Myth No. 5

The highest salaries should go to teachers who have the most years of service and the most academic credits, regardless of their effectiveness as teachers. This takes us full circle to the myth that there are no qualitative differences among teachers and that monetary reward must therefore be based on quantifiable factors that are totally external to teaching itself. This, of course, means that marginal and ineffective teachers get the same rewards as the best teachers.

I accept none of these professional myths; I believe the following:

1. There are qualitative differences among teachers.
2. These differences are recognized by most people, including teachers themselves.
3. The characteristics of effective teaching can be identified and measured.
4. Principals can be credible instructional leaders and reliable evaluators of classroom teaching.
5. The highest salaries should go to the best teachers; marginal teachers should receive assistance, but no raises; and ineffective teachers should be removed.

The crux of the matter is, obviously, the identification of "the best." How it is done, by whom it is done, and when it is done are the process questions to be addressed in individual school systems. The specific procedures are less critical to success than is the underlying conviction that the teaching profession must be freed from the shackles of the last century before we enter the next.

Why is it, then, that schools cling to vestiges of the industrial model? These, for example, are still with us: low pay, minimal academic preparation, lack of decision-making and promotional opportunities for teachers. Eliminating these traces of the past may be easier than eliminating the societal attitude humorously expressed by George Bernard Shaw: "Those who can—do. Those who cannot—teach." Shaw's humor survives, but we should remember that his perspective was nineteenth-century Victorian. Today's classroom is no place for the timid and the fainthearted to hide from life; teaching, today, is for those who can *do*. In the Fairfax County Public Schools, we no longer accept any of these myths, models, or mottoes.

Dispelling the myths began in January 1986 with my appointment of a blue-ribbon Commission on Strengthening the Teaching Profession in Fairfax County Public Schools.

The twelve members of the commission represented the constituencies of public education in Fairfax County—parents, educators, and the community at large. They did not agree on all points, just as any twelve citizens anywhere would be unlikely to agree completely on such debatable issues as teacher preparation and entrance into the profession, the differentiation of roles and responsibilities, compensation and contracts, job satisfaction, status, and professional development. They did, however, come to an informed consensus on certain of these issues after intense study (and equally intense debate) of pertinent factors and forces.

The commission's report did not prescribe one absolute approach to these issues for Fairfax County, because there is no one absolutely right approach, no perfect grand scheme that would be unanimously acclaimed by every teacher, every principal, every parent, every community member.

What the commission did was to begin with a number of beliefs and assumptions on which the members could agree, including these:

- The quality of education in Fairfax County Public Schools is directly related to the quality of its teachers.

- Improvements in teacher preparation and certification, the structure of the profession, the compensation of teachers, and teachers' working conditions are essential if qualified teachers are to be available in the numbers needed in the years ahead.
- Attracting and retaining highly qualified teachers would require aggressive recruiting, salaries competitive with the private and public sectors, a compensation system that rewards excellence and productivity, and a working environment that encourages effective teaching and professional growth.
- The people of Fairfax County were willing to pay more for good teachers if quality control and accountability could be ensured.
- Good management demands, and the taxpaying public expects, a link between pay and performance.
- Good management and public expectations also require stronger action to remove ineffective teachers.

Using these assumptions as a basis for discussion, the commission reviewed various proposals for performance evaluation and career ladders, and endorsed such features as

- internships for new teachers
- peer review and assistance for teachers
- self-appraisal and staff development opportunities
- clearly defined teacher performance standards
- delineation of levels of performance
- involvement of teachers, specialists, and principals in evaluation
- prescriptive supervision for marginal teachers
- involvement of master teachers in activities that would improve instruction.

The commission also endorsed increased training in the supervision and evaluation of instruction for principals, as well as for others involved in the process.

Once the commission had made its report, the school board and I were in a position to move ahead with a broad base of support. The dominant teachers' association, the Fairfax Education Association (FEA), supported the program, while the much smaller Fairfax

County Federation of Teachers (FCFT) opposed it from the beginning. We involved both groups in developing and monitoring the program, which involved a rigorous evaluation program for all teachers and an optional special evaluation for teachers eligible to apply for "Career Level II"—the "merit pay" level. We projected that those who achieved Career Level II would be placed on a separate pay scale 10 percent above that for Career Level I teachers. Extensive training of all school administrators and of hundreds of teachers and other administrators would be required to make the evaluation system effective.

A pilot test in eight schools during the 1986–87 school year was carefully monitored and evaluated. The results showed that the Teacher Performance Evaluation Program (TPEP) was fair, effective in establishing teachers' levels of professional performance, and sustainable with the resources the school system possessed. The school system began a two-year phase-in of TPEP in the fall of 1987; by the spring of 1989 it had evaluated all teachers who were both eligible to try for Career Level II and chose to try for it. This three-year pilot test and phase-in period was an enormous undertaking. Of 6,107 eligible teachers, 3,263 chose Career Level II evaluation, which required at least six separate observations (with required conferences and write-ups) for each eligible teacher. Of the 3,623 evaluated for Career Level II, 2,198 (or approximately 26 percent of the teachers in the school system) were identified as Career Level II teachers. At the other end of the scale, twenty-three, or 0.3 percent of the total number of teachers, were identified as "ineffective" and were recommended for dismissal, and 175, or 2 percent of the teachers, were identified as "marginal" and provided with assistance from three-member intervention teams. Approximately 200 teachers have left the school system as a result of the evaluation process (e.g., resigning before final evaluation) and others, who are not able to improve their "marginal" ratings, will follow.

Perhaps the most important reason for the success of this undertaking was the support of the FEA, which helped gain teacher support for the program and held a number of membership votes on the program and on possible changes in its operation. Both the

FEA and the other teachers' association—the Fairfax County Federation of Teachers (FCFT), which opposed TPEP from the beginning—were represented on the Superintendent's Advisory Council on TPEP, and both recommended changes in procedures during yearly discussions with the school system's personnel services department. The school system made some changes based on these suggestions, and the program did, in fact, work.

In the spring of 1989, after two pilots and two phase-in years, the school system was in a position to recommend additional pay for the 2,198 teachers who had been identified as Career Level II. The superintendent's 1990 budget included a provision for a separate Career Level II pay scale that was an average of 10 percent above the pay scale for Career Level I teachers. In February 1989, the school board considered this proposal and substituted for it a 9-percent bonus that would not be part of base pay. While the difference in take-home pay between the two proposals was minuscule, the bonus would not trigger additional pension credit. The FEA interpreted this change as a betrayal of the agreement they thought they had secured with the superintendent.

Shortly before the February school board vote, Mary Futrell, president of the NEA (of which FEA is an affiliate) had spoken forcefully to the Fairfax County Chamber of Commerce about the importance of that vote; this was surprising, considering the traditional NEA opposition to any kind of "merit pay." After the February school board vote, the FEA held a vote of its membership on merit pay "as amended by the School Board," which predictably drew overwhelming opposition, and both FEA and NEA went into opposition to Career Level II, while continuing to support the rest of TPEP.

At this point the school system has in place a performance-evaluation program that has resulted in highly trained observers and evaluators, much more attention to and discussion of instruction among teachers and administrators, hundreds of teachers either terminated or provided with special help to improve performance, a clear understanding of professional standards among all teachers, and identification of 2,198 teachers as outstanding among their peers. These 2,198 began receiving their 9-percent bonus in their paychecks with the 1989–90 school year. TPEP has already created a more professional atmosphere among teachers and administrators. The "merit pay" element is in place.

While all of this has been going on, the school system has also been developing a program for selecting, training, and evaluating all educational administrators. Those who evaluate must themselves be evaluated, but rigorous selection and comprehensive training will ensure that few, if any, will reach their administrative posts without the wherewithal to handle them at the highest professional level.

The blue-ribbon commission was key to getting past the initial political and financial obstacles to performance evaluation, merit pay, and higher teacher salaries in Fairfax County. The commission's report was a rallying point for various constituencies, and a catalyst for change. Political and financial obstacles are never totally overcome, however; political players change, budgets change, and support for merit pay is always on the same shifting sands as every educational program. All are subject annually to changing political and financial realities in every local community. Real educational innovation typically happens at the local level, and hence is built on these shifting sands. However, when such innovations spread, and become institutionalized at state or national levels, the sands stop shifting. The problem then becomes maintaining the quality and integrity of the program. But the future of our nation depends on the education our children receive, and that education depends on the professional performance and status of our teachers. Many pundits have been telling us for several years that we will not be able, as a nation, to compete on the international scene in the twenty-first century unless we can substantially improve education for all of our students. This is not going to happen unless our teachers are among the very best and brightest of our nation's professionals—unless many of those now going into law and medicine, engineering and finance, go instead into teaching. In a very politically and financially difficult situation, we have been able to establish a performance-evaluation and merit-pay system in Fairfax County, Virginia. It has already paid off, and will provide even greater dividends in future years. More needs to be done, and we will do it, but at some point other school systems need to recognize that teacher professionalism will not develop without some such system. Other school boards and superintendents need to bite the bullet. Teacher unions and educational organizations need to see the benefits of professionalism. Governors and presidents need to see the importance of teacher professionalism to our national future. The future is here in Fairfax County, and spreading.

Perhaps the greatest factor in school reform is public support. If parents and their childless neighbors genuinely want good public schools, almost no force in the country can stop them. If not—well, we have seen how little was accomplished when political leaders in Texas tried to enact reforms that state residents considered unnecessary. In a community like Fairfax County, where schools were good to begin with, residents might be expected to wonder why they should pay for costly reforms. And given the controversy that has surrounded the merit-pay program, the proposed longer school day, and other measures, they might soon tire of the whole subject. The reality is encouragingly different. The following section was written by Marvin Cetron and the staff of Forecasting International.

THE 1990 FAIRFAX COUNTY PUBLIC SCHOOLS SURVEY

Early in 1990, Forecasting International conducted a public-opinion survey for the Fairfax County school system, the third such poll in sixteen years. Our purpose was to learn how strongly Fairfax residents support their schools, how good a job they believe local schools are doing, and where they believe changes are still needed. What we discovered was a community where learning was sure to prosper. In a time when schools across the United States are struggling with low attendance and poor academic performance, Fairfax County's schools work, and area residents know it. What is more, there is no sign that people are growing complacent in their success or are tiring of reform after years of sometimes contentious change.

Community Standing

If parental support is one key to school success, education in Fairfax County has a lot going for it. One parent in four said he or she felt "very involved" with his or her children's schooling, and nearly three-fourths gave themselves at least a 7 or 8 on a ten-point scale of involvement. And this commitment was at its highest among minority populations that in other communities often seem cut off from their schools. Fully 43 percent of Hispanic parents said they felt themselves to be very involved with their children's education, far more than in the overall population. In part, this may be because they have felt themselves handicapped by an inadequate education and thus pay close attention to their children's progress, but the district's human-relations committee deserves credit for actively recruiting minority parents to the cause of schooling.

On the whole, Fairfax County residents rated their public schools very highly. Fully 84 percent of those interviewed considered the quality of the schools to be "excellent" or "good," up from 74 percent sixteen years ago. This is well above the national average. Seventy-seven percent said the schools did "a good job of preparing students for college."

All but 9 percent said that county schools were "getting better," or at least holding their own. Several groups were particularly enthusiastic about the progress of Fairfax County schools in recent years: blacks, Hispanics, and respondents with less than a complete high-school education. This may reflect approval of the special language and minority-aid programs available in this community. Thirty-nine percent of respondents believe that the region's schools will continue to improve, including significant majorities of blacks, Asians, Hispanics, and low-income people.

Yet there were problems as well. Although nearly six out of ten Fairfax residents felt that graduates were well prepared to find a place in the work force, another 24 percent said that their level of readiness was "bad."

More than half of the respondents felt that discipline in the public schools was "not strict enough." Nearly one respondent in four rated student attitudes, behavior, or discipline the worst problem now facing Fairfax schools. Among minority groups, the percentages were even higher. Two-thirds of blacks and more than 60 percent of Hispanics and Asians believed that discipline should be tighter. And some 40 percent rated student drug and alcohol abuse as the worst problem now facing the schools.

In contrast, nearly one-third of respondents cited the quality of teachers as the Fairfax County Public Schools' greatest strength. Instructional programs/curriculum won top honors from 19 percent, while fiscal/financial support was cited by one in ten, up from only 2 percent in the 1981 survey.

Courses and Programs

Fairfax County residents offered strong support for the traditional core curriculum at both elementary and high-school levels. When asked which elementary-school courses were most valuable, arithmetic/math/basic math was the clear winner, selected by 52 percent of the people queried. Reading came in second, with 34 percent, followed by English, at 19 percent. Art, phys-ed, music, health, foreign language, and sex education were all nominated as being least valuable, but none received more than 9 percent of the vote.

Math and science were perceived to be the best-taught courses, chosen by 36 percent and 22 percent of the respondents respectively. Yet these subjects ranked at the top of the list of courses where improvement was needed, with identical ratings of 17 percent. This almost surely reflects the recent wave of publicity about the shortage of trained scientists and technicians in the United States, and the relatively poor performance of American students in these fields compared with their peers in Japan and other countries.

On a scale of 0 to 10, all nine of the special programs and services evaluated were considered important enough to rate an average score of 7 or above. Programs for the disabled topped the list with a composite rating of 8.2. Drug-abuse-prevention efforts came in second on the list, counseling and guidance services third. Extracurricular activities, considered a top priority in the 1974 FCPS survey, are now viewed as one of the least important.

Money Matters

School funding proved to be a major concern, even in well-to-do Fairfax County. Though nearly half of the people surveyed believed that the district's public schools were adequately funded, another 42 percent said that "more funding is needed," including significant majorities of blacks, Asians, Hispanics, parents of intermediate students, and people with less than a full high-school education. Some 45 percent of the survey population said that extra money for the schools should be diverted from other programs; this included comfortable majorities of all sizable ethnic minorities and of people who had a high-school education or less. Only 24 percent said they would be willing to pay higher taxes to provide added school funding.

Reform Efforts

The Fairfax County merit-pay program continues to receive strong support from parents and non-parents alike. Two-thirds of the respondents felt that it would improve the quality of teaching, and fully 71 percent said they approved of the program. Teachers' arguments that teacher evaluation is inherently unfair and likely to cause morale problems seem to carry little weight with the public.

Decentralization proposals were supported even more strongly. Seventy-seven percent of the respondents felt that decentralization in general was a "good idea." Fully 84 percent would grant schools greater flexibility in selecting and assigning staff, while 85 percent would allow them to adapt their instructional methods to meet local student needs. When it came to permitting greater flexibility in the use of school funds, however, the approval rating dropped to 71 percent. In each case, significantly more parents than non-parents approved the proposals.

There was no consensus on whether to lengthen the elementary-school day. Women and elementary-school parents in particular opposed the idea, though by relatively narrow margins, while non-whites, men, those with annual incomes of over $75,000, and those with graduate degrees marginally supported it.

Slightly fewer people approved of extending the school year, though again the vote was almost evenly divided. Only Asian residents clearly favored this change.

Just under 60 percent of respondents endorsed the idea of providing a full day of kindergarten. Most in favor were blacks (73 percent), Hispanics (72 percent), and those who lacked high-school diplomas (78 percent).

With a total approval rating of 70 percent, establishment of a preschool program for four-year-olds was by far the favorite proposal included in the survey. Approval soared to 87 percent among blacks who were polled, and 86 percent among Hispanics. No group gave the idea an approval rating of less than 61 percent.

Conclusions

In all, the 1990 Fairfax County Public Schools Survey paints a very encouraging picture of one local school system. Fairfax County is clearly at the forefront of the school-reform movement in the United States, and residents just as clearly like that idea. The high approval ratings for teacher evaluation and merit pay, decentralization, full-day kindergarten, and a preschool program should encourage the school administration to proceed with these programs as quickly as possible. Even those proposals that respondents rejected—extending the school day and year—might eventually win approval if their merits can be made sufficiently clear to parents. Only one real deficiency appeared in the survey: the perceived weakness in preparing young people for the job market noted by nearly one in four of the people polled. With the support of local residents, school authorities may well repair that weakness before the next poll is due.

For other communities, the dramatic success of the Fairfax County schools offers an encouraging role model. It clearly is possible to improve even relatively good schools. And it is possible to gain broad support for even controversial reforms if school authorities make the effort to explain their proposals to their constituents. Fairfax has done both. What is more, it has maintained its rate of progress for more than a decade, without losing the interest of area residents.

Though Fairfax County's relative wealth and high level of education seem to give it advantages over most other communities, it is in the poorer, less well educated segments of the population that school reform finds its greatest support. This clearly shows the benefits of maintaining good communications between school authorities and the public. If there is a single lesson to be drawn from Fairfax County's experience that other districts can use, this has to be it: If would-be school reformers make sure that local residents know what they are doing, and what benefits any proposed reforms have to offer, then they will give school reform all the support it needs.

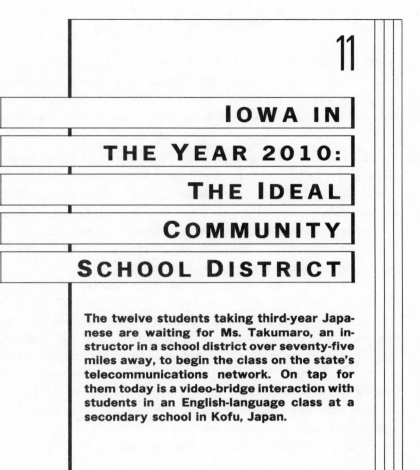

11

IOWA IN THE YEAR 2010: THE IDEAL COMMUNITY SCHOOL DISTRICT

The twelve students taking third-year Japanese are waiting for Ms. Takumaro, an instructor in a school district over seventy-five miles away, to begin the class on the state's telecommunications network. On tap for them today is a video-bridge interaction with students in an English-language class at a secondary school in Kofu, Japan.

Most of the reforms discussed in this book are aimed at one or two aspects of educational reform. Advocates of merit pay hope to improve the pool of teachers; curriculum reformers in general focus on what is to be taught, but ignore the process of teaching itself. Even the most sweeping reforms limit themselves in some way: The Key School's revolutionary program is aimed solely at grade-school students, while the proposals offered by Mortimer Adler and Theodore Sizer inherently deal only with academic learning, not with the job training now expected of our schools. This is not to criticize such tightly focused ideas; to the extent that our schools improve, they will do so by putting such plans into practice. But broader views of the educational landscape are needed as well, to put the welter of programs and proposals into perspective. The following vision of one state's future was supplied by Dr. William L. Lepley, director of the Iowa Department of Education.

I'd like you to forget most of your preconceptions about what an elementary/secondary school district is like. Don't think in terms of enrollment, or grade-school buildings, or 9–12 high schools. I'm going to take you into the year 2010 for a look at the school district of the future. The one concept you can carry twenty years into the future is that our state's commitment to quality education for every person will remain as strong as it is today.

I'd like to call for an educational barn-raising, where all the neighbors gather to build a system geared for the year 2010. We will call it the Ideal Community School District, situated in south-eastern Iowa. This hypothetical district possesses the qualities—including an excellent teaching and administrative staff, the needed community support and resources—that we are striving to create. In a way it is like the famed Lake Wobegon, where all the teachers are well paid and the children are above average. But this scenario is grounded in reality, since many of the initiatives that will create the Ideal Community School District are taking place today.

The Ideal Community
School District

The Ideal Community School District provides a framework of continuous education that spans a person's entire life. Citizens from the Ideal town or city and surrounding areas enter the education system, but are never forced to leave.

The Ideal schools allow students to move in and out of the continuum smoothly and without barriers such as district bound-aries, grade levels, neighborhood locations, or regulatory restrictions. The structure has been created based on what we want the system to deliver—that is, what's best for students.

The Ideal Community School District buildings are not limited by our definition of "school" today. They are hubs of the commu-

nity, since by 2010 society has realized that the school is the only
societal institution that can truly be an advocate, a resource, and a
catalyst for children and families, as well as learners of all ages. As
such, the Ideal school district houses not only educational programs, but a wealth of community resources as well: health services,
job services, and human services agencies. It is the community's
senior-citizen volunteer center. Adults come to Ideal schools for
educational opportunities that range from childbirth and parenting
classes to pre-retirement planning. The buildings are open around
the clock, to accommodate adult and community education classes.
The superintendent is the significant community leader responsible
for coordinating children's and family services of the Ideal community—but he or she is the superintendent of children and family
services, rather than the superintendent of education only.

The Ideal district provides a continuum of education that ranges
from preschool education and child care to elementary education,
to secondary education, to adult education. Iowans in the year 2010
do not think in terms of elementary/secondary versus postsecondary education: They think in terms of a continuum of services for
lifelong learning.

The school year is not limited by artificial restrictions of 180 days
or prescriptions for five-and-a-half-hour instructional days. Flexible
schedules and teacher contracts, enlightened labor-management relations, and year-round learning are emphasized.

An Ideal Professional
Work Environment

As a professional work environment for teachers, the Ideal system
allows teachers to teach at their optimum. Teachers in Ideal have
completed a preparation program that includes college course work
along with an internship or residency in a regional clinical school.
They have had the benefits of mentoring from experienced teachers, and in fact, several Ideal teachers are mentors today for
younger, less-experienced teachers. There are ethnic role models
at each level. Flexible schedules allow teachers in the Ideal system
ample time to prepare for classes, to discuss teaching techniques

with their colleagues in the system, and to enhance their own abilities through continued learning.

Teachers in the Ideal system look back on the work environment of the 1980s and shake their heads. The professional isolation faced by teachers and administrators in the 1980s is a thing of the past, as technology has provided regular and instantaneous communication among teachers and administrators across Iowa and throughout the nation. A science teacher at Ideal High can call upon counterparts anywhere in the nation to trade teaching techniques or to obtain statistics and research. That science teacher can hook up with any of a number of computerized data bases to get up-to-the-minute information for use in tomorrow's physics class. And if this sounds like dreaming to you, it's not. The groundwork for this system is in place today. In fact, by 2010, technology will probably have provided professional opportunities for teachers far beyond what we can now imagine.

The building administrator is an advocate for his staff, a facilitator, a cheerleader for high expectations, with excellent skills in monitoring and reporting student progress on clearly identified learning outcomes. Teachers in the Ideal schools are managers of the learning environment. The teacher has mastered the tools to diagnose learning needs and to prescribe appropriate learning activities, which include direct instruction, computer-assisted instruction, and interaction with peers in the classroom and, electronically, around the nation. Teaching methods are routinely matched to the student's individual learning style. The typical teacher spends only about three hours per day in direct instruction, thanks to a variety of new technological tools, paraprofessionals, volunteers, senior citizens, parents, and other aides.

Teachers use classroom aids and technology to supplement their personal instruction. Each student's desk is an intellectual Adventureland. At each workstation is a microcomputer that links each student to other students, the teacher, powerful instructional data bases worldwide, as well as other diverse cultural classrooms around the country. Students and teachers are well versed in the use of interactive television and videodiscs.

The Ideal curriculum is integrated across subject matter and from prekindergarten through postsecondary education. Students are assessed not on the work they complete but on the skills they master. The curriculum and the teachers set high expectations for students. The Ideal system does not make excuses for why children can't succeed. The basic belief is that each child can learn and each child can succeed. "Pull-out" programs, which remove students from their normal classes for specialized instruction, have been virtually eliminated, lowering class size. Teachers are prepared to deal with children from diverse backgrounds and cultures and with different problems.

The Ideal Student Environment

For students, the Ideal system is also a welcome change. Most Ideal students attended Ideal Preschool from 6:30 A.M. to 6:30 P.M., where play-oriented, developmentally appropriate activities and child care helped to prepare them for all-day, everyday kindergarten. Parents pay according to ability, with state and federal support available for those with the greatest need. The students move from grade level to grade level based not on years, but on abilities. This means that in the Ideal class of what we now call third-graders, children range in age from, say, seven to eleven.

There are no firm boundaries or barriers to prevent children from achieving. Some children who attend Ideal actually live in other districts. Ideal excels in its science and fine-arts programs, and these programs have encouraged some children from surrounding school districts to enroll there. On the reverse side, several children from the Ideal school system have chosen to attend school in a neighboring district that offers a unique instructional program in language arts and communication skills. The key factor is that parents and students in 2010 have choices, and education takes on a more regional look.

Ideal students at the secondary level have an interesting day ahead of them. The twelve students taking third-year Japanese are waiting for Ms. Takumaro, an instructor in a school district over seventy-five miles away, to begin the class on the state's telecommunications network. On tap for them today is a video-bridge interaction with students in an English-language class at a secondary school in Kofu, Japan. Another group of students is heading out into the city for a day of community-service activities, which are required of all students before graduation.

In general, what you can see when looking around the Ideal district on a given day is a curriculum that centers on the use of cooperative learning, individualized instruction, and an experience-based approach to learning. The curriculum emphasizes higher-order thinking and the development of skills needed to make decisions, solve problems, and access information.

The Ideal Educational Neighbor

The Ideal district has an excellent relationship with the nearby area college. Secondary and postsecondary educational opportunities are continuous. Age barriers and access questions are nonexistent, and students of all ages learn from each other. The area college is a valuable part of the Ideal district. Besides offering advanced-placement courses and vocational education, it shares its instructors and helps in meeting the needs of disabled people; it also provides resources for the community education program, partnerships in community and economic development activities, technology enhancements, and assistance with staff-development programs.

One group of students is taking a college-level calculus course at the Ideal school and receiving college-level credit for it. Their instructor is employed by a nearby university. Other students are receiving credit from the local colleges for vocational-education courses. Many Ideal students will graduate from high school already possessing college credit. This is a big change from the 1980s. According to the U.S. Department of Education, Iowa ranked forty-ninth of all states in 1987 in the percentage of high-school students who graduated with advanced-placement credit, at only 2.2 percent; in contrast, Utah, the national leader, graduated 26.6 percent of its students with advanced-placement credit.

Building the Ideal
Community School

What can we do today to help create the Ideal Community School District?

To create the Ideal system, we need to "blur the lines," that is, to lower the educational barriers that regiment our delivery system of education: district boundaries, school calendars and clocks, grade divisions, and lack of linkages with postsecondary education. In Iowa, we are already doing this in a variety of ways. The Post-secondary Enrollment Options Act has eased the transition for high-school students going on to higher education. Parent-choice/open-enrollment legislation has made it possible for students to attend school across city boundaries. School districts are sharing administrators, teachers, grade levels, and technology. One tangible example of "blurring the lines" is provided by area colleges that offer vocational programs for students in high schools.

To create the community-centered school of the Ideal Community School District, we can work to develop a stronger partnership with the community and to create regional access to higher education, including area colleges. Schools can be centers for child care, for preschools, for senior volunteer programs, for community social-service organizations. Indeed, this is already occurring in many forward-looking school districts.

We can apply what we already know about the teaching/learning process to develop clear, integrated curriculum progression based on monitoring of learning objectives so that students see the flexibility in the use of time for adults and for students, and we can work to integrate the use of technology and telecommunications. We need to place our energy into exploring how we can expand the use of technology, rather than trying to control it.

School districts are now in the Dark Ages as regards assessing student progress. We can develop assessment procedures for both students and programs to ensure that that more-flexible system of the year 2010 still provides high-quality education. By issuing state and district "report cards," by using standards that emphasize outcomes, by instituting new techniques to assess student progress, and by creating management-information systems that strengthen our accountability and give local policymakers greater control over the school system, we can thereby improve public support for education.

We can improve the professional workplace for educators by

recognizing different roles and lengths of contracts, recognizing special skills and experience, and paying teachers based on their performance in these new roles. We can pay attention to working conditions and reduce the isolation of the teaching profession. We can recruit minorities and women for teaching and management positions in education. We can improve recruitment, preparation, and continuing education of teachers. The clinical schools that will train teachers in the Ideal Community School District are being developed today. We can continue to develop that concept. While we have already begun development efforts for teachers, we have ignored the development of the administrator who must make the new, more-sophisticated systems work.

I submit to you that Iowa's education system will be strongest when it is not compartmentalized into the categories of preschool, K–8, 9–12, 12–14, and higher education. What separates these aspects of the education system is not nearly as strong as the tie that binds the system together: concern for the future of children, young people, and adults. Educators at all levels need to understand that education is all one system from prekindergarten through graduate school. As with any chain, stress at one link causes stress at all links. If quality declines in the elementary school, quality declines in the pool of college applicants. If quality declines in teacher-education programs, quality declines in the elementary school.

Whether in higher education or K–12, we must work with each other if we want a system that works. Each constituency, each interest group, each profession, each building or college or branch of government has something to say about the outcome, and a legitimate role in shaping that outcome. We need to acknowledge that all of these components are parts of a single system of education. We must not tear down a system that has served us so well, but we must have an educational barn-raising, where we all come together as partners, bringing together our collective commitment, cooperation, and hard work to create an educational system for 2010 that gives us reason to celebrate and be festive because we created it together!

12

ROCHESTER, MINNESOTA: A LESSON IN LONG-TERM PLANNING

[The] continuous process of in-depth analysis, planning, and review has required a major commitment of staff time and resources that might inhibit many school systems from undertaking a similar effort. We firmly believe that the work required is more than justified by the results. . . . [It] makes the difference between the chaos we once faced and the orderly progress we now achieve.

One unhappy characteristic of American government is its focus on the short term. Our leaders spend nearly all their time and effort in putting out whatever fire burns brightest, and relatively little in managing the system to avoid such crises. As a result, the faster they run, the farther behind they get. This is no less true of school systems than it is of the state and federal governments.

In 1984, administrators at the Rochester, Minnesota, community schools decided to break the cycle of reactive, short-term problem-solving and set the stage for lasting improvement. Their approach was to create a systematic process for long-range strategic planning. It worked well, and their experience offers a guide for other educators who would like to make a difference.

The following account of Rochester's forward-thinking way of doing things comes to us from Dr. John M. Schultz, superintendent of the Rochester Community Schools.

Like many other bureaucracies, the Rochester school system had a problem: one hand seldom knew what the other was doing. Each department made its own plans and set out to implement them without coordinating with other departments. The result was chaos. Individual plans were well thought out but wholly incompatible. So the first step was to establish the Superintendent's Cabinet, composed of advisers from each department. Their first task was to set up a long-range plan for the district. Since then, the Cabinet has had to watch developments in such fields as demographics, politics, economics, and technology; figure out how they will affect the schools; and monitor how well the plan is implemented.

It turned out that part of the job had already been done before the formal planning process began. A year earlier, a committee of citizens had evolved a series of fourteen financial recommendations covering almost every area of the school district's operations. Similarly, a committee of teachers and community members, aided by representatives from the Board of Education, had developed a series of "learner goals," a list of things students should know after spending twelve years in the Rochester public schools. These reports became the basis for the district's first five-year plan.

The final plan is broken into two parts. The first part comprises student learner goals adapted from the original committee report, and the second is a series of long-range goals for ten "key result areas." These areas include student learning and growth; financial resources; physical resources (buildings, equipment, and grounds); innovations (new programs and the like); community involvement and relations; organizational management; "marketing" (a combination of consumer surveys among the community and old-fashioned public relations); instructional programs and services, including curriculum materials and classroom equipment; performance training and evaluation; and operational programs and services involving support staff.

The details of the plan are keyed to Rochester's unique circumstances, and would be unlikely to interest those in other areas. For our purposes, the important things are how that plan was hammered out and how it is updated each year.

The Superintendent's Cabinet has developed a standard procedure for long-range analysis, based on the strategic planning methods used in business. Throughout the winter they perform surveys of the key players in the educational system and analyze their findings: in November the Cabinet looks at changes in the community; in December the staff undergoes scrutiny; in January the topic is enrollment projections, followed by student profiles and finance in February and March. The Cabinet develops likely scenarios for each key result area to determine what will happen if nothing occurs to change the current trends. Then it examines each scenario in terms of SWOTs—strengths, weaknesses, opportunities, and threats. From this it establishes the district's long-range goals, concrete operational objectives, and strategies for meeting them.

In the 1988–89 school year the Cabinet added another forecasting tool: a Delphi study that asked experts from around the country for their views on a variety of issues within each key result area. For example, typical questions in the section on student learning and growth asked what factors the respondents felt would have the greatest impact on our students' learning and growth in the 1990s and what changes the school districts would have to make as a result. Influences considered included the growth of high-tech industry, the growth of ethnic minorities, new teaching methods, and the problem of drug abuse.

Each of the multiple-choice questions asked for further comments about each topic.

The goal of the Delphi study was to develop a consensus view of the future, which would be used as a guide in updating our five-year plan. In large part, the idea succeeded. The answers to our questions, and particularly the comments offered by each of the experts polled, now form the basis of our current planning.

This continuous process of in-depth analysis, planning, and review has required a major commitment of staff time and resources that might inhibit many school systems from undertaking a similar effort. We firmly believe that the work required is more than justified by the results. The 1989–90 school year saw the completion of our first full five-year plan. Thanks largely to the feedback gained by each year's re-analysis, we accomplished all of our original goals. Perhaps more important, because we add a new year to our five-year calendar as each old year expires, we still have a firm sense of where we are going in the years ahead.

Strategic planning offers at least four benefits: It forces us to place greater attention to the future implications of today's decisions. It enables the district to identify and prepare for decisions to be made in the future. It helps us to identify the potential opportunities and threats of developments in the community that once might have gone unnoticed until it was too late to plan for them. And it promotes a philosophy of action rather than reaction. In a very real sense, this makes the difference between the chaos we once faced and the orderly progress we now achieve. It is a difference that school districts everywhere should experience for themselves.

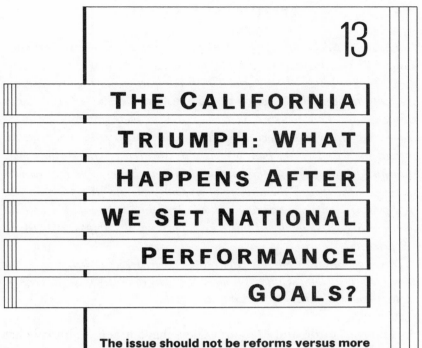

13

THE CALIFORNIA TRIUMPH: WHAT HAPPENS AFTER WE SET NATIONAL PERFORMANCE GOALS?

The issue should not be reforms versus more money, as if spending more money constituted a reform strategy, or as if initiating high-payoff strategies could be done for free. . . . The issue should be, What can the nation buy with additional investments, and how much return can we expect for those expenditures?

One of the best arguments for optimism about American schools is how much some school districts have already achieved. One of the best examples is the state of California. Between 1983 and 1989, twelfth-grade test scores there improved one and a quarter grade equivalents in math and three-fifths grade in reading. Eighth-graders improved one-half grade in all subjects—reading, writing, math, science, and history—in just three years, from 1986 to 1989. Looking at it another way, in 1986 the average Japanese eighth-grader was two years ahead of his American counterpart; California cut the gap by twenty-five percent in just three years.

The state's SAT scores gained almost as dramatically. The proportion of California students scoring over 450 on the verbal portion of the test grew by 19 percent between 1983 and 1989; the fraction scoring over 500 on the math test grew by 28 percent. Average scores went up in every major ethnic group. This occurred though 12 percent more graduates took the test—a less elite group, from whom lower scores might have been expected; though the school system had to cope with an average of 140,000 more students each year; though the number of students living in poverty doubled in the 1980s; though the number of students who did not speak English as a primary language and who are still struggling to cope with it doubled to one in six. And while all this was happening, the dropout rate fell by 18 percent.

Much of the credit for this remarkable progress goes to Bill Honig, the state's widely acclaimed Superintendent of Public Instruction. In this report, he tells how California is rescuing its schools.

As Marvin Cetron and Margaret Gayle have noted, California has made a good start on the task of improving its schools. Our experience may shed some light on what it takes for a reform strategy to work.

First and foremost, it must be comprehensive and spring from what needs to be learned and how best to teach it. The ability to abstract, conceptualize, and solve problems is becoming increasingly important, even for traditionally blue-collar jobs. These skills may best be taught by cooperative learning in the fields of math, science, writing, history, literature, health, and fine arts. The same instructional strategies are also the best way to prepare thinking citizens who understand democracy and its ways, and who possess the wisdom and character to capitalize on the freedom given them.

It took years of heavy lobbying, but this philosophy has now become widely accepted among educators. Our slogan: All students can learn. Our meaning: Virtually all children can learn to think, understand democracy and the culture around them, and become prepared for the changing job market. Our children can learn to be smart and learn to be good.

Second, using experts in each field, we defined the kind of curriculum and instruction necessary to reach these goals—in reading, literature, writing, language skills, science, math, history, foreign language, vocational education, health, and physical education. We obtained consensus by involving large numbers of teachers and educators without watering down the bite of reform. These agreements were embodied in our state framework and curricular guides, which are widely available and used. These guidelines are sufficiently precise to have a definite point of view (e.g., reading instruction should include literature books, and social studies should be history-based and idea-driven), but open enough for teachers to figure out how best to organize instruction.

Third, we changed our state tests to reflect this more-demanding curriculum. We now test in science and history, evaluate writing samples, and assess for higher levels of understanding in reading and math. We also established an accountability system that set specific targets for the state, and gave each school and district information on how it was doing in reaching those targets. We publicize the results annually. More than 700 of our best schools have received Distinguished School Awards given at a prestigious luncheon sponsored by some of education's business friends.

Fourth, we developed specific implementational strategies in each curricular area to get the word out on what the changes were, and why they were needed. For example, in shifting to a more literature-based English curriculum, we developed comprehensive training through the UCLA Literature Project, and produced numerous documents to support our efforts.

Fifth, and crucial to our success, a tremendous effort was made to get local school superintendents and board members to buy into the vision and strategies of reform and, most important, to devote substantial dollars, during tight fiscal times, to staff development. We designed math, history, writing, literature, science, and fine-arts training to fit our revamped curriculum. Many in the corporate world are now saying that investment in their employees is the most critical factor in meeting worldwide competition and continuing productivity growth. Can you imagine IBM or Apple attempting to sell a new product without training its salespeople, or the U.S. Air Force allowing pilots to fly without investing heavily in training them? The concept seems absurd. Yet in many political circles, the obvious reform strategy of heavy investment in teachers to acquaint them with the improvements in each discipline smacks of a boondoggle. The hard reality is that without that investment, large-scale improvements will not occur.

Sixth, California spends nearly $300 million a year for site planning and implementation through our School Improvement Program. This effort provides resources for teachers and principals, with the community's advice, to take the general reform ideas and devise specific strategies for a particular school.

Seventh, we designed and implemented specific strategies to improve the quality of instructional materials (four years ago, California rejected all math books), enhance leadership of principals and superintendents (we are training over 3,000 principals in how to reform their schools), and involve parents (a partnership with the Quality Education Project has trained nearly 200,000 parents and teachers in the state's lowest socioeconomic areas in how to help their children learn). We formed a strong working relationship with the business community, higher education, and law enforcement; and we have initiated hundreds of partnership programs. Finally, we are revamping each special program, such as vocational education, bilingual education, and programs for children at risk of failing, to ensure that these programs will help accomplish the overall reform objectives. We also embarked on a multimillion-dollar program of technology introduction.

How the cumulative effect of these initiatives can produce impressive gains can be seen clearly in our three-year experience with junior-high-school reform. In 1985, when it was apparent that eighth-grade performance was lagging, we called for strengthening academics along the lines suggested in the California frameworks, increasing individual attention to students, and making organizational changes within the schools. Our report was enthusiastically endorsed by educators who knew we were in trouble in those grades. Subsequent surveys found almost every junior high or middle school in the state attempting to implement the report's recommendations.

To further these efforts, a grant from the Carnegie Corporation established a support network of 100 middle-grade schools. We also obtained from the legislature and governor $5 million for planning grants of $30 per student for one-third of California's junior high schools. (This year, every junior high will receive funds.) We strengthened our testing program to cover writing, science, history, problem-solving in math, and more-demanding reading comprehension. Local districts devoted substantial resources to middle-grade improvement, especially in staff development, and alignment of vision, testing, training, and accountability.

The comprehensive approach worked better than any of us had expected—a 25-percent increase in achievement across the board in just three years. The critical elements of such massive change should provide a serviceable blueprint for other efforts: a vision of quality specifically defined; assessment procedures that reinforce that vision; activities to allow people at schools to work through those ideas and plan site-tailored responses and organizational changes; massive investments in staff development; and school and district alignment of curriculum, assessment, and training in a coordinated effort.

National Policy Implications

If the conventional wisdom is way off base, and a significant cadre of educators not only is actually willing and able to improve the schools but also has started to do so, what are the national policy implications? First of all, President Bush can legitimize the successful strategies that many states and districts have used to produce results. His endorsement will provide credibility and accelerate the pace of reform.

Second, the key to success in improving our schools is for our national leaders to invest selectively in strategies that can leverage the whole system and help to upgrade education. The issue should not be reforms versus more money, as if spending more money constituted a reform strategy, or as if initiating high-payoff strategies could be done for free. Some of the educational reforms that worked, such as initiating accountability systems or changing the structural nature of schools, did not require extra funds or required only minimal amounts. But some essential ingredients of reform did necessitate additional capital. Thus, the issue should be, What can the nation buy with additional investments, and how much return can we expect for those expenditures?

What follows are descriptions of the highest-payoff targets of opportunity: goal-setting and strengthened assessment, staff development, development of technology, restructuring schools, parent and business partnerships, and completing the equity agenda.

Set Goals and
Strengthen Assessment

The national goals set by the President's education summit need fleshing out. Performance standards should include increasing the number of seniors who can read at a technologically adept level from 42 percent to 60 percent, who can use numbers to solve moderately complex problems from 51 percent to 75 percent, and who can produce an adequate piece of persuasive writing from 27 percent to 50 percent, based on literacy, mathematics, and writing scales developed by NAEP. Other targets should include increasing proficiency in science and history, increasing the number of students who attend college, and lowering the dropout rate to 10 percent. Standards should be developed at eighth-grade (what reading, writing, mathematics, science, and history performance levels are necessary to make it in high school) and fifth-grade (entry to junior high) levels.

Setting performance standards, however, is only the first step. National goals must be brought home to each school, district, and state. This task can be accomplished by translating the overall target to annual terms (to go from 42 percent to 60 percent in ten years is about a 2-percent improvement a year as a school, district, and state goal). If a typical high school has 300 seniors, 120 of whom are at the adept level, the school must educate another six students a year as its share to reach these national goals. Results could be widely publicized and recognition given for being on target.

In addition, one of the most powerful levers for educational improvement would be to change national and local assessments from mainly multiple-choice, factual-recall questions to more essay, problem-solving, and open-ended items. Local assessments should focus more on achievements in the disciplines than on a narrow range of basic skills. These kinds of tests are used in every other country and are more in line with real-world performance and what teachers should be doing in the classroom. Performance assessment costs more than current assessment, but the expenditure is well worth it.

Invest Sufficient Capital in Staff Development

- **Train our existing teachers to teach a more sophisticated curriculum.** We now know much more about how to teach sophisticated subjects to a diverse student body. Crucial to success is a teacher who knows the material cold. To teach Math A, a course designed to teach sophisticated math to the average junior-high-school or high-school student, teachers have to know as much math as if they were teaching advanced-placement courses for honor students. To get average students to wrestle with the sophisticated ethical, political, and personal issues encountered in literature, teachers must have not only read but also thought about the book and tailored the author's ideas for classroom discussion.

  In California, working with our best teachers and professors, we have designed powerful training strategies in the subject-matter disciplines. Unfortunately, only a lucky few of our teachers have been able to participate. We also need to incorporate more productive training techniques and technologies, similar to those used by our major corporations and other government agencies.

- **Improve recruiting, preparing, inducting, and certifying teachers.** We will need 2 million new teachers by 1999; no strategy will improve our schools' performance more than attracting and retaining top-flight teachers. In 1984, only 45 percent of teachers said they would advise a young person to pursue a career in teaching; today two-thirds say they would. The National Board for Professional Teaching Standards will provide voluntary teacher certification, and a national teachers' corps would encourage talented individuals to enter the profession.

- **Provide leadership training for principals.** Only limited resources are currently allocated to recruit, select, and train principals, who are the key to a good school.

- **Improve technical assistance to school districts.** The best schools are in districts that back up their individual schools with specialized facilities and training that no single institution could justify; yet training in the effective use of these district-level resources is still in its infancy.

Develop and Incorporate Technology

We need a massive software and training effort to assist instructors. According to the federal Office of Technology Assessment, in 1985 there was only $1,000 of capital behind each worker in kindergarten-through-twelfth-grade education. This figure is well below the average of $50,000 per employee in the general economy and between $7,000 and $20,000 for labor-intensive service industries. Because we are asking teachers to teach a more sophisticated curriculum, we need to provide high-quality software that draws upon the nation's best minds to supplement regular classroom instruction. For example, we can provide science software that presents the highest-quality science experiments for elementary-school classrooms. This massive software-development project is ideally undertaken at the federal level; although it will take an initial investment of funds, it can pay huge dividends.

Restructure Schools

We should unleash educators' talents to tackle quality issues and improve student performance, and teachers should participate in creating successful learning environments. Currently, most teachers work in isolation. Overregulation, principal and teacher attitudes, and lack of training and time prevent faculties from organizing schoolwide improvements. We must agree on standards and how to measure them; then we must move out of the schools' way to allow teachers and principals to do their jobs. We should study communities that are restructuring, encourage districts to replicate successful projects, and provide developmental grants that foster team building.

Encourage Parent and Business Partnerships

If parents make sure that their children do their homework, stay on top of their children's performance, and read to their children, student attitudes and performance will soar dramatically. Effective parent-involvement programs have been developed that cost only $10 to $15 per child.

There have been thousands of business-school partnerships, but the most promising ones attempt to change the incentive structure within a high school. Just think of the change if students knew that their grades and effort counted. Businesses could agree to establish common performance standards and allow schools to assess for them. Companies could rely on teacher judgment of quality the way university admissions officers do (this is done in most other countries). Schools could make achievement information available, and build in early counseling for students on what it takes to get hired and receive higher pay, and how far they have to go to reach hiring standards. Then teachers become students' partners to help more of them reach performance levels that pay off. Small developmental grants could encourage this type of partnership, and this strategy could be incorporated in federal training policy and legislation.

Complete the Equity Agenda

We should fully fund programs for at-risk children and youth. We need to expand successful programs that prevent later failure, such as prenatal and neonatal health care, preschool, and coordinated family services.

Model Programs

A perfect example of a successful program made possible by a small initial investment that incorporates every critical component of our effective reform strategies is Project 2000, in the Kern Union High School District in Bakersfield, California. The Ford Motor Company and several other corporations are putting up the initial capital, $400 per student (approximately 10 percent of the state's annual per-pupil expenditure) for 100 students each at four high schools.

The project concentrates on the average child, encouraging that student to take more and harder academic courses and go to college. Students and parents must commit themselves to the project. A team of four teachers (English, science, math, and history) at each school plans the curriculum and organizational changes, with the principal's participation, and stays together during the school year with the 100 students. Teachers have common preparation periods. Each school receives a classroom of Macintosh computers, and the program stresses word processing and writing for freshmen. Students are provided role models and heavy counseling support. Substantial funds are provided for staff development, and teachers tackle the problems of how to make complicated subjects accessible to the average student.

Similar projects, such as AVID in San Diego, have doubled or tripled the college-going rates of minority youth and completely transformed their schools' atmosphere by changing the attitude of many previously apathetic students. The same strategy has worked for potential dropouts in the California Partnership Academies program, which has enjoyed substantial success in increasing graduation rates and community college attendance.

One desperately needed program would supply training for mathematics teachers. Thanks to research performed at the University of Chicago, we now know exactly where we go wrong in math instruction, and there is a consensus on what to do about it. The National Council of Teachers of Mathematics has issued a new set of standards; the University of Chicago has figured out how to teach these complicated standards to the average child; and a major textbook publisher has incorporated these ideas in new materials. Eighth-graders who have used these books have grown four grade levels in one year.

We have set up a university-sponsored California Mathematics Project, which has designed a promising training network and delivered effective training for teams of teachers in successful ideas, methods, and materials. So far, only 5 percent of our teachers have been reached. We are ready to go statewide if given the green light. New Jersey's PRISMS Project has initiated a similar strategy. If our political leaders want to improve math instruction in this country, we have already devised the curriculum and implementational strategies. What we need is a modest infusion of investment capital for significant training and site implementation of these plans.

Funding

Currently we spend approximately $195 billion annually on public schools. Twelve billion dollars of this amount comes from the federal budget (1 percent of the federal budget). If we provided an additional 5 percent of the $195 billion (about $10 billion a year), and invested it in the right activities for five years, we could substantially improve our schools' productivity *and* affect the quality of life and future well-being of our country. A return worth hundreds of billions a year is not a bad payoff for a $10-billion-a-year investment.

Some argue that we already spend a higher percentage of our gross national product on education than other countries do, and that we can fund any needed improvements by making choices within current expenditures. In fact, the statistics show that we rank lower than most industrialized countries on education spending, but there is little point in quoting them here; the whole line of reasoning is specious anyway. If by spending an extra $10 billion we can get five to six times the investment back in improved productivity, comparative percentages of GNP become irrelevant. We can realize such a return, and we must.

A Future Transformation

As educators, we are proud of what we have accomplished so far. Yet we know there is a long way to go. Our plea to our leaders is to make an honest appraisal of what has occurred in our schools since the reform movement was launched. Give us a modicum of respect for what we have accomplished so far, and begin to build on and enhance the effort already made. We know that not every school, district, or even state is participating in the educational reform movement. But there does exist a widespread cadre of educators who are willing to work cooperatively and implement further reforms that, in ten years, will transform our nation's schools into the world-class system our children deserve.

PART IV

TOWARD A
MORE LITERATE
TOMORROW

14

NINE LESSONS
LEARNED

The one reality that teachers everywhere must accept if we are to make any great progress in educational reform is that few students who fail do so because they lack the ability to learn; they fail because teachers fail to teach them.

The story of school reform in the 1980s was largely one of failure. In the three years following publication of *A Nation at Risk,* American educators organized more than 275 task forces, each with the purpose of finding out what was wrong with our schools and devising suitable repairs. Between 1983 and 1985 alone, state legislatures enacted more than 700 laws that specified curricula and course contents, prescribed teaching methods, and established new, more stringent standards for teacher certification. No fewer than forty-three states tightened their standards for high-school graduation, thirty-seven set up new student-testing programs, twenty-nine required new or more difficult teacher-competency tests, twenty-eight changed their teacher-certification requirements, and seventeen raised their college admission standards. Efforts were, if anything, stepped up in the five years that followed. And in 1990 the nation's educational performance was almost unchanged. Standardized test scores had barely risen overall, and had actually continued to fall among some demographic groups. The national literacy rate still declined. Dropout rates held virtually constant.

But of the hundreds of millions of dollars, and equal numbers of man-hours, devoted to rebuilding America's schools during that decade, not all were wasted. As we have seen in the preceding chapters, a few reform efforts have been successful, some of them dramatically so. The lessons learned from them will guide school reconstruction in the 1990s. We can learn from our failures, too, if only by recognizing mistakes to be avoided. The nine key lessons that are summarized in this chapter are distilled from the experiences recounted in previous chapters.

1. Raise Educational Standards at All Levels

There are two halves to this lesson. One is an obvious fact that many of our best educators have been trying to teach their colleagues for years. If virtually all Japanese students make a success of their school careers, then virtually all of them must be capable of learning, at least to that degree required for a sound basic education. And unless we assume that educability is inherited along with the epicanthic fold, virtually all of our own students are capable of learning as well.

It is amazing how few teachers really believe this fundamental premise, without which generalized schooling is a waste of society's resources. In particular, the idea that students from poor and otherwise disadvantaged families will almost inevitably lag behind those whose families occupy the upper end of the socioeconomic scale permeates the educational community.

Few educators are more dedicated to this form of veiled bigotry than those in our inner cities, where endemic social problems, decaying schools, and petrified bureaucracies make it far easier to go along with the system than to attempt the changes required to provide students with a sound education. Numerous studies have shown clearly that too many inner-city teachers by and large expect their students to fail. And when faced with students who, for whatever reason, are not doing well, rather than make a special effort to save them, teachers everywhere tend to abandon their poor performers. They ask less of students who are falling behind the class, are less friendly toward them, and respond less well when lagging students do get something right. The pattern is set during the early days of the school year. After one or two years of experience, a teacher can tell very quickly which students will excel, which will fail, and which will form the midsection of the class who just get by. From that day onward, it becomes very difficult for a student to change his image in the teacher's mind from washout to survivor, survivor to star—or star to survivor. And, of course, children live down to the level expected of them.

This belief in the inevitability of failure is one factor that has diluted educational standards in almost every school district in the country, and most of all those of our inner cities. Where students once were expected to master algebra before high-school graduation, in too many regions it is now enough for them to add and subtract with indifferent accuracy. Where they once would have mastered English grammar, it is now enough that they be able to make themselves approximately understood in conversation. If students cannot master the material, the reasoning goes, ask less of them; that way you avoid traumatizing them with failure—and escape blame for your own failure to teach. That this reasoning has been thoroughly discredited has done little to make it less popular.

There is no excuse for this loss of rigor. We have ample proof that American students *from all socioeconomic strata* can learn just as consistently as Japanese students. We find it in the work of Dr. Mortimer Adler, whose Paideia curriculum, based on the classics, has proved entirely "learnable" by the vast majority of students from virtually all ethnic and socioeconomic backgrounds. We see it too in the record of East Harlem's Central Park East school complex, where children from one of the poorest, most disadvantaged sections of New York City are receiving an education equal to those available in most private schools, and achieving comparable rates of success. If their students can learn, there is no excuse to doubt that others can do so as well.

The one reality that teachers everywhere must accept if we are to make any great progress in educational reform is that few students who fail do so because they lack the ability to learn; they fail because teachers fail to teach them.

That leads to an obvious corollary: Teachers must stop viewing students as statistics, and education as a game of musical chairs in which the slow inevitably lose out.

By definition, teachers today expect some students to fail. That is simply what happens to those who learn more slowly than their peers: when testing time comes around, some students excel, most get by, and some lose out. Many teachers automate this process by the statistical trick of "grading on the curve," giving A's to the top 10 percent of their students and flunking the bottom segment of the class without reference to any absolute measure of how much has been learned. A student who could answer only ten questions out of 100 on a test may receive an A if the remainder of the class answered only eight.

This concern for statistics is an institutional convenience that has nothing to do with providing an education. Instead, its purpose is to let teachers process as many students as possible, thereby minimizing the cost of instruction. Rather than using a wide variety of teaching methods and repeating material from a different angle for those who could not master it the first time around, they can simply lecture for the specified number of hours, give a test, and penalize those who require more time or a different form of teaching. Grading on the curve further ensures that each class will have an adequate supply of both stars and losers to prove that the teacher has been neither so demanding that few students can match his pace nor so lax that few are challenged.

For students and for the cause of learning, this system is every bit as arbitrary as it sounds. The average student who finds himself in a class of slow learners is guaranteed success—not necessarily a sound education, but at least a passing grade—while the same pupil in a class of bright, well-prepared students is doomed to fail. We see this regularly when a child of average ability moves from a school system with few resources and low expectations to a more fortunate district where performance standards are high.

This focus on statistics has nothing to do with the fundamental purpose of schooling. It does nothing to supply students with the fundamental information and skills required to live as responsible, productive, well-rounded adults. That being so, it is no wonder that America's schools often fail to produce the graduates we claim to expect of them, despite a decade of reform efforts.

No standard is good enough if it is built on the idea that some students must inevitably fail. No reform can work if it allows teachers to grade their students by comparing them with their classmates, rather than by evaluating what each student has learned.

2. Make Sure Schools and Teachers Meet New Educational Levels

"Accountability" has been the battle cry of reformers for many years, but we have only just begun to apply it to our educational system. The common thread of many reforms is to make certain that we reward success in educating our students, while punishing—or at least withholding rewards from—those who fail. Merit-pay programs, competency testing, parental choice, performance-based school accreditation, and a host of similar measures all fall into the category of promoting accountability.

Virginia has recently developed one novel program in this field. Its Educational Performance Recognition Program, scheduled to begin operation in the 1991 school year, sets seven objectives that schools should meet, including preparing students for college, preparing them for work, raising the graduation rate, improving the living skills and opportunities of special education students, and educating students at the elementary-, middle-, and secondary-school levels. Each goal is backed by at least six objective measures, and some by as many as fourteen, and schools will be ranked according to how well they rate on these indicators. For example, to determine how well a school is preparing students for college, education-department statisticians will look at the percentage of students taking the SAT and receiving the advanced-studies diploma (separate scores will be kept for minority students), taking advanced placement and college-level courses, completing Algebra I and foreign-language courses by the ninth grade, scoring in the upper quartile of eighth-grade and eleventh-grade tests, and enrolling in remedial college courses. They will also follow the school's graduates to college and look at their grade-point averages. In all, more than sixty indicators have been developed. Schools are free to meet these criteria in any way they can.

The program avoids penalties, but will reward schools that perform well according to the indicators and will provide remedial aid for those which lag behind. The top 5 percent of the state's schools each year will receive a special grant of $4,500 for elementary schools and $10,500 for secondary schools. Another 20 percent will get the opportunity to compete for part of a $100,000 grant fund. The department will seek out the practices that have made grant winners effective, and design workshops around them so that other schools can adopt more effective teaching and management practices. And for the bottom 5 percent each year, the department plans to set up staff training sessions, devise a comprehensive improvement plan for each school, and supply whatever extra money is required to bring deficient schools up to standards.

We have some small qualms about the Virginia proposal. While we agree that rewarding good performance is more likely to improve our schools than punishing failure, ruling out penalties from the start seems needlessly to deprive the state of a tool that it might someday find useful. Yet any attempt to make both schools and their faculties accountable for their performance must improve our chances of getting a good education for our students. Many such programs are sure to be enacted in the 1990s.

3. Spend More Time in School

One of the simplest lessons in our survey emerges, not from American experiments in reform, but from a look at educational practices in Japan. It is that learning is, in a crucial way, no different from digging ditches. All else being equal, the more time you spend at it, the more you will get done. On average, American children spend about 1,170 hours per year in class—180 days of six and a half hours each. Japanese children put in 1,920 hours of class time—240 days of eight hours—or 64 percent more than our students. That comparison neglects the time devoted to homework, which has nearly disappeared from the American student's life, and the fabled Japanese "cram schools"; factor them in, and the most diligent Japanese students spend well over twice as many hours in study each year as ours do. As a result, at graduation, some 98 percent of Japanese children score better on standardized science and math tests than do their American counterparts, and the contrast in other subjects is nearly as great.

Many educators, whose distaste for simple solutions borders on reflex, will argue that what we need is not to keep students in class longer, but to make those classes better at pouring information into the heads of recalcitrant students. In fact, both reforms are needed. It does no good to keep a child in a class where poor teaching methods or disorderly students make it impossible to learn. But in many of our schools, classes already operate with at least the necessary minimum of efficiency. The quickest, easiest way to get their students to learn more is to keep them at work longer. In moving to a seven-period day, Fairfax, Virginia, has taken a step in the right direction. We hope that other districts will follow its lead in the years to come. If by the year 2000 we have managed to stretch our average school year to 210 days of seven hours, it should go a long way toward improving the knowledge and skills with which our students leave high school.

4. Reward Everyone Involved with Education for Performance, Not for Time Served or Other Irrelevancies

It has been said that we have built a Soviet school system, in which no one is rewarded for success and no one is punished for failure. This is not wholly accurate—as we have seen, children are all too often punished for failures that their teachers and "the system" have forced on them—but there is an important truth here. The reward system in our schools is wholly out of touch with the goal of learning. Schools receive accreditation because they offer classes with the appropriate titles, not because students actually learn the subjects that regulators had in mind. Teachers are paid and promoted for their years in the classroom, not for turning out well-educated students. And students are promoted, not for learning, but because they have grown too tall to fit a grammar-school desk. This simply doesn't work.

Linking the reward system in our schools to academic performance will be one of the most difficult reforms to achieve. One reason is that there are so many changes to be made. Another is that so many people have an interest in maintaining the system on which they have based their careers. This is, for example, why teachers' unions across the country have bitterly fought such proposals as merit pay, "master teacher" career ladders, and competency testing; actually having to earn your rewards is a far more difficult proposition than merely serving time.

Further, making such changes is largely an act of faith. There have not yet been enough of these changes to demonstrate clearly that they improve school performance. Only one state has tied school accreditation to student performance, and few districts have adopted merit pay and similar plans. At this point, such proposals are made largely by analogy with private industry, where the "perform or die" philosophy has had a long and successful reign. But as merit pay and other reforms become established, proof of their value will not be difficult to find.

5. Establish a Comprehensive National Program of Preschools and Day-Care Centers

We have known for at least two decades that preschool programs work. When children who spend a year or two in a program like Head Start arrive in kindergarten or first grade, they are better prepared to learn than those who miss that opportunity. Further, they maintain their advantage throughout school and into later life.

One dollar spent on a preschool program saves or earns, on average, at least six dollars in the student's later years. Some of this money comes in the form of income taxes gained because the student who completes school earns far more than one who drops out; the rest represents savings in welfare benefits and prison costs for those who cannot find a place in a society that places an ever-greater premium on education. One of our most urgent needs is to put this knowledge to practical use.

Unfortunately, private preschools are too expensive for many parents to afford. Head Start reaches fewer than 20 percent of the children who need it, and extending its benefits to the remaining 80 percent will not be cheap. In a recent study, the National Research Council cited the need to establish a comprehensive preschool and day-care program as the nation's most pressing child-related issue. However, the group estimated that the cost will reach $5 billion to $10 billion.

The Bush administration's support for an expanded Head Start program is one of the most promising developments in the school reform movement. If preschool programs can be extended to all children, it will eventually do more to improve the success rates of our elementary and secondary schools than anything we can do for students already of school age. However, we do fear that the bill will eventually come much closer to the NRC estimate than to the administration's much lower figures. Whether society will be both willing and able to pay the full cost of preschool for all will be one of the key questions for the next five years.

6. Raise School Budgets So That We Can Pay Our Teachers a Living Wage and Give Them the Equipment They Need to Do Their Jobs

The sorry fact is that until teachers are paid as much as other college-trained professionals, those who enter our schools will be not the best and the brightest, but the worst and the dimmest. And paying teachers a wage high enough to attract talented young people to the profession means adding, on average, perhaps $10,000 per year per teacher to our educational spending.

Raising money for textbooks and other equipment is equally necessary. North Carolina, for example, began its school improvement program years before *A Nation at Risk* woke the rest of us to the need for educational reform. Yet the state department of education recently instructed social-studies teachers to test students as though it were still 1987, before all the changes in Eastern Europe and the Soviet Union began. The reason? The state's textbooks are so dated, and its budget for ancillary materials so low, that students could not be expected to be familiar with events beyond that date. The department could not keep the curriculum current or manage the changes that are necessary.

For science teachers, the situation is, if anything, more critical. The National Governors Association has declared as one of its educational goals that by the year 2000, American students will be the most knowledgeable in the world in the fields of science and mathematics. This is a worthy goal, but science can be taught well only if students have the chance to perform actual experiments. This requires costly laboratories that many of our poorer schools lack, and materials difficult to fit into tight budgets. We have yet to find a trustworthy estimate of how much it will cost to modernize our grammar- and high-school science courses. We predict that the total will stun budget-weary legislators.

That said, one more lesson is that money is not everything. Despite the Reagan administration's tight-money talk, spending on education, adjusted for inflation and the shrinking class size of the "baby bust" generation, grew in the 1980s by about 24 percent—half again as much as in the previous decade. Instructional spending, that part of the budget not devoted to school construction and similar expenditures, went up by 31 percent during the decade—this while students' test scores continued their decline. At least three-fourths of the studies that have compared school spending and student performance have found no correlation between them; two or three have even suggested that school districts that spend more on their students actually get less performance in return. One reason for this may be that about half of our national education budget goes to pay for the bloated bureaucracy that administers our schools. In Europe, the figure is only 20 percent. *Our problem is less how much money we spend for schooling than how we spend it.*

7. Use Computers Both to Make Up for the Shortage of Human Teachers and to Take Advantage of Their Own Unique Benefits

We have little to add here to what was said in chapter 8. There is more than ample evidence that computerized instruction can go a long way toward making up for a shortage of teachers, and that it can speed up learning in almost any field. Their benefits can only grow as the technology becomes more powerful and as we develop more skill at integrating it into our curricula.

Again, the question here is financial, not educational. Our schools can profitably use many more computers than they can now afford. Finding the money to buy more is yet another pressing budgetary need.

8. Seek Help from Business Whenever It Can Be Had

In this book, we have been able to survey only a tiny fraction of the nearly 150,000 reform initiatives in which business has donated its considerable resources to the cause of school improvement. America's companies, and some foreign corporations doing business here, have donated people and money to build new schools, tutor inner-city students, provide scholarships, give management advice, and bolster school-reform efforts in virtually every school district in the land. For many schools and students, they have made a crucial difference between success and failure. At this point there is hardly any need for schools to search for business help; most major companies are actively seeking every promising opportunity they can find to aid our schools. But districts that work to build a close relationship between their schools and local employers will have a major advantage over those that simply take whatever help is offered them. It is a resource that no one can afford to overlook.

9. In Any Effort to Rebuild a Failing School System, Make Certain That Everyone Involved Has "Bought Into" the Program

One last, indisputably clear lesson is that it is seldom possible to impose reform from on high. Even the most promising reform efforts easily fall apart unless everyone concerned is behind them. Dr. Theodore Sizer's groundbreaking Coalition for Essential Schools is a case in point. We noted several of its disappointing failures in chapter 9: a faculty that voted to leave the program, not because it failed to help their students, but in large part because teachers in elective courses feared for their jobs; a school where one pupil in four transferred back to the less-demanding traditional curriculum; and a Texas school system where parents rejected the program because it would have devoted to academic study class time that their children now use to practice football.

There have been others. One school system rejected Coalition membership because many of their students were already going on to college. Sizer could not convince teachers there that the chance to do an even better job of waking student minds was worth the effort of scrapping career-long educational habits. At Hope High School, in Providence, Rhode Island, teachers in the regular program harbor such hostility toward those who volunteered for the Sizer-esque Hope Essential High School that the dramatically successful program has been unable to grow beyond its original 100-student limit. And at New York's famed Central Park East Secondary School, state regulations that specify both curriculum and testing procedures may put an end to the interdisciplinary classes and "exhibitions" central to the Coalition concept. Rather than dilute the program, principal Deborah Meier has vowed to close the school unless it is exempted from the new rules.

From all these cases, a simple pattern emerges. In each school system, someone crucial to the Coalition program's success has not "bought into" the project. In that Texas town, it was the parents who considered football practice more important than their children's education. At Hope High School, teachers seem to have voted for the experiment—by a tiny majority—largely in hopes that it would fail and thereby validate their determination to stick with business as usual. And at Central Park East, the state education department has proved to be, if not actually hostile to the Coalition program, then at least too distant or too inflexible to make allowances for it when setting regulations for the state as a whole. Like any other large enterprise, and particularly those with a component of government funding and control, education is too complex to operate efficiently by fiat. Almost any disaffected participant can bring the process to a halt when reforms conflict with their real goals—and too often those goals have more to do with personal convenience or turf disputes than with education.

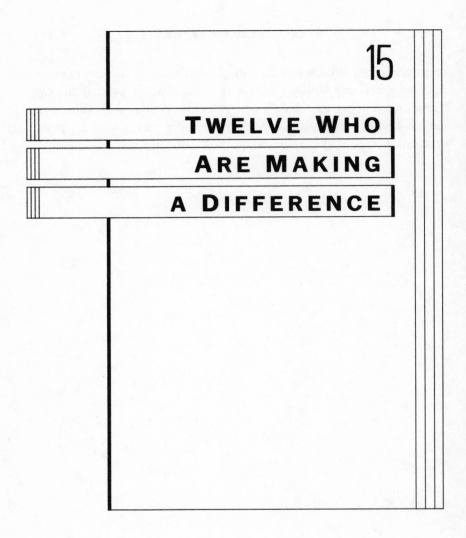

15

TWELVE WHO
ARE MAKING
A DIFFERENCE

No reform movement can alter the status quo if it consists only of good ideas. Not even general public and political support will turn theoretical insights into the effective policies and daily actions that constitute real change. That final step depends on committed people who recognize the need for new ways of doing things and have both the imagination to create them and the power to put them into effect. Fortunately, American education has such people in abundance at all levels of the system.

Some of the most influential are the superintendents, the men and women whose job it is to set policy for entire districts. A reluctant or ineffective superintendent can stifle change even when everyone else in the district is committed to it. A good one can move reluctant staff members, earn the cooperation of recalcitrant unions, bring skeptical politicians into line, and enlist the support of business and community leaders.

The National Association of School Administrators provided us with a list of the most farsighted and effective superintendents in the United States. What follows is a look at the challenges facing twelve of the best, and the responses that have earned them the respect of their peers. In many cases, in small districts and large, their experiences are remarkably similar.

James Buchanan
Fremont, Nebraska

"Single individuals do not accomplish great things in a school system," says Dr. Buchanan, and he may have a point. Yet, much as he credits the success of Fremont schools to the group effort that goes into long-range planning, he seems to prove himself wrong. It was, after all, Dr. Buchanan himself who set up the planning system, soon after he took over the schools.

Fremont is a small farming community of 25,000 people, 99 percent of them white, about thirty-five miles from Omaha. Its economic base depends on meat packing, feed-corn production, grain farming, and a growing portion of light and medium manufacturing. A growing number of residents face significant money problems. There are some 4,500 schoolchildren, spread through thirteen small schools.

Many of Fremont's school-improvement methods can be found in any diligent, progressive district. The town tests its students regularly and uses modern teaching methods to make sure that each lives up to his or her potential. Recently it has begun the transition to site-based management, a significant change for staff members, many of whom have worked in the town for twenty-five years or more.

What makes Fremont different, Dr. Buchanan says, is its focus on future needs. Each year he meets with a planning team that includes teachers, administrative staffers, and representatives from the school board. They look back at the previous twelve months to review their progress, then look ahead eighteen months to examine community trends and the impact they will have on the schools. The plans that emerge from this process change with circumstances, the superintendent notes. When the team began work in 1986, its first plan contained five strategic objectives. Two focused on finance, a problem that prevented much emphasis on program development in the community. In 1990 there were six objectives; only one dealt with finance, while four involved new programs.

This systematic approach has served the town well. Fremont students now rank above the national average on standardized test scores, a significant improvement. But that is not enough for Dr. Buchanan; scores are still slightly below the average of comparable school districts in Nebraska. "By 1995," the superintendent says, "we want to have the highest student achievement scores in the state."

Blanche Fraser, Mount Clemens, Michigan

In the 1940s and 1950s, Mount Clemens enjoyed a reputation as one of the state's most successful school districts, but the community has fallen on hard times since then. Beginning in the late 1960s, the student population fell from 8,800 to only 3,300. More than one-third belong to ethnic minorities, and 60 percent are poor enough to qualify for a free or reduced-price lunch. Both local property-tax revenues and state support fell as well, and academic standards sank along with them.

Having arrived in Mount Clemens only recently, in 1988, Dr. Fraser credits her predecessor with making many of the hard decisions needed to salvage the Detroit suburb's schools. Yet it is clear that she inherited a difficult situation. When she arrived, the district had just closed four of its seven elementary schools, combined two middle schools into one, and shrunk the high school to half a building. The contraction had cost jobs among the system's aging staff, and there had been teachers' strikes in 1986 and 1987. The students' math and reading scores in the Michigan Education Assessment Program were among the lowest in the state, and the dropout rate among seniors was about 15 percent.

Things have changed dramatically in the last two years. Reading and math scores are still a little below the state average, yet are dramatically better than they were. The dropout rate is down to 6 percent. And the district managed to sign a three-year contract with the teachers' union in June—the first time in at least twenty years that a contract had been signed so early.

Dr. Fraser attributes this success to a variety of policy changes. One is a strong new emphasis on staff development. In past years, the money needed for teacher training had gone instead to patch up decaying buildings. Teaching methods were antiquated as well as unsupervised. In 1989 the superintendent managed to find $125,000 for staff training, up from only $15,000 the year before, and modern teaching methods are entering the system.

Another is a revised curriculum. When Dr. Fraser took over, teachers made up their own courses, so what was taught had little to do with state standards; achievement scores were predictably low. Worse, teachers seldom coordinated their classes, as a result of which many spent half the year on material that should have been learned in prior courses. Dr. Fraser says that she has made at least a beginning at solving all these problems, and the results seem to bear her out.

One more important feature of her tenure is an open management style. When someone has a problem to discuss, her door is always open. As a result, not only was there no strike last year, but for the first time in living memory no one even filed a grievance. And she spends each Monday visiting classrooms; she sees each class at least once a year, and many of them two or three times. In her follow-up notes to teachers, she is careful to find something to praise ("Sometimes it isn't easy," she comments), but she also points out problems before they get too big to handle with friendly advice.

Arthur W. Gosling
Arlington, Virginia

When Dr. Gosling arrived here in 1985, he found that a host of problems had grown from an unrecognized transition that had overtaken the community. Arlington was once a rich, white suburb of Washington, D.C., home to executives and middle-level bureaucrats, and local leaders still thought of it that way. In fact, half of the students belonged to ethnic minorities, and a significant inner city had grown up. School facilities had been neglected, and neither the school board nor the community had much confidence in the staff.

Dr. Gosling set out to change the situation with what he calls some "awareness raising." He invited guest speakers to inform the staff about the problems they faced, sent people to conferences, and set up a series of small programs for ethnic and language minorities. Staff members and parents at the seven elementary schools with the greatest ethnic diversity were trained to write project proposals, and the new superintendent persuaded the school board to set aside money to fund their ideas. One of their projects set up a science center with a curriculum that integrates both math and language instruction around the core concept of science. Another established an all-day kindergarten—Arlington's kindergartens usually run only half the day—and evaluated the performance of graduates when they entered first grade.

Since then, there have been other changes. The middle and high schools have shifted from six fifty-six-minute periods each day to seven periods of forty-eight minutes each. Children at risk of dropping out now attend an afternoon program at the University of Virginia. A Spanish-language immersion program at one high school is recruiting native English-speakers for intensive foreign-language training. And the district has expanded its summer programs for gifted children, setting up three- and four-week "institutes" around unifying themes. One typical institute asked children to speculate about life in the year 2000. Another focused on the ways in which water affects our lives. Dr. Gosling has made a special effort to recruit ethnic minorities to the institutes. In 1989 there were only ten nonwhite participants; a year later there were 110.

At this point the problems Dr. Gosling found waiting for him have largely been solved. Arlington's schools are now designed for today's student body, not for one that vanished more than a decade ago, and both the school board and the community now know that their teachers have what it takes to succeed in the difficult business of education. But the superintendent is far from satisfied. "We have persistent difficulty in seeing substantial progress for minority kids," he says. "Either we are going to make a constructive difference for substantial numbers of them, or we will have failed in our jobs."

Donald W. Ingwerson
Jefferson County, Kentucky

The 1970s were a difficult time for Louisville and the surrounding Jefferson County. Teachers went on strike, school superintendents were fired, and there were riots so bad the National Guard had to be called in to control them.

When Don Ingwerson arrived there in 1981, after twenty years in the Los Angeles area, he found that all the turmoil had taken its toll. Test scores were often below the national average, dropout rates were high, teachers and administrators "did not speak the same language," and the district was still trying to cope with a court-ordered desegregation plan that remains among the most rigorous ever established.

"The district lacked political muscle," he says. "We had to set up an organization to work within the authority of the school district to wrest power from special interest groups and put the board of education in control." It took long hours of classical grassroots politicking, but Jefferson County now has a school system in which education, not power-brokering, comes first.

To solve many of the district's other problems, Dr. Ingwerson went to the community. Over the years he has built more than 600 partnerships with local businesses and community organizations. Area firms have given the schools one computer for every eleven students; in 1992, district high schools will graduate the first class in which all students are competent in the use of computers. A program modeled on the famed Boston Compact provides jobs for graduates—not just openings for unskilled labor, but executive-trainee positions with a promising future. The effort has cut the dropout rate to 2.5 percent per year. And the Gheens Foundation now provides $500,000 per year to support the Public School/ Gheens Professional Development Academy for staff training.

Several years ago, Dr. Ingwerson negotiated the beginnings of a site-based management system into the district's union contract. The union gave up many of its hard-won rights—limits on the number of students teachers can take, length of day, and similar work rules—and teachers received the right to help in the management of their schools. Two dozen schools were allowed to enter the program the first year, with twenty-four more to be added each year until all schools whose teachers want to join in have done so. Site-based management has proved so popular that some teachers who voted to enter the program but were blocked by the twenty-four-school limit have threatened to sue for admission.

It is too soon to tell exactly how site-based management will change Jefferson County schools, but Dr. Ingwerson is encouraged by the results to date. He cites one school in which teachers decided that none of their students would be allowed to fail. Now, when students neglect to turn assignments in, their teachers stay with them after school until the job is done. And in 1989, when twenty-seven students had not completed their courses at year's end, their teachers gave up vacation time to work with them until all twenty-seven were ready for the next grade.

There is more to come. At the top of Dr. Ingwerson's current list is the task of eliminating drugs from Jefferson County's schools. He is now working to set up a community drug-assessment program to evaluate and treat children caught with drugs, keeping them out of school until they are free of the problem.

But already the results almost speak for themselves. In 1989 the district's scores on the Scholastic Aptitude Test and other achievement tests all averaged above the national norm. Some 95 percent of students now attend school each day, and the dropout rate is lower than that of any comparable city in the United States. And fully 78 percent of the 1989 graduating class went on to college or specialized career training.

Louisville's remarkable progress has captured attention far beyond Kentucky's borders. *Newsweek, The New York Times,* public television, and ABC News have all reported on developments in

Jefferson County. And recently Dr. Ingwerson was called in to help with Chicago's new site-based management program.

John A. Murphy
Prince Georges County, Maryland

Prince Georges County is an anomaly. There is no single large city in the region, just outside Washington, D.C.; instead, the entire county is covered with an all-but-continuous urban sprawl. Two-thirds of the county's inhabitants are black. There are neighborhoods of great wealth, but also areas of abject poverty where the rates of violent crime and drug problems are every bit as high as in the worst slums of Washington itself.

When John Murphy took over the school system in 1984, academic performance there was every bit as bad as many people have come to expect from inner-city schools. Student performance on the California Achievement Test was below the national average. There was a 25-percentile gap between the average scores of black and white students. School administrators were reporting a dropout rate of only 3 percent; the truth was closer to 25 percent.

Dr. Murphy swore that things would change in Prince Georges County, and quickly. He set himself two major goals: to raise the system's academic performance into the top 25 percent of the nation's schools, and to reduce the gap between the performance of black and white students. Within five years, he vowed, county schools would be the equal of the best white, suburban school systems in the country.

He succeeded to an extent that other educators find amazing. By the time his deadline ran out, Dr. Murphy had established thirteen new magnet programs spread over forty-seven schools, put computer-assisted instruction in grades two through four, set up an in-school university for principals and teachers, recruited new teachers from around the country, and set up a program to make both students and teachers more accountable for learning. And by the 1989 school year, more than 70 percent of middle-school children were taking algebra, up from only 27 percent—and seven out of eight pass the course. Achievement-test scores were up sharply, the gap between black and white students was shrinking, and fully 60 percent of students were going on to higher education.

There are more changes to come. Dr. Murphy's current goals include converting to site-based management, raising the number of middle-school children who take algebra to 85 percent, and toughening the science curriculum. (Already, a *Challenger* Space Center set up by the families of the ill-fated *Challenger* shuttle crew, is taking thirty children per day for a simulated ride into space and raising the demand for more science courses.)

Though community leaders give Dr. Murphy full credit for the remarkable improvement of schools in Prince Georges County— "He has more energy than any four people I know," one comments—the superintendent denies that there is anything unique about his achievement. "Urban education is being thrown away because people do not believe that black children can perform as well as whites," he says. "But I believe that any major school system in this country could be turned around in five years, given the appropriate conditions. All it takes is for politicians to stay out of the game and let educators get the job done."

Thomas Payzant
San Diego, California

At age fifty, Dr. Payzant is the model of a big-city school superintendent. A graduate of Williams College, he has advanced degrees from both Williams and Harvard University. When he arrived in San Diego in 1982, he brought with him over twelve years of experience as a school superintendent, first in Springfield Township, Pennsylvania; then in Eugene, Oregon; and finally in Oklahoma City. Yet, he says, he still finds San Diego an enormously challenging place to work.

Well he might. With 155 schools and more than 122,000 students, San Diego qualifies as one of the largest school districts in the nation. It is also one of the most diversified. Only 39 percent of the students there are white; 16 percent are African Americans, 26 percent Hispanic, and 19 percent Asian. Many of the Hispanic and Asian students are recent arrivals, many with only a tenuous grasp of English and some illiterate even in their native languages.

Many students subsist at or below the poverty line, yet some of the city's neighborhoods easily qualify as wealthy.

With such a mix of students, Dr. Payzant says, equity issues are a major factor in managing his district. San Diego operates under a court-ordered integration plan that may be unique among major cities, because it functions largely by parental choice. Students are free to attend whatever school they wish, so long as it still has openings and the move does not disturb the institution's racial balance. A wide variety of magnet schools makes daily travel more appealing for many students.

Like many other school systems, San Diego is deep into the process of restructuring. Most schools either have set up their own management teams or are now doing so, and such responsibilities as budget allocation, selection of principals, and scheduling are being shifted down to them from the district level as quickly as possible.

Curriculum reform is more difficult to delegate, because the framework for each subject is set largely at the state level. However, many schools are experimenting with team teaching and inter-disciplinary classes, presenting ideas in new ways while still devoting the required amount of time to each topic. The entire district is adopting a new reading/language-arts program that is based on literature and requires students to do far more writing than they did in the past.

So far, the results seem promising. In 1989 the scores of San Diego's twelfth-graders went up fifteen points on the California Assessment Program writing test, compared with only six points for the state as a whole. "It's hard to draw a cause-and-effect relationship," Dr. Payzant says, "but we think this work is beginning to pay off."

Gerald O. Skaar
Pardeeville, Wisconsin

When Dr. Skaar arrived in Pardeeville in 1982, the schools in the tiny Madison suburb were, he says, "horrendous." In the high school, discipline had broken down completely. Twelve percent or more of the system's 800-odd students were absent each day. Those who actually tried to learn were ridiculed by their peers; as a result, even the seniors were virtually illiterate. The situation was little better in junior high school, where students scored around the thirty-fifth percentile on standardized reading tests. Throughout the system, the curriculum and textbooks were fifteen years or more out of date. No one had evaluated staff performance in perhaps twenty years.

To some extent, a weak high-school principal was to blame for some of the problems; Dr. Skaar's first official act was to hire a new one. But many more grew from the community itself. The area's largest employers are an Oscar Meyer meat-packing plant and four prisons, and though most Pardeeville residents enjoy a middle-class income, they have achieved a comfortable life without spending any great effort on their own education. Parents thus showed little interest in their children's schooling.

Turning Pardeeville around seemed to require almost a miracle; in fact, it took years of hard, grinding work. "It took five to six years to get teachers to hold students more accountable," Dr. Skaar recalls. "The freshman class almost had to graduate before we could accomplish anything."

One part of Dr. Skaar's formula was a series of new disciplinary and performance standards. He raised the academic standards required for participation in school sports. The conference allows team members to fail one or two courses; Pardeeville students must now pass all their classes. He also replaced the old shirt-sleeves graduation with a much more formal ceremony; it took three or four years to eliminate the catcalls that accompanied each senior to the front of the hall.

Dr. Skaar also put in a comprehensive supervisory and evaluation program, something he had done in two previous districts. Teachers are now evaluated frequently, and poor ones receive intensive counseling; one who relied on ridicule to enforce discipline retired early after several such sessions. Four to six teachers every year are sent for outside classes in learning theory and practice, while the rest receive in-service training. Each year, teachers must write a brief statement of their philosophy and grading criteria. Over the years, their grading criteria have changed; classroom rules, like not being tardy, have been replaced by objective measures of learning.

The curriculum has changed as well. The antiquated textbooks are gone now, replaced by modern materials. A few courses have been added, others revised or eliminated. For several years, Pardeeville bused students to a neighboring school, where extra language courses were available; the program is now being replaced by a television hookup. A new course in developmental reading and writing for junior-high students has markedly improved writing performance in high school.

Dr. Skaar was also able to recruit several local businesses to the cause. They now provide small scholarships each year to help local students go on to college. The encouragement seems to help, he says.

All this effort has paid off. Scores on standardized achievement tests are up a bit. Nearly 60 percent of the recent high-school graduating class went on to postsecondary education, almost twice as many as in 1982. And discipline problems are rare now. "When students realized that they were doing better, that they were able to meet higher standards, it seemed to change their attitudes," the superintendent reports.

Pardeeville may never be hailed as one of the Midwest's foremost centers of learning, but Dr. Skaar has clearly moved the system in the right direction.

Margaret A. Smith
Hempfield Area School District, Pennsylvania

There was not much obviously wrong with this 7,300-student district in 1986, when Dr. Smith left her job as Pennsylvania Secretary of Education to take over as superintendent. A rural and suburban area with a small minority population and a broad socioeconomic mix, it had missed many of the problems facing nearby Pittsburgh and other cities. True, the high-school building needed major renovations, a $22-million project finished in mid-1990. But beyond that, it was a typical medium-sized school system, perhaps a bit set in its ways.

That changed rapidly when Dr. Smith arrived. She has spent the last four years restructuring grade levels, adding middle schools to the system, and moving ninth grade into the senior high school.

Her curriculum reforms have been even more sweeping. Ele-

mentary schools are focusing more now on early-childhood education, with a "transitional first class" for students who need more
help to succeed. Middle schools have added both a "self-esteem"
program to help teens cope with the problems of adolescence and
exploratory foreign-language courses to prepare for more-intensive
high school programs. The high schools have more required course
work these days, so the difference between the academic and college preparatory tracks and those for employment-bound students
has shrunk markedly. There is a new computer laboratory, backed
by extra computers available in all subject areas and computer-
literacy courses from elementary school on. And the high schools
now provide advanced-placement, college-credit courses in all curriculum areas.

Dr. Smith has also been building coalitions with local businesses
and nearby colleges and universities. Many firms provide mentors
for high-school students, supply part-time teachers with practical
workplace experience, and host field trips from area schools. The
five colleges and universities in the district take in students for
remedial reading courses. And a separate education foundation run
by community leaders raises money to support special projects
suggested by students and teachers.

Early in Dr. Smith's tenure, there were people who wondered
whether all this change was really needed—but not anymore.
Scores on standardized tests and state achievement exams are rising
quickly. And about 80 percent of students now go on to advanced
education, about 60 percent of them to four-year colleges. Even for
a school system that was already doing reasonably well, these are
dramatic gains.

Franklin L. Smith
Dayton, Ohio

Not long ago, Dayton was one of the nation's foremost manufacturing centers. For that matter, it still is, but with computers displacing
skilled workers from once-secure assembly-line jobs, that no longer
guarantees a strong industrial labor market. That has been clear at
least since the early 1980s. Yet when Dr. Smith took over the
29,000-student school system early in 1986, most parents were still

convinced that their children could graduate from high school and find a good job, just as they themselves had done a generation earlier. The task of modernizing the antiquated school policies that grew from that delusion has taken up the new superintendent's time ever since.

Five years ago, Dayton's schools were still designed to churn out the relatively uneducated workers needed by an industrial society, not the well-educated, highly skilled technicians of the high-tech world. There were many remedial classes, but few enrichment courses. High-school students could graduate after having passed only a basic math course; algebra was not required. And standardized test scores barely matched the national averages; some were significantly below.

All that has changed since Dr. Smith arrived, and a good deal more. Would-be employers wanted Dayton's students to be proficient in algebra and geometry; those subjects are now required for graduation, and all math courses now conform to the standards of the National Council of Teachers of Math. All schools have at least one computer lab, most have two, and computers are now entering individual classrooms. IBM's famed "Writing to Read" program is now a key part of the elementary-school curriculum. The old reading books have been replaced by more modern texts, and the curriculum has been revised to concentrate more on the skills of critical thinking. All teachers have gone through thirty-hour workshops in learning theory and teaching methods.

Other changes are even more dramatic. A magnet-school grant from the federal government paid to turn all of the high schools and half of the elementary schools into magnet schools. Students can attend the school of their choice, so long as space is available and they do not throw off the institution's racial balance. School themes include a Montessori program, performing arts, computer science, environmental science, professional studies (designed for would-be doctors and dentists), and international studies. Students can enter their chosen theme in elementary school—many children and their families know what interests them surprisingly early in life, Dr. Smith notes—and are guaranteed a space in the program through high-school graduation, so long as they remain within their theme.

And, like many other districts, Dayton is now moving to site-based management, beginning with seven of the city's fifty-three schools. In these schools, teachers, administrators, and parents will control the budget, hiring and firing of staff members, curriculum revisions, and other critical issues. The district administration will measure student performance and let schools do as they will, so long as it works.

Dr. Smith is not content with the system's progress to date, but he admits that the results have been encouraging. Standardized test scores have risen every year, even though tests are now scored according to stricter standards than in the past.

What he seems most proud of, though, is the extent to which he has gotten virtually the entire community to "buy into" his program. Businesses all over town are now sponsoring field trips, providing mentors for at-risk students, and contributing to support the administrators' off-hours planning sessions. Voters have backed the new regime as they never supported the old one. In the past, school levies totaling only $3 million were regularly voted down; recently they passed a levy of $15.37 million!

But the move that paid off best may have been a party that Dr. Smith and his wife gave when they arrived in Dayton. "We had four hundred administrators and their wives at our house for a reception at Christmas in 1985," he recalls. "It was hell trying to bring it off, but I still get comments from people that it was the first time anyone had treated them as human beings."

Robert R. Spillane
Fairfax County, Virginia

In 1985, "Bud" Spillane made a change that many big-city superintendents must have envied. He left the beleaguered Boston school system and moved to Fairfax County. In Boston, over a period of five years, he had spearheaded a major administrative reorganization, revised the curriculum, survived a budget shortfall that forced layoffs of over 1,800 staff members, and established the famed "Boston Compact." In the wealthy Washington suburb, some may have thought, he could take a well-earned rest.

It has not worked out that way. Throughout his tenure, Dr.

Spillane has labored to build an already excellent school system into the best in the country. Many people would say he has succeeded.

After our accounts of Fairfax County's schools in earlier chapters, that should come as no surprise. We have already looked closely at the controversial teacher-evaluation program enacted under Dr. Spillane's tenure, and at his attempt to lengthen the school week, which is still pending. But it seems worth noting what these efforts have bought the community.

The answer should be encouraging for school reformers elsewhere. Fairfax County students excel on the Scholastic Aptitude Test. In 1989 the district's average SAT scores were 36 points higher than the national average on the verbal test and 44 points higher on the math test—even though the number of students taking the test has risen from 70 percent in 1980 to a phenomenal 85 percent in 1989. (The national average is 40 percent; among Virginia school districts, the average is 59 percent.) No less than 90 percent of the 1989 graduating class went on to higher education, including 85 percent of black students. And, at the other end of the educational spectrum, 85 percent of the special-education students who have graduated from Fairfax County schools are employed, compared with only one-third nationally. All this has been accomplished with the lowest increase in the school operating budget of any comparable community in the region.

There is not much we can say about a record like that. Like John Murphy's work in Prince Georges County, Maryland, Dr. Spillane's record serves as a model for other superintendents and school districts. It is a difficult one to match.

John A. Stewart
Polk County, Florida

Lakeland, Winter Haven, and their surrounding communities form a strange district, with extremes of wealth and poverty, Dr. Stewart comments. The economy is based largely on citrus groves and phosphate mining, and in recent years they have proved frail supports. Years of heavy freezes and canker have taken their toll on local groves, and the bottom has dropped out of the market for phosphates. So Polk County has one of the highest unemployment rates in the country. With hundreds of migrant citrus workers making what pass for homes there, it also has one of the largest programs teaching English as a second language. With 62,000 students, and another 6,000 in vocational and adult programs, it is a major responsibility. And the school superintendent is elected, not appointed; if his actions ruffle enough feathers, he can soon find himself looking for other employment.

When Dr. Stewart took over the district in 1983—he was a high-school principal in Winter Haven when his predecessor as superintendent died in office—a vitriolic election had left Polk County schools with a serious morale problem. His first efforts were aimed at restoring the teachers' outlook. His "I Make a Difference" campaign stressed the role of individual staff members in education and provided small awards to those who had done outstanding work. A state academic tournament hosted by Walt Disney World got students interested in education; now there are both state and national tournaments each year.

A wide variety of measures have been aimed to promote better education more directly. Computer labs are in place from elementary school through senior high. Two career-development centers take middle-school students by referral and work with them to keep potential dropouts in school; a third center is scheduled to open soon. And a new high school for the visual and performing arts opened in 1989, with about 200 students specializing in theater, music, and fine arts. Throughout the system, every student has a full four-year educational plan, computer-accessible in the guidance counselor's office to make sure he or she is on track.

But in Polk County, even the strongest of regular school programs would leave a major "market segment" unserved. So Dr. Stewart has reached out to both ends of the age spectrum. A prekindergarten intervention program makes sure that children of poorly educated, low-income residents are ready to begin school when they reach age five. And the county literacy center he established provides adult education. This and other programs have brought many dropouts from long ago back to earn their diplomas.

In 1988 the Florida legislature mandated a restructuring program designed to bring site-based management to the state's schools. Polk County was almost left behind, because the changes contemplated were barred by court desegregation orders left over from the late 1960s. But, with the exception of the county's two largest cities, the courts have relented, and ten of the region's schools will soon begin to run their own programs. Budgeting will remain much as it was, Dr. Stewart notes; that has always been site-based in Polk County. But school committees will now be able to select personnel, including the principal; change the curriculum (within some state guidelines); and alter the school calendar. A special task force is now looking at the possibility of keeping schools open year-round, using a flexible calendar to fit students' individual needs and make the best use of the available buildings.

Dr. Stewart does not claim to have achieved miracles with all his innovations. Scores on the Scholastic Aptitude Test and other standardized exams are going up slowly, though the number of students taking them is rising quickly. Dropout rates are within 1 or 2 percent of the state average, though withdrawals of children of migrant workers, "no-shows" of students registered automatically, and similar losses bring the high-school graduation rate down to just under 70 percent of the nominal freshman class. But in a fast-growing district facing the social challenges of Polk County, just standing still would have seemed miracle enough.

Robert D. Tschirki,
Cherry Creek, Colorado

Now in his first year at Cherry Creek, Dr. Tschirki faces a challenge that many of his colleagues would envy: Rather than having to rescue a failing district, his task is to make one of the nation's truly outstanding school systems even better.

Cherry Creek is a rich suburban area, with thirty-eight schools and 28,000 students. Its high schools all provide some 300 to 400 course offerings. Most of the district's students take the Scholastic Aptitude Test, scoring well above the state and national averages. Most go on to college. Only 3 percent drop out before graduation. Even school restructuring is a non-issue here; the district converted to exclusively site-based management no less than twenty years ago.

Yet Cherry Creek does face some challenges. According to local realtors, the community's excellent school system has made it a favorite destination for people moving from nearby cities. As a result, the student population is growing by 800 to 1,000 each year. The number of minority students has grown from virtually none five years ago to about 12 percent today. And Dr. Tschirki says the district's staff development program is weak, its decision-making process inconsistent.

These are problems that he is well prepared to solve. In his last assignment, he spent eight years as superintendent in nearby Littleton, Colorado, a town that presented greater challenges.

When Dr. Tschirki took over the Littleton schools in 1981, three-fourths of the town's 15,000 students went on to college; yet the system itself was in decline. Enrollment was shrinking, the community aging. In the mid-1960s, fully 70 percent of Littleton's adults were parents. By the early 1980s the number had fallen to 30 percent. With the region's economy in trouble, the state could not contribute much to pay for schooling. Yet local officials had not dared to hold a budget election in twelve years, fearing that childless voters would reject the needed appropriations. Though most of Littleton's teachers had spent over twenty years in the system, the district could not afford staff-development courses to update their subject knowledge and teaching methods. And the curriculum covered only the basics; there was no money for electives or other frills.

Dr. Tschirki did the only thing possible: He took his case to the people. And after some intensive lobbying, he got voters to pass three budget elections and a bond issue. He added foreign languages to the curriculum and supported advanced-placement programs in all major subject areas. He worked for eighteen months to explain teen development and the needs of modern young people to skeptical older adults, then set up a junior-high-school program for grades seven through nine. And he dramatically raised the staff development budget; all teachers now go through in-service training, while administrators attend classes in problem-solving, decision-making, and conflict resolution.

After only three months at Cherry Creek, Dr. Tschirki had already begun to follow the pattern he set in Littleton. One of the community's high schools now offers courses in Chinese, while another is due to open with an interdisciplinary program and a strong focus on international affairs. And he is quickly beefing up the staff-development program for both teachers and administrators.

"We are now going through an intensive cultural inventory," he reports. "We are asking ourselves what we believe and what we would like to become. Going back to the beginning like this is the only way to make sure that we still have the best possible schools ten years from now."

16

FROM HERE
TO LITERACY

In the end, how much our schools improve is up to us. If our school systems are to recover their lost quality, if the United States is to survive as an economic leader, parents—and everyone who reads this book—must accept responsibility for the performance of their local school systems.

In the near future, American schools will have changed dramatically, and so will our relationship to them. On the outside, most will still be the same brick-and-glass structures—literally the same, half of them nearing seventy-five years old. But on the inside, the changes will be clear: Classrooms will be full of personal computers and other high-tech teaching aids. Teaching methods will have changed to reflect our growing understanding of the learning process. Teachers will be backed up by volunteers from the community and from local businesses. Most of all, educational standards will be more demanding, and they will be enforced. We will be asking far more of our schools a few short years from now, and giving them more as well. And we will be getting more in return.

In one sense, our renewed concern for education comes at an opportune time. Reforming our schools requires more than merely voting for the most plausible politicians or levying extra taxes to pay for more teachers and new classroom equipment; it will take a personal commitment of time, energy, and dedication from a large number of people outside the professional education community. Not even large-scale adoption of computerized learning will reduce that need, for in addition to passing knowledge on to children who desperately need it, we have set out to give them the wisdom that will allow them to live responsibly in a democratic society. That task requires mentors and role models, and it will fall to the baby-boom generation to fill that need.

No generation in history has been more likely to handle such a role well. Its major qualification is, ironically enough, the same penchant for public causes that made it so uncomfortable to have around twenty years ago. We have heard relatively little from the boomers of late, save for the faintly ridiculous spectacle of flower children-turned-yuppies accumulating wealth even more eagerly than their parents once did. But this says nothing about their personal commitment to their vision of the national welfare, only that they grew up, acquired families, and developed a taste for comfort. This remains the same generation that marched for civil rights when such activism was genuinely dangerous, that protested the Vietnam War, spearheaded the environmental movement, and, albeit, in reduced numbers, still pickets against nuclear power. They did not retire from activism when the Nixon administration declared that it had won "peace with honor" in Vietnam; they merely took time out to get their own houses in order. Nearly two decades later, they have accomplished that goal. Their personal economies are on a firm footing, their children grown or nearly so. It is time for them to find new causes, and there is no public mission more necessary or closer to home than the cause of education. School reform will be the civil-rights movement of the 1990s.

This help will come at a price, however. To gain it, the professional educators will have to surrender their control over our schools. They have lost much of it already. In the 1950s and 1960s, school boards were for the most part a fairly benign power, as far as teachers and school administrators were concerned. They established budgets, negotiated contracts, and set broad policies, but in large part left the day-to-day matters of administration and teaching to the administrators and teachers. Parents joined the PTA and in some areas voted on school appropriations, but they too left the classroom to the professionals. This is not something the baby boomers are prepared to do. In the 1980s they put the issue of schools at the center of many local political debates, and they demanded and won a broader role in school policy.

In the 1990s, both parents and citizens without children in school will take an even more active role in formulating curricula, establishing teaching methods, hiring and firing teachers, and many other functions that until recently have been the province of the school staff. This trend can be seen clearly in the Chicago public schools, where the cause of local control has put parents and disinterested citizens on the governing boards of each institution. This change from professional to political control of the schools will quickly spread to districts throughout the nation. Those educators who still retain their autonomy will soon grow accustomed to having their policies debated, often acrimoniously, in local elections, town meetings, and other public forums. They will have to accept that they can no longer act even in small matters without the advice and consent of the community.

The coming debate will probably slow the school-reform movement, just as public argument has made it impossible to set a policy and implement it efficiently in many other areas of government. However, it will ensure that a comprehensive reform is eventually enacted. In the 1990s, the political price of inaction on this issue will be very high.

That much could have been forecast a decade ago; another factor that will ease the task of rebuilding our schools in this decade comes as more of a surprise. This is the outbreak of freedom and goodwill in eastern Europe. Though budget-conscious Washington has downplayed the role of money in rebuilding our schools, the fact is that progress will not come free, or even cheaply. There are too many teachers and early-childhood specialists to hire, too many textbooks to replace, too many computers to buy and laboratories to equip for new funding to be anything less than a major factor in the process. Washington has also downplayed the prospects for a large "peace dividend," the money to be saved from military spending because we no longer have to treat Europe as an armed garrison with implacable enemies camped on its eastern frontier. Yet with less fear of war, our leaders will inevitably take a substantial portion of the military budget and devote it to social problems. School reform will be a major beneficiary of this change, and it will be much easier to accomplish as a result.

As we have seen, in most areas the first experiments in reconstruction have already begun. From them, we have learned more than enough to heal the ills that now affect our national school system. Our task in the 1990s is to put those lessons into practice.

So far, our record in this crucial step is mixed. One reason is that reforms to date have occurred largely in isolation, so that planners in one part of the country often are unaware of the measures that have brought success elsewhere; this book is one attempt to solve that problem. Another cause of delay, and one that seems a far greater cause for concern, is that relatively few political leaders have yet moved school reform far enough up on their agendas to ensure fast, effective action. In almost every state, we find both promising developments and evidence that needed improvements remain on the back burner.

We have already described some of the sweeping reforms enacted in Texas during the 1980s, and the flagrant backsliding that followed them. This may be the nation's worst example of deranged educational priorities and the political process gone wrong.

North Dakota has enacted several worthwhile reforms. In 1987 it set up twelve "technology consortia" designed to bring computer networks, two-way interactive television, and other high-tech facilities to nearly 100 school districts. Two years later, the state tightened its school-accreditation standards and tied school funding to them. But the legislature rejected both a major school-reorganization bill and a reform plan that would have offered incentive payments for local educational reforms.

One of the more disappointing performances we have seen

comes from Tennessee, where the Department of Education has been formulating a paper entitled "21st Century Challenge: State-wide Goals and Objectives for Educational Excellence." We admire the department's intentions and effort; some such plan is needed in every school district in the country. And the proposal has features of merit. Among the recommended goals, the department offers to set up early childhood programs for all students, provide special help for pregnant teens, and reward schools, teachers, and administrators for meeting objective performance standards—worthy objectives all.

But other statements force us to wonder whether the state's educational leaders really understand how urgently reforms are needed and how radical they must be. Among its major goals, all to be accomplished "by no later than the first day of the twenty-first century," the paper proposes to reduce the state's dropout rate to 20 percent and to raise student achievement levels so that Tennessee ranks in the top one-third of states in the Southeast. These aims do qualify as improvements over the state's current performance; its dropout rate in 1987 was just over 32 percent. But the loss of one student in five and a standing in the top third of one of the nation's least successful regions remain grossly inadequate, and there is something very wrong about establishing them as the targets on which nearly a decade of work will focus. The Tennessee authorities may have been trying to set their goals realistically, at a level they were sure they could reach. They should have aimed far higher.

We have similar qualms about the education goals published by the National Governors' Association early in 1990. Where Tennessee's objectives were specific but painfully modest, the governors' targets are ambitious, but painfully nonspecific. We would have been happier if their final report had included more limited goals and given a plausibly detailed plan for achieving them. We do not wish to be too critical, however. The governors' report at least gave us a valuable summary of what remains to be accomplished if we are to build an educational renaissance.

As a forecast of things to come, it was less successful, though our reservations concern their schedule more than their substance. If we look at the goals as do-or-die marching orders to be accomplished in full during the remainder of this decade, they form a daunting list:

Goal 1. By the year 2000, all children in America will start school ready to learn.

Goal 2. By the year 2000, the high-school graduation rate will increase to at least 90 percent.

Goal 3. By the year 2000, American students will leave grades 4, 8, and 12 having demonstrated competency over challenging subject matter, including English, math, science, history, and geography, and every school in America will ensure that all students learn to use their minds well, so they may be prepared for responsible citizenship, further learning, and productive employment in our modern economy.

Goal 4. By the year 2000, U.S. students will be the first in the world in mathematics and science achievement.

Goal 5. By the year 2000, every adult American will be literate and will possess the knowledge and skills necessary to compete in a global economy and exercise the rights and responsibilities of citizenship.

Goal 6. By the year 2000, every school in America will be free of drugs and violence, and will offer a disciplined environment conducive to learning.

Let us look at each goal in turn.

Regarding Goal 1, we discussed the problems of our preschoolers in detail in chapter 4. We can make certain that the vast majority of kindergarten-age children are ready to begin their studies, and probably before 2000—if we are willing to pay the price. That price is the establishment of a nationwide system of preschools open to all children and attended by them. Developing such a system will not be easy, because it requires us to train far more early-childhood specialists than our current educational system can supply. We expect to see rapid progress in this area, but it is still too early to forecast total success.

What of cutting the dropout rate to 10 percent? This one is more difficult still, because it is far more complex. Children are not stupid, and they have even less tolerance for wasting their time than do most adults. To keep them in school, they must be convinced both that getting an education is worth the effort required—a realistic look at the help-wanted ads might accomplish that once they were old enough, but by then it is too late—and that they can succeed in learning. This is a hope that many youngsters today gave up early in their school careers.

The only thing that will keep tomorrow's high-school students from making the same decision is a record of success in learning established early in their school careers. A year or two of preschool will provide a good start, but more is required. In fact, almost every initiative mentioned in this book holds some part of the answer to this problem, from replacing vacuous textbooks with pithier reading to the Key School's new, psychology-based brand of pedagogy. We will still be working to meet this goal as the new century dawns.

Goal 3 is the critical issue. In this, the governors have given us a summary of everything that parents and educators now hope for. Meet this goal, and by definition we will have solved all the problems that now confront us. We only wish it were possible. We have no doubt that by 2000 our schools will have made enormous progress in improving the competence of the graduates in all these fields; in fact, we are more optimistic about the years to come than are most reformers. But unless we declare that students will remain in those grades until they have met the required standards, no matter how long it takes them, progress is all we can hope for. Absolute success is, in this decade, far beyond our reach.

Unfortunately, we have not the slightest hope of making our students first in science and mathematics in the time available. We lack both the necessary supply of competent math and science teachers and, in many districts, the laboratories and equipment without which it is not possible to provide sound training in biology and chemistry. Finding enough teachers will take time, and producing well-equipped laboratories for every high school in the nation demands funding that will be difficult to provide in today's tight-budget environment. Yet we do expect to make considerable progress in this field. If our students are not the world's most capable young scientists and mathematicians by the year 2000, they will at least be, on average, a good deal better than their elder brothers and sisters have had the opportunity to become.

There is little cause for optimism with regard to Goal 5—universal adult literacy. It will not be achieved, or even approached, at any time during the foreseeable future.

One reason is the vast number of adults who are illiterate today, and who lack the knowledge and skills required for a productive role in the modern world. If it has proved difficult to give children an adequate education when most are, by law, a captive audience for their teachers, it can only be far more difficult to supply adults with the learning they missed during their first brush with the school system. The task is so great, and their time and motivation often so slight, that there is little prospect of making more than a small improvement in this generation.

Add to that the vast wave of immigration now reaching our shores. By far the largest fraction of new Americans come here from Central and South America, driven by political turmoils and economic hardship. And the majority of them are illiterate, or nearly so, even in their native languages. If all adults within our borders today were magically given the power to read, write, and reason, and the knowledge expected of adults in the industrialized West, by the year 2000 there would again be several million of us in need of the same spell.

A national literacy program provided direct to the home using computer-assisted instruction may make major inroads into this enormous problem. Yet this is one area in which it will be difficult even to hold our own.

In some ways, the final goal—ridding our schools of drugs and violence—seems the most complex and difficult task of all, for it implies that students will arrive at school both drug-free and safe from violence, and will return to neighborhoods and homes where they are secure from these ills. Anything less must surely leave our schools prey to the evils around them. And to clean up the schools, much less their surroundings, requires an enormous commitment to effective antidrug education. This is one form of education that seldom appeals to our legalistic, punishment-oriented society.

Yet we believe the outlook here is better than it first appears.

One reason is simply the level of interest this issue inspires among the American electorate. The other is the clear efficacy of antidrug efforts within schools. In those rare instances where a courageous and determined school administration has set out to eliminate drugs and violence from its institution, it has generally managed to do the job. Simply providing students with an island of safety has proved to be enough to raise their academic performance and reduce drop-out rates dramatically, even when nothing else in their environments has changed. And this is something that most schools can accomplish fairly quickly when principals, faculty, and parents make up their minds to do it. In this respect, our schools should be much healthier and more productive places ten years from now.

In all, the governors have chosen an admirable, if slightly vague, set of goals for American education, though we are unlikely to meet most of them within the time available. But then, goals are not forecasts, no matter how sincerely they are offered or how diligently they are pursued. Goals are targets that, whether they are hit or not, at least give us a reasonable place to focus our efforts. Even if we come nowhere near meeting the goals of the National Governors' Association, that role alone is enough to justify the effort that went into formulating them. And if we can manage to close by half the gap that now separates us from them, we will have done more to solve the problems of our schools than we have accomplished in the last twenty years.

In the end, how much our schools improve is up to us. If our school systems are to recover their lost quality, if the United States is to survive as an economic leader, parents—and everyone who reads this book—must accept responsibility for the performance of their local school system. We must offer ourselves as part-time teachers and teaching assistants, and work with local political leaders to raise school budgets and with school administrators to see that the money is used to promote effective classes in the core subjects. Above all, we must make certain that our own children understand the importance of a good education and have the support required for the difficult job of learning. In the years to come, more and more of us will accept this challenge. The trend has clearly begun.

From Here to Literacy   **217**

To make your own start, we recommend looking at the appendices that conclude this book. You might begin with a look at Appendix B, "Fifty States: Educational and Demographic Profiles." The profiles in this section will give you a good sense of how well your own state's educational system performs, and some indication of its strengths and weaknesses. If your state ranks in the top five in its graduation rate and SAT scores, you can probably turn your attention to specialized needs, such as programs for the gifted or handicapped, or to the kind of incremental improvements that make a good system better. If it rates in the bottom five, you know there is major work to be done. Somewhere in the United States, someone has already developed and tested a reform program that can help. You may well have read about it in preceding chapters.

There is nothing to prevent school districts across the country from adopting the reforms that have proved successful in other areas—nothing but the inertia of 16,000 school districts. That is rapidly disappearing in the face of political pressure from enraged parents.

In the decade to come, a new wave of educational reform will sweep across the land. It will flow outward from the growing minority of creative, experimental, and highly successful schools like the ones described in this book. Bringing all our schools up to the standard set by these few will not be an easy task. Neither will it be done by the year 2000. But it will occur far faster than most school planners would dare to hope. You and your neighbors will make it happen. Our children, and our nation, will be the better for it.

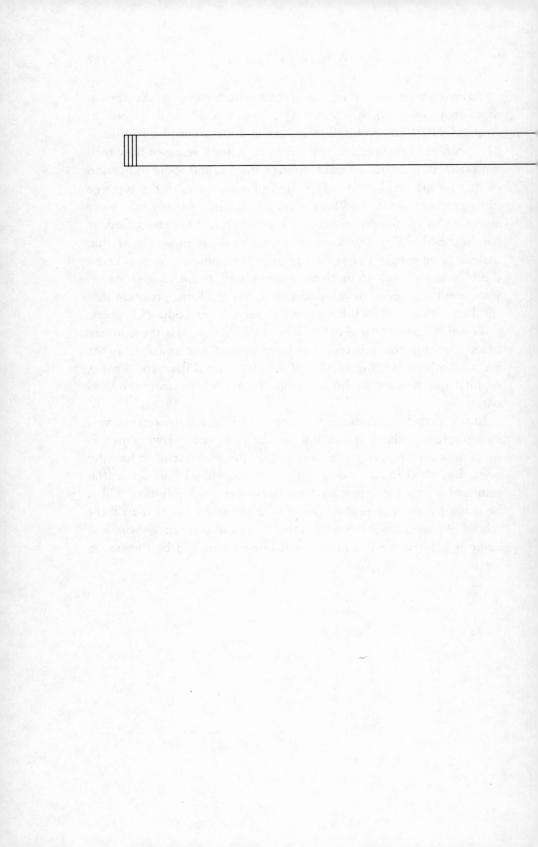

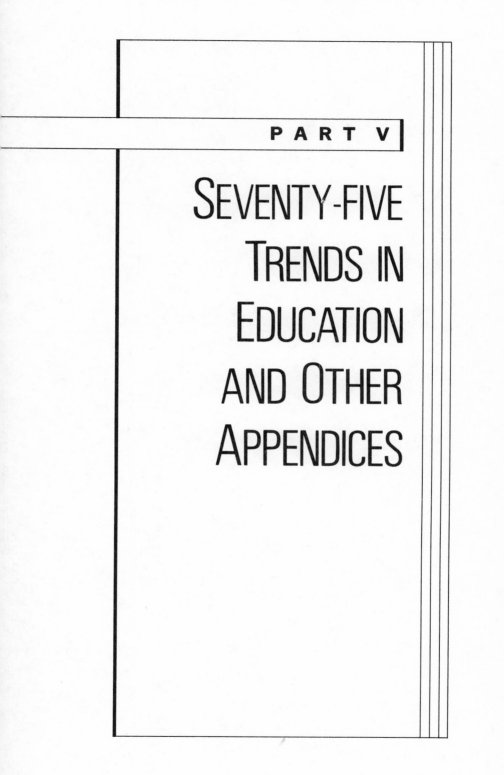

PART V

SEVENTY-FIVE TRENDS IN EDUCATION AND OTHER APPENDICES

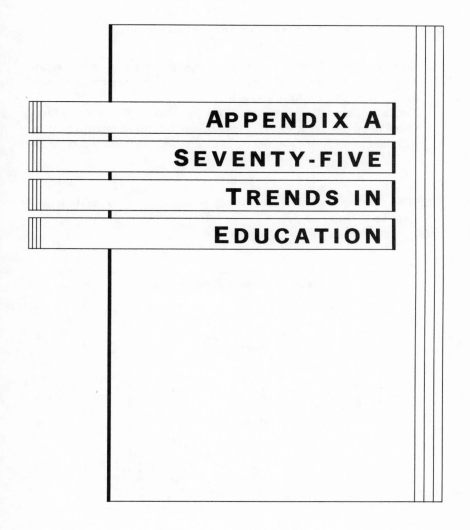

APPENDIX A
SEVENTY-FIVE
TRENDS IN
EDUCATION

1. Education will be the major public agenda item into the twenty-first century.
2. Education will continue to be viewed as the key to economic growth.
3. Technology, coupled with flexible home, work, and learning schedules, will provide more productive time for schooling, training, and working.
4. There is a growing mismatch between the literacy (vocabulary, reading and writing skills) of the labor force and the competency required by the jobs available.

- Both ill-prepared new entrants and employed workers, who cannot adapt to changing requirements that new technologies bring to their jobs, contribute to this mismatch.
- The mismatch will be greatest among the "best" jobs, where educational demands are greatest. Three-quarters of new entrants will be qualified for only 40% of new jobs created between 1985 and 2000.

Students

5. The number of public-school enrollments will increase to 43.8 million by 2000.

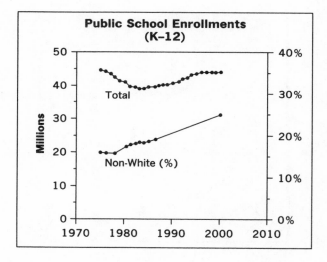

6. American education in the 1990s, in its concern for the quality of education for all students, will emphasize the development of "youth schools" modeled on those of Europe, which use terms of community service, challenging outdoor experiences, and similar activities to build confidence, problem-solving abilities, and leadership skills. Such programs, many of them resembling the well-known Outward Bound schools, are now available in about twelve states.

7. One million youth will continue to drop out of school annually, at an estimated cost of $240 billion in lost earnings and forgone taxes over their lifetimes.

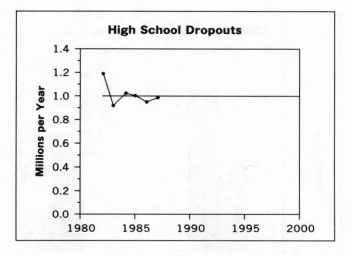

8. The majority of students will continue to be at risk of dropping out of school during the 1990s. The at-risk population may be described by the following characteristics:

• About half of high-school graduates do not go on to college (four-year or two-year).

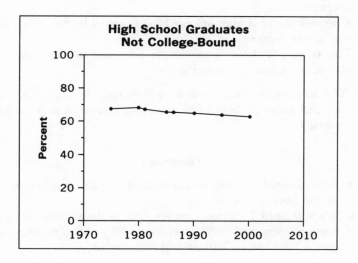

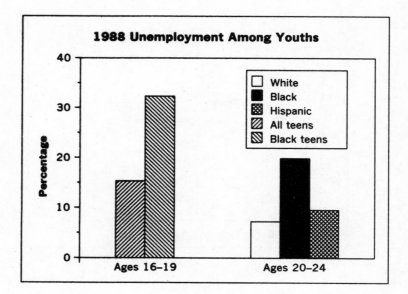

- One-third of all high-school students work part-time.
- Three-fourths of high school seniors work 16–20 hours per week, average.
- Unemployment is high among 16–24-year-olds, the group containing recent dropouts.
- The same population experiences increases in drug abuse, child abuse, and especially mortality rates.

9. The number of at-risk students will increase as academic standards rise and social problems (such as drug abuse, teenage pregnancy) intensify.

Teachers

10. Education will be respected as a valuable and prestigious profession by the twenty-first century.
11. We will need 2 million new teachers in the public-school system between now and 1995, but historical projections indicate that only a little over a million will materialize.

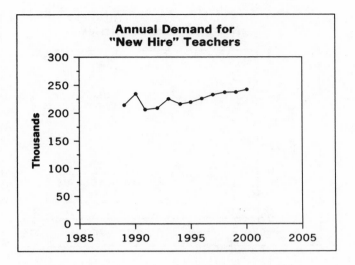

Annual Demand for "New Hire" Teachers

12. Class-size policies, school enrollment projections, and the expected attrition of the aging teaching force will be major factors determining the numbers of new teachers required to staff the nation's schools.

13. The supply of newly graduated teaching candidates is expected to satisfy only about 60% of the "new hire" demand over the next ten years.

14. The current shortage of minority teachers will continue into the 1990s while the minority student population increases. This will be particularly acute in the Southern states, where minority enrollment ranges from 25% to 56% and the proportion of minority teachers ranges from 4% to 35%.

15. By 1995, most states will implement alternative routes to certification (see chapter 3) as a solution to teacher shortages, especially in the sciences.

16. We will see a return to teaching laboratories or development schools in the 1990s, as university programs and teaching professionals develop a new vision for schooling from the ground up.

17. Teachers' salaries will continue to be debated in the 1990s while research regarding the relationship of financial incentives to retention of qualified teachers continues. Teacher salaries will need to increase by as much as $10,000 per teacher if the profession is to be able to attract talented individuals with skills commensurate to other like professions.

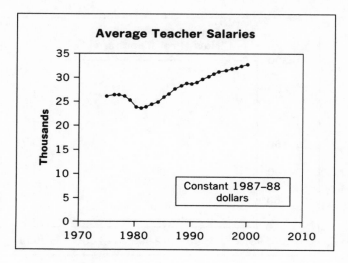

Average Teacher Salaries

Constant 1987–88 dollars

18. Teaching will become recognized as a bona fide profession; teacher unions will behave more like their counterparts in other professions.

Curriculum and Instruction

19. Lifelong learning will generate birth-to-death curriculum and delivery systems.
20. A core curriculum for all students will emerge as concerned people, through dialogue and debate, determine what the important things for the learning enterprise are; basic skills versus artistic and vocational education will be a major part of the debate.
21. The focus on thinking globally will make foreign languages, particularly French, German, Spanish, Russian and Japanese, a requirement for all students who are entering college programs.
22. Foreign-language and bilingual instruction will become a necessity for all students for the twenty-first century. All states will initiate programs or expand existing ones to prepare students for a worldwide marketplace.

Higher Education

23. Only 15% of the jobs of the future will require a college diploma, but more than half of all jobs will require postsecondary education and training.

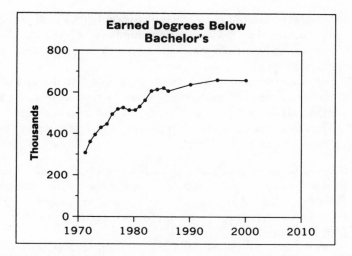

24. There will continue to be an "oversupply" of college graduates, especially in liberal arts. A liberal-arts background is valued in principle, but not in pay or in competition for jobs that require skills.

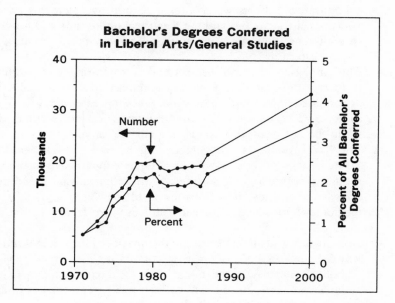

25. Community colleges and technical institutes will become major determinants of technological growth in communities and within regions.

26. Vocational education, with emphasis on higher technical literacy, will be required for increasing numbers of students. Access to state-of-the-art vocational education will be demanded by more parents and clients.

27. Secondary students will come to value vocational education more highly as reform efforts bring about a restructuring of schools, especially an integration of academic and technical skills.

28. The crisis in educating and preparing minority students to be teachers will peak in the 1990s:

• Current minority enrollment in teacher education is insufficient even to replace the minority teachers who are leaving the profession.

• Fewer than half of all minority teacher candidates, prepared by colleges and universities, pass the required certification tests in some forty-five states.

• High failure rates on standardized tests and teacher certification examinations are also reducing the pool of available minority teachers.

School Reform and Restructuring

29. School-reform efforts will continue to improve elements of the educational system, but without a national philosophy and funding commitment, the American schools will remain inferior to those of other western nations.

30. The emphasis on school reform and restructuring will continue throughout the 1990s, but with little impact on the national averages related to standardized testing. Since a greater majority of all students will take exams like the SATs, performance will increase while the average will virtually remain the same.

31. The "back to basics" movement will become the "forward to future basics" movement, which will include the use of telecommunications technologies, together with other advanced science knowledge and technical skills, in problem-solving.

32. Flexible school scheduling will result in more learning time for students.

33. Accountability at all levels will be the buzzword for the 1990s; but will the impetus be top-down or bottom-up? The trend toward school-based management suggests that local schools can carry out national standards. Accountability issues will create major conflict among federal, state, and local agencies.

34. Increased accountability and higher-paid education personnel will produce more professional approaches and solutions to educating a democratic and pluralistic society.

Governance and Leadership

35. All community stakeholders (parents, students, teachers, business leaders, and others) will continue to demand more involvement in the decisions governing education, but they will have little knowledge about what should be done to restructure; much is done with little research basis.

36. Centralized control of curriculum, teacher training, and achievement standards will continue, but decentralization of school and classroom management will increase.

37. The current shortage of qualified candidates for school administration positions will continue well into the twenty-first century. Three-quarters of American school superintendents, and as many as half of all principals, will retire by 1994.

38. The principal will become the major change agent for schools. He or she will bear tremendous leadership responsibility in sharing governance with the staff of the school. This school-based-management trend will create a need for quality professionals in school administration, projected shortages and the present low test scores of candidates notwithstanding.

39. Educational bureaucracies, local school boards, and other regulatory agencies will lose their power as the second wave of reforms takes hold during the 1990s.

40. The educational system will become more fragmented in the next decade. Implementation of numerous schooling alternatives will erode the traditional schooling pattern.

41. Exploration of research topics on governance will be undertaken that go beyond centralization and decentralization to, for instance, distribution of authority among government, teaching professionals, and families.

School Finance

42. A wide spectrum of school-finance initiatives and experiments will be undertaken. These will range from extreme centralization and financial control at the state level on one end, to privatization on the other, where the states will finance education through vouchers to parents (based on their choices of schools) rather than by directly financing schools. Between these extremes, there will be many traditional programs, but with an increasing number of private-sector partnerships.

43. Employers spend $210 billion annually on training. The number and effectiveness of business-education partnerships, to reduce remediation costs and to develop technical skills, will increase.

44. Regional disparities in educational resources will increase. As economies in coastal states flourish, so too will schools. Central and southern states will see their school systems lag behind.

School Law

45. Making public education work for everyone, especially for minorities and those with low incomes, will be the challenge for the 1990s. Parents and special-interest groups will raise legal challenges to curriculum, methodology, expenditures, access, and a host of other issues.
46. Equity issues, particularly among rich and poor school districts, will become the major problems faced by policymakers. Legal challenges will increase as standards are raised.
47. A new set of lawsuits, like those in Kentucky and Texas, will redefine equity in education in terms of how much is spent per pupil, not per property taxes of a school district.

THE CONNECTION TO JOBS AND WORK

48. From maternity leaves to longer school hours, personnel directors will face enormously difficult decisions in the 1990s because of the educational, social, economic, and technological changes in the workplace, home, and school.
49. Lifetime employment in the same job or company is a thing of the past. Workers will change jobs or careers five or more times; this will require lifelong training and learning.
50. The major management issues of the 1990s will be quality, productivity, and the decline of the work ethic.
51. The decline of employment in agricultural and manufacturing industries will continue, but by 2001, manufacturing productivity will have increased 500% in those industries that have become more automated, added robotics, and remained flexible in their management and production.

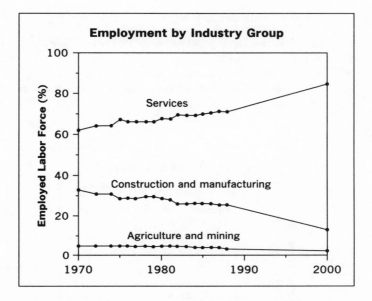

Employment by Industry Group

52. The emerging service economy will provide jobs for 85% of the work force by 2000.

53. A new category of "knowledge workers" has resulted from the unprecedented growth of information and knowledge industries. Information processing (collecting, analyzing, synthesizing, structuring, storing, or retrieving data, text, or graphics), as a basis of knowledge, is becoming important in more and more jobs; by 2000, knowledge workers will fill 43% of available jobs.

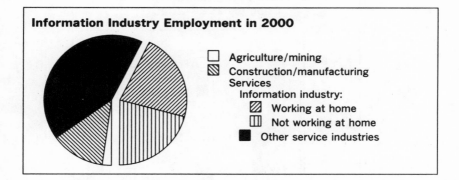

Information Industry Employment in 2000

- Agriculture/mining
- Construction/manufacturing
- Services
  Information industry:
    - Working at home
    - Not working at home
  - Other service industries

54. Work at home will increase as office automation becomes more portable and powerful; 22% of the labor force will work at home by the year 2000.

55. The profile of the labor force is changing rapidly:

- 52% of workers entering between 1988 and 2000 will be women; 33% will be minorities.
- Whites and men will constitute the largest groups leaving the labor force in the 1988–2000 period; their places will be taken by minorities and women.

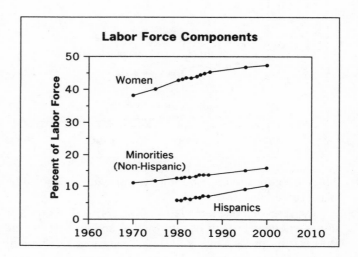

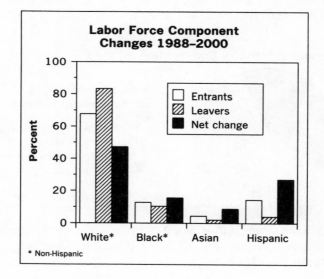

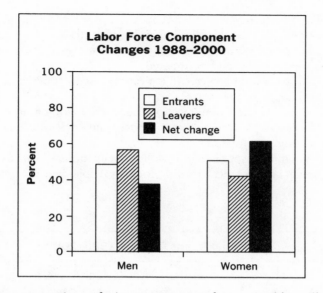

56. The proportion of sixteen-to-twenty-four-year-olds will shrink from 20% of the labor force in 1985 to only 16% in 2000.

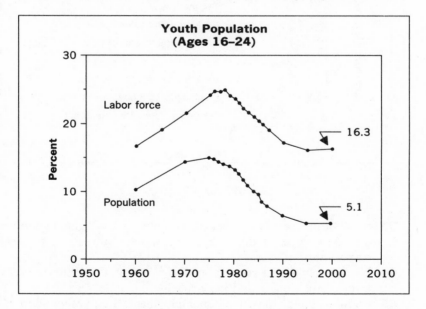

57. A shortage of entry-level workers, especially in the service sector, will create competition among business, the military, and institutions of higher learning for the youth labor force.

58. The National Science Foundation projects a shortage of 1 million professional scientists and engineers by 2010.

59. The impact of high-technology industries on the workplace will continue to be underestimated.

60. Computer competence will approach close to 100% in urban areas by 2000.

61. Interactive telecommunications networks linking homes, cars, and offices will provide customer services and employee education and training.

62. Eight million jobs in highly skilled occupations—executive, professional, and technical—will become available over the next decade.

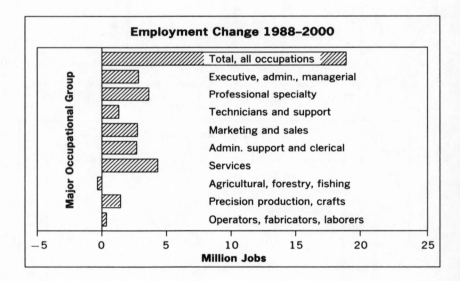

63. Small businesses (fewer than 100 employees) will employ most of the labor force by the year 2000. Many of these will be small manufacturing firms.

64. Biotechnology will generate major growth in the 1990s as breakthroughs in cloning and gene-splicing continue.

65. Continued high levels of unemployment (i.e., competition for jobs) in some states will force overqualified workers to take available jobs, displacing less-qualified workers who will experience longer periods of unemployment.

66. The mandatory retirement age, perhaps as high as seventy or seventy-two, will rise as senior citizens become needed and wanted in the workplace.

67. The growth in numbers of part-time workers and workers who moonlight will continue into the twenty-first century as two incomes within a family become increasingly needed to maintain quality-of-life expectations.

68. Day care will become the major fringe-benefit issue of the 1990s. Other important employee-benefit issues will include flexible schedules and job sharing, maternity and paternity leave, and health care.

THE FAMILY CONNECTION

69. Factors affecting the family will continue to show a dramatic change from the "Norman Rockwell" family (male breadwinner, homemaker wife, typically two children) of the past. By 2000, fewer than 4% of families will fit the "Norman Rockwell" mold.

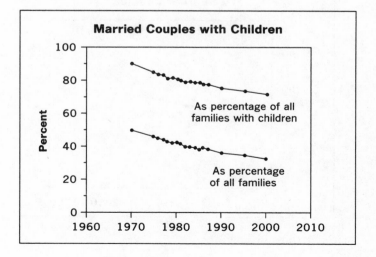

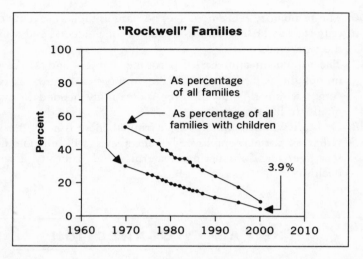

70. There will be more multi-families, i.e., children living with adults who are not related.
71. Legal redefinitions of "family" will have an impact on schools. For example, more and more schools will take care of children during after-school hours while the single parent is still at work.
72. By 2000, 75% of three-year-olds will attend nurseries (day-care centers or nursery schools).
73. Both partners in most family units (married and unmarried) will work; this figure could rise to 75% by 2000.

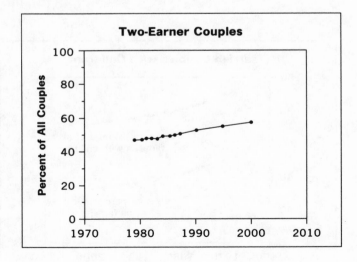

74. The number of single-parent families is steadily growing in size and importance. The major reason why white children are living with only one parent is divorce; for black and Hispanic children it is because the parent was never married. If current trends continue, by 2000:

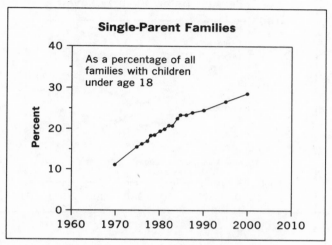

- 11% of white children will be living with a divorced mother (10% in 1988).
- 42% of black children will be living with a never-married mother (29% in 1988).
- 17% of Hispanic children will be living with a never-married mother (10% in 1988).

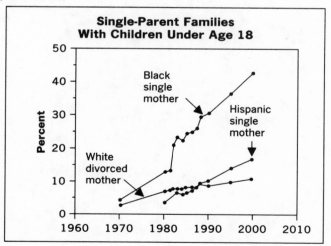

75. The number of people below the poverty level is not improving; among woman-headed families (no husband present) the rates are rising, especially for children.

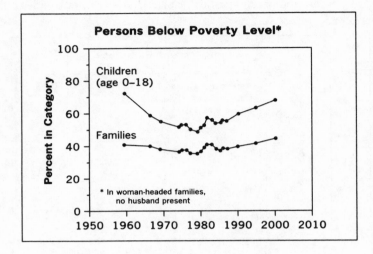

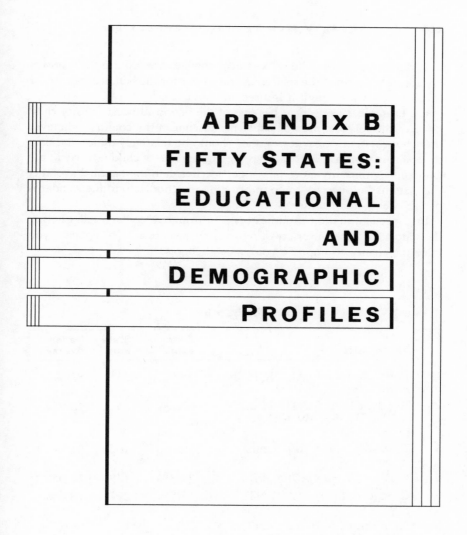

APPENDIX B
FIFTY STATES:
EDUCATIONAL
AND
DEMOGRAPHIC
PROFILES

According to tradition, the Chinese used to say that a journey of a thousand miles begins with a single step. In the case of educational reform, that step is figuring out the strengths and weaknesses of your local and state school systems.

What follows is a data base for would-be reformers. In it you will find a host of statistics about the economies, demographics, and educational systems of all fifty states. A few minutes with the profile of your state should give you a good idea of the areas in which your schools are at their best, and those in which improvements are needed. If your state ranks in the top five in, say, SAT scores, it is probably doing a good job of preparing young people for college; whatever changes are required will probably appear in some of the specialized programs for the handicapped or for students for whom English is a second language.

For example, Connecticut has one of the nation's lowest rates of child poverty and the best ratio of pupils-per-teacher in the country; whatever the school system's weaknesses, they should be relatively minor and easy to repair. In contrast, Alabama has the highest rate of child poverty in the land and significantly more pupils per teacher than the national average; this state has a long way to go in bringing its schools up to the standards of the twenty-first century.

Pay special attention to indicators 27 through 33, which tell whether the state has enacted a variety of reforms. Anywhere a "No" appears, you have the chance to improve your state's schools.

Alabama

	Vital Statistic	State Value	State Rank	National Average
1	POPULATION CHANGE [1980–88]	6.0%	23	8.5%
2	Resident POPULATION in METROPOLITAN AREAS [1987]	67.2%	25	76.9%
3	TAXES per $1,000 personal income [1986]	$91	46	$106
4	POVERTY rate [1984–86]	21.5%	47	14.0%
5	Change in EMPLOYMENT [1979–89]	15.5%	27	18.6%
6	Short-term EMPLOYMENT GROWTH [1986–87]	2.9%	17	N.A.
7	UNEMPLOYMENT RATE [November 1989]	6.3%	45	5.2%
8	UNEMPLOYED more than 27 weeks [1987]	14.6%	32	N.A.
9	UNIONIZATION rate [1984]	22%	26	23%
10	Average annual PAY [1987]	$18,318	36	$20,855
11	Change in PERSONAL INCOME [1979–89]	103.9%	28	112.1%
12	Per capita INCOME [1988]	$12,604	44	$16,444
13	JOB GENERATION SCORE [2/84–2/88]	19.14	22	18.38

Alabama *(continued)*

Vital Statistic	State Value	State Rank	National Average
14 NEW BUSINESSES SCORE [1/84–1/88]	18.40	16	15.17
15 YOUNG-COMPANY GROWTH SCORE [1/84–1/88]	14.68	28	15.34
16 ECONOMIC SUCCESS TOTAL SCORE [1984–88]	52.21	20	54.26
17 Child POVERTY [1983–87 average]	31.7%	50	20.9%
18 MINORITY school enrollment [1987]	38.0%	11	30.0%
19 HANDICAPPED school enrollment [1989]	14.2%	5	11.3%
20 PUPIL-TEACHER RATIO [1989]	18.7	43	17.4
21 EXPENDITURES PER PUPIL [1988]	$2,718	48	$4,243
22 TEACHER SALARY [1989]	$25,190	37	$29,567
23 GRADUATION RATE [1988]	74.9%	23	71.2%
24 SAT SCORES [1990] (rank, out of 21 states + DC)	N.A.		900
25 ACT SCORES [1989] (rank, out of 28 states)	17.9	19	18.6
26 GRADUATES TAKING 1989 SAT(S) or ACT(A) tests	53.4%	A	N.A.
Education System Measures			
27 PERFORMANCE indicators [1988]	No	N.A.	N.A.
28 School INCENTIVES [1988]	No	N.A.	N.A.
29 Alternate CERTIFICATION [1989]	No	N.A.	N.A.
30 Teacher INCENTIVES [1988]	No	N.A.	N.A.
31 Teacher MENTORS [1988]	No	N.A.	N.A.
32 High school COMPETENCY TESTS [1989]	No	N.A.	N.A.
33 PRESCHOOL programs [1989]	No	N.A.	N.A.

Alaska

	Vital Statistic	State Value	State Rank	National Average
1	POPULATION CHANGE [1980–88]	27.7%	2	8.5%
2	Resident POPULATION in METROPOLITAN AREAS [1987]	42.4%	41	76.9%
3	TAXES per $1,000 personal income [1986]	$245	1	$106
4	POVERTY rate [1984–86]	10.4%	8	14.0%
5	Change in EMPLOYMENT [1979–89]	30.5%	9	18.6%
6	Short-term EMPLOYMENT GROWTH [1986–87]	−3.2%	49	N.A.
7	UNEMPLOYMENT RATE [November 1989]	6.0%	42	5.2%
8	UNEMPLOYED more than 27 weeks [1987]	17.7%	42	N.A.
9	UNIONIZATION rate [1984]	34%	4	23%
10	Average annual PAY [1987]	$28,008	2	$20,855
11	Change in PERSONAL INCOME [1979–89]	112.0%	22	112.1%
12	Per capita INCOME [1988]	$19,514	5	$16,444
13	JOB GENERATION SCORE [2/84–2/88]	5.38	49	18.38
14	NEW BUSINESSES SCORE [1/84–1/88]	6.70	44	15.17
15	YOUNG-COMPANY GROWTH SCORE [1/84–1/88]	2.60	48	15.34
16	ECONOMIC SUCCESS TOTAL SCORE [1984–88]	14.67	49	54.26
17	Child POVERTY [1983–87 average]	12.7%	3	20.9%
18	MINORITY school enrollment [1987]	34.0%	14	30.0%
19	HANDICAPPED school enrollment [1989]	13.9%	6	11.3%
20	PUPIL-TEACHER RATIO [1989]	17.0	26	17.4
21	EXPENDITURES PER PUPIL [1988]	$7,971	1	$4,243

Alaska *(continued)*

	Vital Statistic	State Value	State Rank	National Average
22	TEACHER SALARY [1989]	$41,693	1	$29,567
23	GRADUATION RATE [1988]	65.5%	43	71.2%
24	SAT SCORES [1990] (rank, out of 21 states + DC)	N.A.		900
25	ACT SCORES [1989] (rank, out of 28 states)	17.9	19	18.6
26	GRADUATES TAKING 1989 SAT(S) or ACT(A) tests	36.4%	A	N.A.
	Education System Measures			
27	PERFORMANCE indicators [1988]	No	N.A.	N.A.
28	School INCENTIVES [1988]	No	N.A.	N.A.
29	Alternate CERTIFICATION [1989]	Yes	N.A.	N.A.
30	Teacher INCENTIVES [1988]	No	N.A.	N.A.
31	Teacher MENTORS [1988]	No	N.A.	N.A.
32	High school COMPETENCY TESTS [1989]	No	N.A.	N.A.
33	PRESCHOOL programs [1989]	No	N.A.	N.A.

Arizona

	Vital Statistic	State Value	State Rank	National Average
1	POPULATION CHANGE [1980–88]	27.5%	3	8.5%
2	Resident POPULATION in METROPOLITAN AREAS [1987]	76.2%	20	76.9%
3	TAXES per $1,000 personal income [1986]	$109	16	$106
4	POVERTY rate [1984–86]	13.4%	26	14.0%
5	Change in EMPLOYMENT [1979–89]	45.4%	3	18.6%
6	Short-term EMPLOYMENT GROWTH [1986–87]	33.0%	14	N.A.

Arizona *(continued)*

	Vital Statistic	State Value	State Rank	National Average
7	UNEMPLOYMENT RATE [November 1989]	4.4%	20	5.2%
8	UNEMPLOYED more than 27 weeks [1987]	6.3%	4	N.A.
9	UNIONIZATION rate [1984]	16%	37	23%
10	Average annual PAY [1987]	$19,610	21	$20,855
11	Change in PERSONAL INCOME [1979–89]	152.5%	3	112.1%
12	Per capita INCOME [1988]	$14,887	31	$16,444
13	JOB GENERATION SCORE [2/84–2/88]	21.66	16	18.38
14	NEW BUSINESSES SCORE [1/84–1/88]	21.94	13	15.17
15	YOUNG-COMPANY GROWTH SCORE [1/84–1/88]	21.78	11	15.34
16	ECONOMIC SUCCESS TOTAL SCORE [1984–88]	65.38	11	54.26
17	Child POVERTY [1983–87 average]	21.2%	32	20.9%
18	MINORITY school enrollment [1987]	38.0%	11	30.0%
19	HANDICAPPED school enrollment [1989]	9.6%	43	11.3%
20	PUPIL-TEACHER RATIO [1989]	18.2	37	17.4
21	EXPENDITURES PER PUPIL [1988]	$3,744	34	$4,243
22	TEACHER SALARY [1989]	$28,684	23	$29,567
23	GRADUATION RATE [1988]	61.1%	48	71.2%
24	SAT SCORES [1990] (rank, out of 21 states + DC)	N.A.		900
25	ACT SCORES [1989] (rank, out of 28 states)	19.0	12	18.6
26	GRADUATES TAKING 1989 SAT(S) or ACT(A) tests	35.7%	A	N.A.
	Education System Measures			
27	PERFORMANCE indicators [1988]	No	N.A.	N.A.

Arizona *(continued)*

	Vital Statistic	State Value	State Rank	National Average
28	School INCENTIVES [1988]	Yes	N.A.	N.A.
29	Alternate CERTIFICATION [1989]	Yes	N.A.	N.A.
30	Teacher INCENTIVES [1988]	No	N.A.	N.A.
31	Teacher MENTORS [1988]	No	N.A.	N.A.
32	High school COMPETENCY TESTS [1989]	Yes	N.A.	N.A.
33	PRESCHOOL programs [1989]	Yes	N.A.	N.A.

Arkansas

	Vital Statistic	State Value	State Rank	National Average
1	POPULATION CHANGE [1980–88]	5.9%	24	8.5%
2	Resident POPULATION in METROPOLITAN AREAS [1987]	39.5%	42	76.9%
3	TAXES per $1,000 personal income [1986]	$92	45	$106
4	POVERTY rate [1984–86]	22.4%	48	14.0%
5	Change in EMPLOYMENT [1979–89]	17.6%	24	18.6%
6	Short-term EMPLOYMENT GROWTH [1986–87]	2.3%	24	N.A.
7	UNEMPLOYMENT RATE [November 1989]	6.1%	44	5.2%
8	UNEMPLOYED more than 27 weeks [1987]	11.3%	24	N.A.
9	UNIONIZATION rate [1984]	16%	37	23%
10	Average annual PAY [1987]	$16,529	46	$20,855
11	Change in PERSONAL INCOME [1979–89]	102.2%	29	112.1%
12	Per capita INCOME [1988]	$12,172	48	$16,444
13	JOB GENERATION SCORE [2/84–2/88]	19.40	21	18.38

Arkansas *(continued)*

	Vital Statistic	State Value	State Rank	National Average
14	NEW BUSINESSES SCORE [1/84–1/88]	10.55	40	15.17
15	YOUNG-COMPANY GROWTH SCORE [1/84–1/88]	6.42	43	15.34
16	ECONOMIC SUCCESS TOTAL SCORE [1984–88]	36.37	40	54.26
17	Child POVERTY [1983–87 average]	29.0%	46	20.9%
18	MINORITY school enrollment [1987]	25.0%	21	30.0%
19	HANDICAPPED school enrollment [1989]	10.9%	29	11.3%
20	PUPIL-TEACHER RATIO [1989]	15.7	15	17.4
21	EXPENDITURES PER PUPIL [1988]	$2,989	47	$4,243
22	TEACHER SALARY [1989]	$21,692	50	$29,567
23	GRADUATION RATE [1988]	77.2%	17	71.2%
24	SAT SCORES [1990] (rank, out of 21 states + DC)	N.A.		900
25	ACT SCORES [1989] (rank, out of 28 states)	17.6	25	18.6
26	GRADUATES TAKING 1989 SAT(S) or ACT(A) tests	58.6%	A	N.A.
	Education System Measures			
27	PERFORMANCE indicators [1988]	Yes	N.A.	N.A.
28	School INCENTIVES [1988]	Yes	N.A.	N.A.
29	Alternate CERTIFICATION [1989]	Yes	N.A.	N.A.
30	Teacher INCENTIVES [1988]	Yes	N.A.	N.A.
31	Teacher MENTORS [1988]	No	N.A.	N.A.
32	High school COMPETENCY TESTS [1989]	Yes	N.A.	N.A.
33	PRESCHOOL programs [1989]	Yes	N.A.	N.A.

California

	Vital Statistic	State Value	State Rank	National Average
1	POPULATION CHANGE [1980–88]	19.0%	6	8.5%
2	Resident POPULATION in METROPOLITAN AREAS [1987]	95.7%	3	76.9%
3	TAXES per $1,000 personal income [1986]	$103	25	$106
4	POVERTY rate [1984–86]	13.4%	26	14.0%
5	Change in EMPLOYMENT [1979–89]	27.8%	10	18.6%
6	Short-term EMPLOYMENT GROWTH [1986–87]	3.9%	8	N.A.
7	UNEMPLOYMENT RATE [November 1989]	4.9%	30	5.2%
8	UNEMPLOYED more than 27 weeks [1987]	10.8%	21	N.A.
9	UNIONIZATION rate [1984]	27%	15	23%
10	Average annual PAY [1987]	$23,100	6	$20,855
11	Change in PERSONAL INCOME [1979–89]	130.5%	14	112.1%
12	Per capita INCOME [1988]	$18,855	9	$16,444
13	JOB GENERATION SCORE [2/84–2/88]	21.33	18	18.38
14	NEW BUSINESSES SCORE [1/84–1/88]	22.86	9	15.17
15	YOUNG-COMPANY GROWTH SCORE [1/84–1/88]	22.49	8	15.34
16	ECONOMIC SUCCESS TOTAL SCORE [1984–88]	66.69	10	54.26
17	Child POVERTY [1983–87 average]	21.4%	35	20.9%
18	MINORITY school enrollment [1987]	46.0%	6	30.0%
19	HANDICAPPED school enrollment [1989]	9.3%	45	11.3%
20	PUPIL-TEACHER RATIO [1989]	22.7	50	17.4
21	EXPENDITURES PER PUPIL [1988]	$3,840	31	$4,243

California *(continued)*

	Vital Statistic	State Value	State Rank	National Average
22	TEACHER SALARY [1989]	$35,285	5	$29,567
23	GRADUATION RATE [1988]	65.9%	42	71.2%
24	SAT SCORES [1990] (rank, out of 21 states + DC)	903	4	900
25	ACT SCORES [1989] (rank, out of 28 states)	N.A.		18.6
26	GRADUATES TAKING 1989 SAT(S) or ACT(A) tests	42.1%	S	N.A.
	Education System Measures			
27	PERFORMANCE indicators [1988]	Yes	N.A.	N.A.
28	School INCENTIVES [1988]	No	N.A.	N.A.
29	Alternate CERTIFICATION [1989]	No	N.A.	N.A.
30	Teacher INCENTIVES [1988]	No	N.A.	N.A.
31	Teacher MENTORS [1988]	No	N.A.	N.A.
32	High school COMPETENCY TESTS [1989]	No	N.A.	N.A.
33	PRESCHOOL programs [1989]	Yes	N.A.	N.A.

Colorado

	Vital Statistic	State Value	State Rank	National Average
1	POPULATION CHANGE [1980–88]	13.8%	11	8.5%
2	Resident POPULATION in METROPOLITAN AREAS [1987]	81.7%	13	76.9%
3	TAXES per $1,000 personal income [1986]	$98	36	$106
4	POVERTY rate [1984–86]	10.8%	10	14.0%
5	Change in EMPLOYMENT [1979–89]	18.2%	23	18.6%
6	Short-term EMPLOYMENT GROWTH [1986–87]	−0.2%	45	N.A.

Colorado *(continued)*

Vital Statistic	State Value	State Rank	National Average
7 UNEMPLOYMENT RATE [November 1989]	4.8%	27	5.2%
8 UNEMPLOYED more than 27 weeks [1987]	15.2%	36	N.A.
9 UNIONIZATION rate [1984]	18%	31	23%
10 Average annual PAY [1987]	$20,736	12	$20,855
11 Change in PERSONAL INCOME [1979–89]	112.6%	21	112.1%
12 Per capita INCOME [1988]	$16,417	19	$16,444
13 JOB GENERATION SCORE [2/84–2/88]	11.06	45	18.38
14 NEW BUSINESSES SCORE [1/84–1/88]	17.93	17	15.17
15 YOUNG-COMPANY GROWTH SCORE [1/84–1/88]	10.15	38	15.34
16 ECONOMIC SUCCESS TOTAL SCORE [1984–88]	39.14	37	54.26
17 Child POVERTY [1983–87 average]	16.2%	16	20.9%
18 MINORITY school enrollment [1987]	21.0%	26	30.0%
19 HANDICAPPED school enrollment [1989]	9.5%	44	11.3%
20 PUPIL-TEACHER RATIO [1989]	17.8	34	17.4
21 EXPENDITURES PER PUPIL [1988]	$4,462	16	$4,243
22 TEACHER SALARY [1989]	$29,558	17	$29,567
23 GRADUATION RATE [1988]	74.7%	24	71.2%
24 SAT SCORES [1990] (rank, out of 21 states + DC)	N.A.		900
25 ACT SCORES [1989] (rank, out of 28 states)	19.6	5	18.6
26 GRADUATES TAKING 1989 SAT(S) or ACT(A) tests	59.7%	A	N.A.

Education System Measures

27 PERFORMANCE indicators [1988]	Yes	N.A.	N.A.

Colorado *(continued)*

	Vital Statistic	State Value	State Rank	National Average
28	School INCENTIVES [1988]	Yes	N.A.	N.A.
29	Alternate CERTIFICATION [1989]	Yes	N.A.	N.A.
30	Teacher INCENTIVES [1988]	No	N.A.	N.A.
31	Teacher MENTORS [1988]	Yes	N.A.	N.A.
32	High school COMPETENCY TESTS [1989]	No	N.A.	N.A.
33	PRESCHOOL programs [1989]	Yes	N.A.	N.A.

Connecticut

	Vital Statistic	State Value	State Rank	National Average
1	POPULATION CHANGE [1980–88]	4.3%	32	8.5%
2	Resident POPULATION in METROPOLITAN AREAS [1987]	92.6%	5	76.9%
3	TAXES per $1,000 personal income [1986]	$100	31	$106
4	POVERTY rate [1984–86]	7.2%	2	14.0%
5	Change in EMPLOYMENT [1979–89]	21.0%	19	18.6%
6	Short-term EMPLOYMENT GROWTH [1986–87]	1.3%	36	N.A.
7	UNEMPLOYMENT RATE [November 1989]	3.4%	5	5.2%
8	UNEMPLOYED more than 27 weeks [1987]	9.6%	12	N.A.
9	UNIONIZATION rate [1984]	23%	24	23%
10	Average annual PAY [1987]	$24,322	4	$20,855
11	Change in PERSONAL INCOME [1979–89]	136.0%	11	112.1%
12	Per capita INCOME [1988]	$22,761	1	$16,444
13	JOB GENERATION SCORE [2/84–2/88]	17.42	31	18.38

Connecticut *(continued)*

	Vital Statistic	State Value	State Rank	National Average
14	NEW BUSINESSES SCORE [1/84–1/88]	13.78	26	15.17
15	YOUNG-COMPANY GROWTH SCORE [1/84–1/88]	22.76	7	15.34
16	ECONOMIC SUCCESS TOTAL SCORE [1984–88]	53.96	18	54.26
17	Child POVERTY [1983–87 average]	11.8%	2	20.9%
18	MINORITY school enrollment [1987]	23.0%	23	30.0%
19	HANDICAPPED school enrollment [1989]	13.7%	8	11.3%
20	PUPIL-TEACHER RATIO [1989]	13.1	1	17.4
21	EXPENDITURES PER PUPIL [1988]	$6,230	4	$4,243
22	TEACHER SALARY [1989]	$37,339	3	$29,567
23	GRADUATION RATE [1988]	84.9%	7	71.2%
24	SAT SCORES [1990] (rank, out of 21 states + DC)	901	6	900
25	ACT SCORES [1989] (rank, out of 28 states)	N.A.		18.6
26	GRADUATES TAKING 1989 SAT(S) or ACT(A) tests	70.3%	S	N.A.
	Education System Measures			
27	PERFORMANCE indicators [1988]	Yes	N.A.	N.A.
28	School INCENTIVES [1988]	No	N.A.	N.A.
29	Alternate CERTIFICATION [1989]	Yes	N.A.	N.A.
30	Teacher INCENTIVES [1988]	No	N.A.	N.A.
31	Teacher MENTORS [1988]	Yes	N.A.	N.A.
32	High school COMPETENCY TESTS [1989]	No	N.A.	N.A.
33	PRESCHOOL programs [1989]	Yes	N.A.	N.A.

Delaware

	Vital Statistic	State Value	State Rank	National Average
1	POPULATION CHANGE [1980–88]	11.0%	16	8.5%
2	Resident POPULATION in METROPOLITAN AREAS [1987]	66.0%	29	76.9%
3	TAXES per $1,000 personal income [1986]	$107	19	$106
4	POVERTY rate [1984–86]	11.3%	14	14.0%
5	Change in EMPLOYMENT [1979–89]	33.1%	7	18.6%
6	Short-term EMPLOYMENT GROWTH [1986–87]	3.4%	12	N.A.
7	UNEMPLOYMENT RATE [November 1989]	2.8%	1	5.2%
8	UNEMPLOYED more than 27 weeks [1987]	10.4%	20	N.A.
9	UNIONIZATION rate [1984]	25%	19	23%
10	Average annual PAY [1987]	$20,764	11	$20,855
11	Change in PERSONAL INCOME [1979–89]	130.0%	15	112.1%
12	Per capita INCOME [1988]	$17,699	10	$16,444
13	JOB GENERATION SCORE [2/84–2/88]	25.43	5	18.38
14	NEW BUSINESSES SCORE [1/84–1/88]	17.63	18	15.17
15	YOUNG-COMPANY GROWTH SCORE [1/84–1/88]	29.33	2	15.34
16	ECONOMIC SUCCESS TOTAL SCORE [1984–88]	72.39	7	54.26
17	Child POVERTY [1983–87 average]	15.3%	10	20.9%
18	MINORITY school enrollment [1987]	3.2%	15	30.0%
19	HANDICAPPED school enrollment [1989]	14.4%	4	11.3%
20	PUPIL-TEACHER RATIO [1989]	16.4	23	17.4
21	EXPENDITURES PER PUPIL [1988]	$5,017	11	$4,243

Delaware *(continued)*

	Vital Statistic	State Value	State Rank	National Average
22	TEACHER SALARY [1989]	$31,605	11	$29,567
23	GRADUATION RATE [1988]	71.7%	33	71.2%
24	SAT SCORES [1990] (rank, out of 21 states + DC)	903	4	900
25	ACT SCORES [1989] (rank, out of 28 states)	N.A.		18.6
26	GRADUATES TAKING 1989 SAT(S) or ACT(A) tests	65.0%	S	N.A.
	Education System Measures			
27	PERFORMANCE indicators [1988]	Yes	N.A.	N.A.
28	School INCENTIVES [1988]	Yes	N.A.	N.A.
29	Alternate CERTIFICATION [1989]	Yes	N.A.	N.A.
30	Teacher INCENTIVES [1988]	Yes	N.A.	N.A.
31	Teacher MENTORS [1988]	Yes	N.A.	N.A.
32	High school COMPETENCY TESTS [1989]	Yes	N.A.	N.A.
33	PRESCHOOL programs [1989]	Yes	N.A.	N.A.

District of Columbia

	Vital Statistic	State Value	State Rank	National Average
1	POPULATION CHANGE [1980–88]	−2.9%	50	8.5%
2	Resident POPULATION in METROPOLITAN AREAS [1987]	100.0%	1	76.9%
3	TAXES per $1,000 personal income [1986]	$146	4	$106
4	POVERTY rate [1984–86]	N.A.		14.0%
5	Change in EMPLOYMENT [1979–89]	12.1%	33	18.6%
6	Short-term EMPLOYMENT GROWTH [1986–87]	N.A.		N.A.

District of Columbia *(continued)*

	Vital Statistic	State Value	State Rank	National Average
7	UNEMPLOYMENT RATE [November 1989]	4.7%	25	5.2%
8	UNEMPLOYED more than 27 weeks [1987]	N.A.		N.A.
9	UNIONIZATION rate [1984]	N.A.		23%
10	Average annual PAY [1987]	$28,477	1	$20,855
11	Change in PERSONAL INCOME [1979–89]	90.1%	34	112.1%
12	Per capita INCOME [1988]	$21,667	3	$16,444
13	JOB GENERATION SCORE [2/84–2/88]	N.A.		18.38
14	NEW BUSINESSES SCORE [1/84–1/88]	N.A.		15.17
15	YOUNG-COMPANY GROWTH SCORE [1/84–1/88]	N.A.		15.34
16	ECONOMIC SUCCESS TOTAL SCORE [1984–88]	N.A.		54.26
17	Child POVERTY [1983–87 average]	31.3%	49	20.9%
18	MINORITY school enrollment [1987]	96.0%	1	30.0%
19	HANDICAPPED school enrollment [1989]	8.5%	49	11.3%
20	PUPIL-TEACHER RATIO [1989]	13.3	2	17.4
21	EXPENDITURES PER PUPIL [1988]	$6,132	5	$4,243
22	TEACHER SALARY [1989]	$37,504	2	$29,567
23	GRADUATION RATE [1988]	58.2%	50	71.2%
24	SAT SCORES [1990] (rank, out of 21 states + DC)	850	18	900
25	ACT SCORES [1989] (rank, out of 28 states)	N.A.		18.6
26	GRADUATES TAKING 1989 SAT(S) or ACT(A) tests	55.4%	S	N.A.
	Education System Measures			
27	PERFORMANCE indicators [1988]	N.A.	N.A.	N.A.

District of Columbia *(continued)*

	Vital Statistic	State Value	State Rank	National Average
28	School INCENTIVES [1988]	N.A.	N.A.	N.A.
29	Alternate CERTIFICATION [1989]	N.A.	N.A.	N.A.
30	Teacher INCENTIVES [1988]	N.A.	N.A.	N.A.
31	Teacher MENTORS [1988]	N.A.	N.A.	N.A.
32	High school COMPETENCY TESTS [1989]	N.A.	N.A.	N.A.
33	PRESCHOOL programs [1989]	N.A.	N.A.	N.A.

Florida

	Vital Statistic	State Value	State Rank	National Average
1	POPULATION CHANGE [1980–88]	27.0%	4	8.5%
2	Resident POPULATION in METROPOLITAN AREAS [1987]	90.8%	7	76.9%
3	TAXES per $1,000 personal income [1986]	$87	49	$106
4	POVERTY rate [1984–86]	13.3%	25	14.0%
5	Change in EMPLOYMENT [1979–89]	54.8%	1	18.6%
6	Short-term EMPLOYMENT GROWTH [1986–87]	5.3%	2	N.A.
7	UNEMPLOYMENT RATE [November 1989]	5.6%	37	5.2%
8	UNEMPLOYED more than 27 weeks [1987]	8.6%	7	N.A.
9	UNIONIZATION rate [1984]	12%	47	23%
10	Average annual PAY [1987]	$18,674	32	$20,855
11	Change in PERSONAL INCOME [1979–89]	166.7%	2	112.1%
12	Per capita INCOME [1988]	$16,546	18	$16,444
13	JOB GENERATION SCORE [2/84–2/88]	26.60	2	18.38

Florida *(continued)*

	Vital Statistic	State Value	State Rank	National Average
14	NEW BUSINESSES SCORE [1/84–1/88]	29.17	2	15.17
15	YOUNG-COMPANY GROWTH SCORE [1/84–1/88]	17.79	21	15.34
16	ECONOMIC SUCCESS TOTAL SCORE [1984–88]	74.39	5	54.26
17	Child POVERTY [1983–87 average]	21.1%	31	20.9%
18	MINORITY school enrollment [1987]	35.0%	13	30.0%
19	HANDICAPPED school enrollment [1989]	12.1%	17	11.3%
20	PUPIL-TEACHER RATIO [1989]	17.1	28	17.4
21	EXPENDITURES PER PUPIL [1988]	$4,092	25	$4,243
22	TEACHER SALARY [1989]	$26,648	30	$29,567
23	GRADUATION RATE [1988]	58.0%*	51	71.2%
24	SAT SCORES [1990] (rank, out of 21 states + DC)	884	12	900
25	ACT SCORES [1989] (rank, out of 28 states)	N.A.		18.6
26	GRADUATES TAKING 1989 SAT(S) or ACT(A) tests	47.5%	S	N.A.
	Education System Measures			
27	PERFORMANCE indicators [1988]	No	N.A.	N.A.
28	School INCENTIVES [1988]	Yes	N.A.	N.A.
29	Alternate CERTIFICATION [1989]	Yes	N.A.	N.A.
30	Teacher INCENTIVES [1988]	No	N.A.	N.A.
31	Teacher MENTORS [1988]	Yes	N.A.	N.A.
32	High school COMPETENCY TESTS [1989]	Yes	N.A.	N.A.
33	PRESCHOOL programs [1989]	No	N.A.	N.A.

*71.6% by Florida's unique definition of graduation rate.

Georgia

	Vital Statistic	State Value	State Rank	National Average
1	POPULATION CHANGE [1980–88]	17.2%	8	8.5%
2	Resident POPULATION in METROPOLITAN AREAS [1987]	64.6%	31	76.9%
3	TAXES per $1,000 personal income [1986]	$95	42	$106
4	POVERTY rate [1984–86]	15.6%	36	14.0%
5	Change in EMPLOYMENT [1979–89]	38.3%	5	18.6%
6	Short-term EMPLOYMENT GROWTH [1986–87]	2.4%	22	N.A.
7	UNEMPLOYMENT RATE [November 1989]	5.7%	38	5.2%
8	UNEMPLOYED more than 27 weeks [1987]	6.2%	2	N.A.
9	UNIONIZATION rate [1984]	15%	42	23%
10	Average annual PAY [1987]	$19,651	20	$20,855
11	Change in PERSONAL INCOME [1979–89]	149.4%	6	112.1%
12	Per capita INCOME [1988]	$14,980	29	$16,444
13	JOB GENERATION SCORE [2/84–2/88]	24.36	8	18.38
14	NEW BUSINESSES SCORE [1/84–1/88]	28.25	3	15.17
15	YOUNG-COMPANY GROWTH SCORE [1/84–1/88]	21.78	11	15.34
16	ECONOMIC SUCCESS TOTAL SCORE [1984–88]	74.39	5	54.26
17	Child POVERTY [1983–87 average]	24.2%	43	20.9%
18	MINORITY school enrollment [1987]	39.0%	10	30.0%
19	HANDICAPPED school enrollment [1989]	8.5%	49	11.3%
20	PUPIL-TEACHER RATIO [1989]	18.5	41	17.4
21	EXPENDITURES PER PUPIL [1988]	$3,434	39	$4,243

Georgia *(continued)*

	Vital Statistic	State Value	State Rank	National Average
22	TEACHER SALARY [1989]	$28,038	25	$29,567
23	GRADUATION RATE [1988]	61.0%	49	71.2%
24	SAT SCORES [1990] (rank, out of 21 states + DC)	844	19	900
25	ACT SCORES [1989] (rank, out of 28 states)	N.A.		18.6
26	GRADUATES TAKING 1989 SAT(S) or ACT(A) tests	60.3%	S	N.A.
	Education System Measures			
27	PERFORMANCE indicators [1988]	Yes	N.A.	N.A.
28	School INCENTIVES [1988]	Yes	N.A.	N.A.
29	Alternate CERTIFICATION [1989]	Yes	N.A.	N.A.
30	Teacher INCENTIVES [1988]	No	N.A.	N.A.
31	Teacher MENTORS [1988]	Yes	N.A.	N.A.
32	High school COMPETENCY TESTS [1989]	Yes	N.A.	N.A.
33	PRESCHOOL programs [1989]	No	N.A.	N.A.

Hawaii

	Vital Statistic	State Value	State Rank	National Average
1	POPULATION CHANGE [1980–88]	13.3%	12	8.5%
2	Resident POPULATION in METROPOLITAN AREAS [1987]	76.7%	19	76.9%
3	TAXES per $1,000 personal income [1986]	$122	6	$106
4	POVERTY rate [1984–86]	9.9%	6	14.0%
5	Change in EMPLOYMENT [1979–89]	24.1%	16	18.6%
6	Short-term EMPLOYMENT GROWTH [1986–87]	5.5%	1	N.A.

Hawaii *(continued)*

	Vital Statistic	State Value	State Rank	National Average
7	UNEMPLOYMENT RATE [November 1989]	2.8%	1	5.2%
8	UNEMPLOYED more than 27 weeks [1987]	9.6%	12	N.A.
9	UNIONIZATION rate [1984]	28%	12	23%
10	Average annual PAY [1987]	$19,091	25	$20,855
11	Change in PERSONAL INCOME [1979–89]	117.9%	18	112.1%
12	Per capita INCOME [1988]	$16,898	14	$16,444
13	JOB GENERATION SCORE [2/84–2/88]	22.81	12	18.38
14	NEW BUSINESSES SCORE [1/84–1/88]	23.48	8	15.17
15	YOUNG-COMPANY GROWTH SCORE [1/84–1/88]	18.32	17	15.34
16	ECONOMIC SUCCESS TOTAL SCORE [1984–88]	64.61	12	54.26
17	Child POVERTY [1983–87 average]	16.7%	19	20.9%
18	MINORITY school enrollment [1987]	77.0%	2	30.0%
19	HANDICAPPED school enrollment [1989]	7.3%	51	11.3%
20	PUPIL-TEACHER RATIO [1989]	21.1	49	17.4
21	EXPENDITURES PER PUPIL [1988]	$3,919	29	$4,243
22	TEACHER SALARY [1989]	$30,778	15	$29,567
23	GRADUATION RATE [1988]	69.1%	38	71.2%
24	SAT SCORES [1990] (rank, out of 21 states + DC)	885	11	900
25	ACT SCORES [1989] (rank, out of 28 states)	N.A.		18.6
26	GRADUATES TAKING 1989 SAT(S) or ACT(A) tests	50.5%	S	N.A.
	Education System Measures			
27	PERFORMANCE indicators [1988]	No	N.A.	N.A.

Hawaii *(continued)*

	Vital Statistic	State Value	State Rank	National Average
28	School INCENTIVES [1988]	No	N.A.	N.A.
29	Alternate CERTIFICATION [1989]	No	N.A.	N.A.
30	Teacher INCENTIVES [1988]	Yes	N.A.	N.A.
31	Teacher MENTORS [1988]	Yes	N.A.	N.A.
32	High school COMPETENCY TESTS [1989]	Yes	N.A.	N.A.
33	PRESCHOOL programs [1989]	No	N.A.	N.A.

Idaho

	Vital Statistic	State Value	State Rank	National Average
1	POPULATION CHANGE [1980–88]	5.8%	25	8.5%
2	Resident POPULATION in METROPOLITAN AREAS [1987]	19.6%	51	76.9%
3	TAXES per $1,000 personal income [1986]	$94	43	$106
4	POVERTY rate [1984–86]	16.4%	40	14.0%
5	Change in EMPLOYMENT [1979–89]	6.2%	42	18.6%
6	Short-term EMPLOYMENT GROWTH [1986–87]	0.2%	40	N.A.
7	UNEMPLOYMENT RATE [November 1989]	4.4%	20	5.2%
8	UNEMPLOYED more than 27 weeks [1987]	11.4%	25	N.A.
9	UNIONIZATION rate [1984]	18%	31	23%
10	Average annual PAY [1987]	$17,062	45	$20,855
11	Change in PERSONAL INCOME [1979–89]	86.2%	39	112.1%
12	Per capita INCOME [1988]	$12,657	43	$16,444
13	JOB GENERATION SCORE [2/84–2/88]	15.12	41	18.38

Idaho *(continued)*

	Vital Statistic	State Value	State Rank	National Average
14	NEW BUSINESSES SCORE [1/84–1/88]	7.00	43	15.17
15	YOUNG-COMPANY GROWTH SCORE [1/84–1/88]	5.26	45	15.34
16	ECONOMIC SUCCESS TOTAL SCORE [1984–88]	27.39	43	54.26
17	Child POVERTY [1983–87 average]	21.7%	36	20.9%
18	MINORITY school enrollment [1987]	7.0%	43	30.0%
19	HANDICAPPED school enrollment [1989]	9.1%	46	11.3%
20	PUPIL-TEACHER RATIO [1989]	20.6	48	17.4
21	EXPENDITURES PER PUPIL [1988]	$2,667	49	$4,243
22	TEACHER SALARY [1989]	$22,860	44	$29,567
23	GRADUATION RATE [1988]	75.4%	22	71.2%
24	SAT SCORES [1990] (rank, out of 21 states + DC)	N.A.		900
25	ACT SCORES [1989] (rank, out of 28 states)	19.1	9	18.6
26	GRADUATES TAKING 1989 SAT(S) or ACT(A) tests	57.5%	A	N.A.
	Education System Measures			
27	PERFORMANCE indicators [1988]	Yes	N.A.	N.A.
28	School INCENTIVES [1988]	Yes	N.A.	N.A.
29	Alternate CERTIFICATION [1989]	No	N.A.	N.A.
30	Teacher INCENTIVES [1988]	No	N.A.	N.A.
31	Teacher MENTORS [1988]	No	N.A.	N.A.
32	High school COMPETENCY TESTS [1989]	No	N.A.	N.A.
33	PRESCHOOL programs [1989]	Yes	N.A.	N.A.

Illinois

	Vital Statistic	State Value	State Rank	National Average
1	POPULATION CHANGE [1980–88]	1.0%	45	8.5%
2	Resident POPULATION in METROPOLITAN AREAS [1987]	82.5%	12	76.9%
3	TAXES per $1,000 personal income [1986]	$100	31	$106
4	POVERTY rate [1984–86]	15.0%	33	14.0%
5	Change in EMPLOYMENT [1979–89]	5.5%	45	18.6%
6	Short-term EMPLOYMENT GROWTH [1986–87]	1.7%	30	N.A.
7	UNEMPLOYMENT RATE [November 1989]	6.3%	45	5.2%
8	UNEMPLOYED more than 27 weeks [1987]	17.9%	43	N.A.
9	UNIONIZATION rate [1984]	30%	8	23%
10	Average annual PAY [1987]	$22,250	9	$20,855
11	Change in PERSONAL INCOME [1979–89]	87.9%	38	112.1%
12	Per capita INCOME [1988]	$17,611	12	$16,444
13	JOB GENERATION SCORE [2/84–2/88]	16.77	36	18.38
14	NEW BUSINESSES SCORE [1/84–1/88]	11.78	33	15.17
15	YOUNG-COMPANY GROWTH SCORE [1/84–1/88]	14.59	29	15.34
16	ECONOMIC SUCCESS TOTAL SCORE [1984–88]	43.13	33	54.26
17	Child POVERTY [1983–87 average]	22.8%	38	20.9%
18	MINORITY school enrollment [1987]	30.0%	19	30.0%
19	HANDICAPPED school enrollment [1989]	13.7%	8	11.3%
20	PUPIL-TEACHER RATIO [1989]	17.1	28	17.4
21	EXPENDITURES PER PUPIL [1988]	$4,369	19	$4,243

Illinois *(continued)*

	Vital Statistic	State Value	State Rank	National Average
22	TEACHER SALARY [1989]	$31,195	13	$29,567
23	GRADUATION RATE [1988]	75.6%	21	71.2%
24	SAT SCORES [1990] (rank, out of 21 states + DC)	N.A.		900
25	ACT SCORES [1989] (rank, out of 28 states)	18.8	16	18.6
26	GRADUATES TAKING 1989 SAT(S) or ACT(A) tests	61.3%	A	N.A.
	Education System Measures			
27	PERFORMANCE indicators [1988]	Yes	N.A.	N.A.
28	School INCENTIVES [1988]	Yes	N.A.	N.A.
29	Alternate CERTIFICATION [1989]	No	N.A.	N.A.
30	Teacher INCENTIVES [1988]	No	N.A.	N.A.
31	Teacher MENTORS [1988]	Yes	N.A.	N.A.
32	High school COMPETENCY TESTS [1989]	Yes	N.A.	N.A.
33	PRESCHOOL programs [1989]	Yes	N.A.	N.A.

Indiana

	Vital Statistic	State Value	State Rank	National Average
1	POPULATION CHANGE [1980–88]	1.5%	43	8.5%
2	Resident POPULATION in METROPOLITAN AREAS [1987]	68.0%	23	76.9%
3	TAXES per $1,000 personal income [1986]	$94	43	$106
4	POVERTY rate [1984–86]	12.2%	19	14.0%
5	Change in EMPLOYMENT [1979–89]	9.8%	38	18.6%
6	Short-term EMPLOYMENT GROWTH [1986–87]	0.1%	42	N.A.

Indiana (continued)

	Vital Statistic	State Value	State Rank	National Average
7	UNEMPLOYMENT RATE [November 1989]	4.8%	27	5.2%
8	UNEMPLOYED more than 27 weeks [1987]	14.8%	34	N.A.
9	UNIONIZATION rate [1984]	30%	8	23%
10	Average annual PAY [1987]	$19,692	19	$20,855
11	Change in PERSONAL INCOME [1979–89]	89.0%	36	112.1%
12	Per capita INCOME [1988]	$14,721	33	$16,444
13	JOB GENERATION SCORE [2/84–2/88]	21.80	15	18.38
14	NEW BUSINESSES SCORE [1/84–1/88]	13.78	26	15.17
15	YOUNG-COMPANY GROWTH SCORE [1/84–1/88]	16.54	23	15.34
16	ECONOMIC SUCCESS TOTAL SCORE [1984–88]	52.12	21	54.26
17	Child POVERTY [1983–87 average]	18.4%	23	20.9%
18	MINORITY school enrollment [1987]	11.0%	36	30.0%
19	HANDICAPPED school enrollment [1989]	11.4%	22	11.3%
20	PUPIL-TEACHER RATIO [1989]	17.8	34	17.4
21	EXPENDITURES PER PUPIL [1988]	$3,794	32	$4,243
22	TEACHER SALARY [1989]	$28,664	24	$29,567
23	GRADUATION RATE [1988]	76.3%	19	71.2%
24	SAT SCORES [1990] (rank, out of 21 states + DC)	867	17	900
25	ACT SCORES [1989] (rank, out of 28 states)	N.A.		18.6
26	GRADUATES TAKING 1989 SAT(S) or ACT(A) tests	55.6%	S	N.A.
	Education System Measures			
27	PERFORMANCE indicators [1988]	Yes	N.A.	N.A.

Indiana *(continued)*

Vital Statistic	State Value	State Rank	National Average
28 School INCENTIVES [1988]	No	N.A.	N.A.
29 Alternate CERTIFICATION [1989]	No	N.A.	N.A.
30 Teacher INCENTIVES [1988]	Yes	N.A.	N.A.
31 Teacher MENTORS [1988]	No	N.A.	N.A.
32 High school COMPETENCY TESTS [1989]	No	N.A.	N.A.
33 PRESCHOOL programs [1989]	Yes	N.A.	N.A.

Iowa

Vital Statistic	State Value	State Rank	National Average
1 POPULATION CHANGE [1980–88]	−2.7%	49	8.5%
2 Resident POPULATION in METROPOLITAN AREAS [1987]	43.1%	40	76.9%
3 TAXES per $1,000 personal income [1986]	$106	21	$106
4 POVERTY rate [1984–86]	16.5%	41	14.0%
5 Change in EMPLOYMENT [1979–89]	5.0%	46	18.6%
6 Short-term EMPLOYMENT GROWTH [1986–87]	2.2%	26	N.A.
7 UNEMPLOYMENT RATE [November 1989]	4.1%	13	5.2%
8 UNEMPLOYED more than 27 weeks [1987]	15.8%	38	N.A.
9 UNIONIZATION rate [1984]	22%	26	23%
10 Average annual PAY [1987]	$17,292	43	$20,855
11 Change in PERSONAL INCOME [1979–89]	70.3%	48	112.1%
12 Per capita INCOME [1988]	$14,764	32	$16,444
13 JOB GENERATION SCORE [2/84–2/88]	18.97	24	18.38

Iowa *(continued)*

	Vital Statistic	State Value	State Rank	National Average
14	NEW BUSINESSES SCORE [1/84–1/88]	4.39	46	15.17
15	YOUNG-COMPANY GROWTH SCORE [1/84–1/88]	10.68	36	15.34
16	ECONOMIC SUCCESS TOTAL SCORE [1984–88]	34.03	41	54.26
17	Child POVERTY [1983–87 average]	21.3%	33	20.9%
18	MINORITY school enrollment [1987]	5.0%	47	30.0%
19	HANDICAPPED school enrollment [1989]	12.0%	18	11.3%
20	PUPIL-TEACHER RATIO [1989]	15.8	16	17.4
21	EXPENDITURES PER PUPIL [1988]	$4,124	24	$4,243
22	TEACHER SALARY [1989]	$25,884	33	$29,567
23	GRADUATION RATE [1988]	85.8%	5	71.2%
24	SAT SCORES [1990] (rank, out of 21 states + DC)	N.A.		900
25	ACT SCORES [1989] (rank, out of 28 states)	20.1	1	18.6
26	GRADUATES TAKING 1989 SAT(S) or ACT(A) tests	60.0%	A	N.A.
	Education System Measures			
27	PERFORMANCE indicators [1988]	Yes	N.A.	N.A.
28	School INCENTIVES [1988]	No	N.A.	N.A.
29	Alternate CERTIFICATION [1989]	No	N.A.	N.A.
30	Teacher INCENTIVES [1988]	No	N.A.	N.A.
31	Teacher MENTORS [1988]	No	N.A.	N.A.
32	High school COMPETENCY TESTS [1989]	No	N.A.	N.A.
33	PRESCHOOL programs [1989]	No	N.A.	N.A.

Kansas

	Vital Statistic	State Value	State Rank	National Average
1	POPULATION CHANGE [1980–88]	5.2%	27	8.5%
2	Resident POPULATION in METROPOLITAN AREAS [1987]	52.8%	36	76.9%
3	TAXES per $1,000 personal income [1986]	$96	39	$106
4	POVERTY rate [1984–86]	11.2%	12	14.0%
5	Change in EMPLOYMENT [1979–89]	11.0%	36	18.6%
6	Short-term EMPLOYMENT GROWTH [1986–87]	2.9%	17	N.A.
7	UNEMPLOYMENT RATE [November 1989]	3.9%	10	5.2%
8	UNEMPLOYED more than 27 weeks [1987]	9.7%	15	N.A.
9	UNIONIZATION rate [1984]	15%	42	23%
10	Average annual PAY [1987]	$18,424	35	$20,855
11	Change in PERSONAL INCOME [1979–89]	88.5%	37	112.1%
12	Per capita INCOME [1988]	$15,905	22	$16,444
13	JOB GENERATION SCORE [2/84–2/88]	17.23	32	18.38
14	NEW BUSINESSES SCORE [1/84–1/88]	10.85	37	15.17
15	YOUNG-COMPANY GROWTH SCORE [1/84–1/88]	11.21	35	15.34
16	ECONOMIC SUCCESS TOTAL SCORE [1984–88]	39.30	36	54.26
17	Child POVERTY [1983–87 average]	14.5%	7	20.9%
18	MINORITY school enrollment [1987]	14.0%	33	30.0%
19	HANDICAPPED school enrollment [1989]	10.2%	39	11.3%
20	PUPIL-TEACHER RATIO [1989]	15.2	12	17.4
21	EXPENDITURES PER PUPIL [1988]	$4,076	26	$4,243

Kansas *(continued)*

	Vital Statistic	State Value	State Rank	National Average
22	TEACHER SALARY [1989]	$27,401	27	$29,567
23	GRADUATION RATE [1988]	80.2%	9	71.2%
24	SAT SCORES [1990] (rank, out of 21 states + DC)	N.A.		900
25	ACT SCORES [1989] (rank, out of 28 states)	19.1	9	18.6
26	GRADUATES TAKING 1989 SAT(S) or ACT(A) tests	66.2%	A	N.A.
	Education System Measures			
27	PERFORMANCE indicators [1988]	Yes	N.A.	N.A.
28	School INCENTIVES [1988]	Yes	N.A.	N.A.
29	Alternate CERTIFICATION [1989]	Yes	N.A.	N.A.
30	Teacher INCENTIVES [1988]	No	N.A.	N.A.
31	Teacher MENTORS [1988]	Yes	N.A.	N.A.
32	High school COMPETENCY TESTS [1989]	No	N.A.	N.A.
33	PRESCHOOL programs [1989]	Yes	N.A.	N.A.

Kentucky

	Vital Statistic	State Value	State Rank	National Average
1	POPULATION CHANGE [1980–88]	1.6%	41	8.5%
2	Resident POPULATION in METROPOLITAN AREAS [1987]	45.8%	39	76.9%
3	TAXES per $1,000 personal income [1986]	$98	36	$106
4	POVERTY rate [1984–86]	18.5%	44	14.0%
5	Change in EMPLOYMENT [1979–89]	11.8%	35	18.6%
6	Short-term EMPLOYMENT GROWTH [1986–87]	0.2%	41	N.A.

Kentucky (continued)

	Vital Statistic	State Value	State Rank	National Average
7	UNEMPLOYMENT RATE [November 1989]	5.2%	33	5.2%
8	UNEMPLOYED more than 27 weeks [1987]	21.2%	48	N.A.
9	UNIONIZATION rate [1984]	24%	21	23%
10	Average annual PAY [1987]	$18,008	38	$20,855
11	Change in PERSONAL INCOME [1979–89]	89.7%	35	112.1%
12	Per capita INCOME [1988]	$12,795	39	$16,444
13	JOB GENERATION SCORE [2/84–2/88]	21.06	19	18.38
14	NEW BUSINESSES SCORE [1/84–1/88]	14.70	19	15.17
15	YOUNG-COMPANY GROWTH SCORE [1/84–1/88]	14.32	31	15.34
16	ECONOMIC SUCCESS TOTAL SCORE [1984–88]	50.08	25	54.26
17	Child POVERTY [1983–87 average]	23.6%	41	20.9%
18	MINORITY school enrollment [1987]	11.0%	36	30.0%
19	HANDICAPPED school enrollment [1989]	12.0%	18	11.3%
20	PUPIL-TEACHER RATIO [1989]	17.8	34	17.4
21	EXPENDITURES PER PUPIL [1988]	$3,011	46	$4,243
22	TEACHER SALARY [1989]	$24,920	40	$29,567
23	GRADUATION RATE [1988]	69.0%	39	71.2%
24	SAT SCORES [1990] (rank, out of 21 states + DC)	N.A.		900
25	ACT SCORES [1989] (rank, out of 28 states)	17.8	22	18.6
26	GRADUATES TAKING 1989 SAT(S) or ACT(A) tests	58.2%	A	N.A.
	Education System Measures			
27	PERFORMANCE indicators [1988]	Yes	N.A.	N.A.

Kentucky *(continued)*

	Vital Statistic	State Value	State Rank	National Average
28	School INCENTIVES [1988]	Yes	N.A.	N.A.
29	Alternate CERTIFICATION [1989]	Yes	N.A.	N.A.
30	Teacher INCENTIVES [1988]	No	N.A.	N.A.
31	Teacher MENTORS [1988]	Yes	N.A.	N.A.
32	High school COMPETENCY TESTS [1989]	Yes	N.A.	N.A.
33	PRESCHOOL programs [1989]	Yes	N.A.	N.A.

Louisiana

	Vital Statistic	State Value	State Rank	National Average
1	POPULATION CHANGE [1980–88]	5.1%	28	8.5%
2	Resident POPULATION in METROPOLITAN AREAS [1987]	69.0%	22	76.9%
3	TAXES per $1,000 personal income [1986]	$112	12	$106
4	POVERTY rate [1984–86]	20.8%	46	14.0%
5	Change in EMPLOYMENT [1979–89]	−0.1%	48	18.6%
6	Short-term EMPLOYMENT GROWTH [1986–87]	−0.6%	47	N.A.
7	UNEMPLOYMENT RATE [November 1989]	7.2%	50	5.2%
8	UNEMPLOYED more than 27 weeks [1987]	25.0%	49	N.A.
9	UNIONIZATION rate [1984]	16%	37	23%
10	Average annual PAY [1987]	$18,707	31	$20,855
11	Change in PERSONAL INCOME [1979–89]	78.9%	45	112.1%
12	Per capita INCOME [1988]	$12,193	47	$16,444
13	JOB GENERATION SCORE [2/84–2/88]	5.44	48	18.38

Louisiana *(continued)*

	Vital Statistic	State Value	State Rank	National Average
14	NEW BUSINESSES SCORE [1/84–1/88]	12.70	30	15.17
15	YOUNG-COMPANY GROWTH SCORE [1/84–1/88]	8.82	41	15.34
16	ECONOMIC SUCCESS TOTAL SCORE [1984–88]	26.95	44	54.26
17	Child POVERTY [1983–87 average]	30.6%	48	20.9%
18	MINORITY school enrollment [1987]	43.0%	8	30.0%
19	HANDICAPPED school enrollment [1989]	8.8%	48	11.3%
20	PUPIL-TEACHER RATIO [1989]	18.2	37	17.4
21	EXPENDITURES PER PUPIL [1988]	$3,138	43	$4,243
22	TEACHER SALARY [1989]	$22,470	45	$29,567
23	GRADUATION RATE [1988]	61.4%	47	71.2%
24	SAT SCORES [1990] (rank, out of 21 states + DC)	N.A.		900
25	ACT SCORES [1989] (rank, out of 28 states)	17.1	27	18.6
26	GRADUATES TAKING 1989 SAT(S) or ACT(A) tests	62.3%	A	N.A.
	Education System Measures			
27	PERFORMANCE indicators [1988]	Yes	N.A.	N.A.
28	School INCENTIVES [1988]	No	N.A.	N.A.
29	Alternate CERTIFICATION [1989]	No	N.A.	N.A.
30	Teacher INCENTIVES [1988]	Yes	N.A.	N.A.
31	Teacher MENTORS [1988]	Yes	N.A.	N.A.
32	High school COMPETENCY TESTS [1989]	Yes	N.A.	N.A.
33	PRESCHOOL programs [1989]	No	N.A.	N.A.

Maine

	Vital Statistic	State Value	State Rank	National Average
1	POPULATION CHANGE [1980–88]	7.2%	21	8.5%
2	Resident POPULATION in METROPOLITAN AREAS [1987]	36.1%	45	76.9%
3	TAXES per $1,000 personal income [1986]	$110	14	$106
4	POVERTY rate [1984–86]	11.1%	11	14.0%
5	Change in EMPLOYMENT [1979–89]	26.9%	13	18.6%
6	Short-term EMPLOYMENT GROWTH [1986–87]	5.3%	2	N.A.
7	UNEMPLOYMENT RATE [November 1989]	4.3%	19	5.2%
8	UNEMPLOYED more than 27 weeks [1987]	10.8%	21	N.A.
9	UNIONIZATION rate [1984]	24%	21	23%
10	Average annual PAY [1987]	$17,447	42	$20,855
11	Change in PERSONAL INCOME [1979–89]	138.6%	8	112.1%
12	Per capita INCOME [1988]	$14,976	30	$16,444
13	JOB GENERATION SCORE [2/84–2/88]	24.19	9	18.38
14	NEW BUSINESSES SCORE [1/84–1/88]	11.16	35	15.17
15	YOUNG-COMPANY GROWTH SCORE [1/84–1/88]	21.87	10	15.34
16	ECONOMIC SUCCESS TOTAL SCORE [1984–88]	57.22	16	54.26
17	Child POVERTY [1983–87 average]	16.0%	14	20.9%
18	MINORITY school enrollment [1987]	2.0%	49	30.0%
19	HANDICAPPED school enrollment [1989]	13.1%	11	11.3%
20	PUPIL-TEACHER RATIO [1989]	14.6	7	17.4
21	EXPENDITURES PER PUPIL [1988]	$4,258	20	$4,243

Maine *(continued)*

	Vital Statistic	State Value	State Rank	National Average
22	TEACHER SALARY [1989]	$24,933	39	$29,567
23	GRADUATION RATE [1988]	74.4%	25	71.2%
24	SAT SCORES [1990] (rank, out of 21 states + DC)	886	10	900
25	ACT SCORES [1989] (rank, out of 28 states)	N.A.		18.6
26	GRADUATES TAKING 1989 SAT(S) or ACT(A) tests	60.2%	S	N.A.
Education System Measures				
27	PERFORMANCE indicators [1988]	No	N.A.	N.A.
28	School INCENTIVES [1988]	No	N.A.	N.A.
29	Alternate CERTIFICATION [1989]	No	N.A.	N.A.
30	Teacher INCENTIVES [1988]	Yes	N.A.	N.A.
31	Teacher MENTORS [1988]	Yes	N.A.	N.A.
32	High school COMPETENCY TESTS [1989]	Yes	N.A.	N.A.
33	PRESCHOOL programs [1989]	Yes	N.A.	N.A.

Maryland

	Vital Statistic	State Value	State Rank	National Average
1	POPULATION CHANGE [1980–88]	10.1%	18	8.5%
2	Resident POPULATION in METROPOLITAN AREAS [1987]	92.9%	4	76.9%
3	TAXES per $1,000 personal income [1986]	$103	25	$106
4	POVERTY rate [1984–86]	8.5%	3	14.0%
5	Change in EMPLOYMENT [1979–89]	25.6%	15	18.6%
6	Short-term EMPLOYMENT GROWTH [1986–87]	2.3%	24	N.A.

Maryland *(continued)*

	Vital Statistic	State Value	State Rank	National Average
7	UNEMPLOYMENT RATE [November 1989]	3.6%	8	5.2%
8	UNEMPLOYED more than 27 weeks [1987]	9.5%	10	N.A.
9	UNIONIZATION rate [1984]	23%	24	23%
10	Average annual PAY [1987]	$21,324	10	$20,855
11	Change in PERSONAL INCOME [1979–89]	137.4%	10	112.1%
12	Per capita INCOME [1988]	$19,314	6	$16,444
13	JOB GENERATION SCORE [2/84–2/88]	22.02	14	18.38
14	NEW BUSINESSES SCORE [1/84–1/88]	27.33	5	15.17
15	YOUNG-COMPANY GROWTH SCORE [1/84–1/88]	26.40	3	15.34
16	ECONOMIC SUCCESS TOTAL SCORE [1984–88]	75.75	4	54.26
17	Child POVERTY [1983–87 average]	13.0%	4	20.9%
18	MINORITY school enrollment [1987]	40.0%	9	30.0%
19	HANDICAPPED school enrollment [1989]	13.0%	12	11.3%
20	PUPIL-TEACHER RATIO [1989]	16.8	25	17.4
21	EXPENDITURES PER PUPIL [1988]	$5,201	9	$4,243
22	TEACHER SALARY [1989]	$33,700	8	$29,567
23	GRADUATION RATE [1988]	74.1%	27	71.2%
24	SAT SCORES [1990] (rank, out of 21 states + DC)	908	3	900
25	ACT SCORES [1989] (rank, out of 28 states)	N.A.		18.6
26	GRADUATES TAKING 1989 SAT(S) or ACT(A) tests	57.6%	S	N.A.
	Education System Measures			
27	PERFORMANCE indicators [1988]	No	N.A.	N.A.

Maryland *(continued)*

	Vital Statistic	State Value	State Rank	National Average
28	School INCENTIVES [1988]	Yes	N.A.	N.A.
29	Alternate CERTIFICATION [1989]	Yes	N.A.	N.A.
30	Teacher INCENTIVES [1988]	Yes	N.A.	N.A.
31	Teacher MENTORS [1988]	No	N.A.	N.A.
32	High school COMPETENCY TESTS [1989]	No	N.A.	N.A.
33	PRESCHOOL programs [1989]	Yes	N.A.	N.A.

Massachusetts

	Vital Statistic	State Value	State Rank	National Average
1	POPULATION CHANGE [1980–88]	2.3%	37	8.5%
2	Resident POPULATION in METROPOLITAN AREAS [1987]	90.7%	8	76.9%
3	TAXES per $1,000 personal income [1986]	$110	14	$106
4	POVERTY rate [1984–86]	8.8%	4	14.0%
5	Change in EMPLOYMENT [1979–89]	20.8%	20	18.6%
6	Short-term EMPLOYMENT GROWTH [1986–87]	1.5%	32	N.A.
7	UNEMPLOYMENT RATE [November 1989]	4.0%	12	5.2%
8	UNEMPLOYED more than 27 weeks [1987]	9.3%	9	N.A.
9	UNIONIZATION rate [1984]	25%	19	23%
10	Average annual PAY [1987]	$22,486	8	$20,855
11	Change in PERSONAL INCOME [1979–89]	137.8%	7	112.1%
12	Per capita INCOME [1988]	$20,701	4	$16,444
13	JOB GENERATION SCORE [2/84–2/88]	16.92	35	18.38

Massachusetts *(continued)*

	Vital Statistic	State Value	State Rank	National Average
14	NEW BUSINESSES SCORE [1/84–1/88]	14.24	22	15.17
15	YOUNG-COMPANY GROWTH SCORE [1/84–1/88]	23.74	5	15.34
16	ECONOMIC SUCCESS TOTAL SCORE [1984–88]	54.90	17	54.26
17	Child POVERTY [1983–87 average]	14.1%	6	20.9%
18	MINORITY school enrollment [1987]	16.0%	30	30.0%
19	HANDICAPPED school enrollment [1989]	18.2%	1	11.3%
20	PUPIL-TEACHER RATIO [1989]	13.7	5	17.4
21	EXPENDITURES PER PUPIL [1988]	$5,471	6	$4,243
22	TEACHER SALARY [1989]	$31,670	10	$29,567
23	GRADUATION RATE [1988]	74.4%	25	71.2%
24	SAT SCORES [1990] (rank, out of 21 states + DC)	900	7	900
25	ACT SCORES [1989] (rank, out of 28 states)	N.A.		18.6
26	GRADUATES TAKING 1989 SAT(S) or ACT(A) tests	71.5%	S	N.A.
	Education System Measures			
27	PERFORMANCE indicators [1988]	Yes	N.A.	N.A.
28	School INCENTIVES [1988]	Yes	N.A.	N.A.
29	Alternate CERTIFICATION [1989]	Yes	N.A.	N.A.
30	Teacher INCENTIVES [1988]	No	N.A.	N.A.
31	Teacher MENTORS [1988]	No	N.A.	N.A.
32	High school COMPETENCY TESTS [1989]	No	N.A.	N.A.
33	PRESCHOOL programs [1989]	Yes	N.A.	N.A.

Michigan

	Vital Statistic	State Value	State Rank	National Average
1	POPULATION CHANGE [1980–88]	0.4%	47	8.5%
2	Resident POPULATION in METROPOLITAN AREAS [1987]	80.2%	16	76.9%
3	TAXES per $1,000 personal income [1986]	$115	9	$106
4	POVERTY rate [1984–86]	14.4%	30	14.0%
5	Change in EMPLOYMENT [1979–89]	6.3%	41	18.6%
6	Short-term EMPLOYMENT GROWTH [1986–87]	3.6%	11	N.A.
7	UNEMPLOYMENT RATE [November 1989]	6.9%	47	5.2%
8	UNEMPLOYED more than 27 weeks [1987]	16.5%	40	N.A.
9	UNIONIZATION rate [1984]	37%	2	23%
10	Average annual PAY [1987]	$23,081	7	$20,855
11	Change in PERSONAL INCOME [1979–89]	81.1%	43	112.1%
12	Per capita INCOME [1988]	$16,387	20	$16,444
13	JOB GENERATION SCORE [2/84–2/88]	18.50	25	18.38
14	NEW BUSINESSES SCORE [1/84–1/88]	11.78	33	15.17
15	YOUNG-COMPANY GROWTH SCORE [1/84–1/88]	18.32	17	15.34
16	ECONOMIC SUCCESS TOTAL SCORE [1984–88]	48.59	27	54.26
17	Child POVERTY [1983–87 average]	22.7%	37	20.9%
18	MINORITY school enrollment [1987]	24.0%	22	30.0%
19	HANDICAPPED school enrollment [1989]	10.3%	37	11.3%
20	PUPIL-TEACHER RATIO [1989]	19.8	45	17.4
21	EXPENDITURES PER PUPIL [1988]	$4,692	15	$4,243

Michigan *(continued)*

	Vital Statistic	State Value	State Rank	National Average
22	TEACHER SALARY [1989]	$34,419	6	$29,567
23	GRADUATION RATE [1988]	73.6%	30	71.2%
24	SAT SCORES [1990] (rank, out of 21 states + DC)	N.A.		900
25	ACT SCORES [1989] (rank, out of 28 states)	18.6	18	18.6
26	GRADUATES TAKING 1989 SAT(S) or ACT(A) tests	57.0%	A	N.A.
	Education System Measures			
27	PERFORMANCE indicators [1988]	No	N.A.	N.A.
28	School INCENTIVES [1988]	Yes	N.A.	N.A.
29	Alternate CERTIFICATION [1989]	No	N.A.	N.A.
30	Teacher INCENTIVES [1988]	No	N.A.	N.A.
31	Teacher MENTORS [1988]	No	N.A.	N.A.
32	High school COMPETENCY TESTS [1989]	No	N.A.	N.A.
33	PRESCHOOL programs [1989]	Yes	N.A.	N.A.

Minnesota

	Vital Statistic	State Value	State Rank	National Average
1	POPULATION CHANGE [1980–88]	5.6%	26	8.5%
2	Resident POPULATION in METROPOLITAN AREAS [1987]	66.2%	28	76.9%
3	TAXES per $1,000 personal income [1986]	$114	11	$106
4	POVERTY rate [1984–86]	11.5%	15	14.0%
5	Change in EMPLOYMENT [1979–89]	17.0%	26	18.6%
6	Short-term EMPLOYMENT GROWTH [1986–87]	1.2%	38	N.A.

Minnesota *(continued)*

	Vital Statistic	State Value	State Rank	National Average
7	UNEMPLOYMENT RATE [November 1989]	3.5%	6	5.2%
8	UNEMPLOYED more than 27 weeks [1987]	12.5%	28	N.A.
9	UNIONIZATION rate [1984]	26%	16	23%
10	Average annual PAY [1987]	$20,450	15	$20,855
11	Change in PERSONAL INCOME [1979–89]	106.4%	27	112.1%
12	Per capita INCOME [1988]	$16,787	16	$16,444
13	JOB GENERATION SCORE [2/84–2/88]	19.14	22	18.38
14	NEW BUSINESSES SCORE [1/84–1/88]	10.70	39	15.17
15	YOUNG-COMPANY GROWTH SCORE [1/84–1/88]	15.12	25	15.34
16	ECONOMIC SUCCESS TOTAL SCORE [1984–88]	44.97	30	54.26
17	Child POVERTY [1983–87 average]	16.3%	17	20.9%
18	MINORITY school enrollment [1987]	6.0%	45	30.0%
19	HANDICAPPED school enrollment [1989]	11.2%	26	11.3%
20	PUPIL-TEACHER RATIO [1989]	17.0	26	17.4
21	EXPENDITURES PER PUPIL [1988]	$4,386	18	$4,243
22	TEACHER SALARY [1989]	$31,500	12	$29,567
23	GRADUATION RATE [1988]	90.9%	1	71.2%
24	SAT SCORES [1990] (rank, out of 21 states + DC)	N.A.		900
25	ACT SCORES [1989] (rank, out of 28 states)	19.7	4	18.6
26	GRADUATES TAKING 1989 SAT(S) or ACT(A) tests	46.4%	A	N.A.
	Education System Measures			
27	PERFORMANCE indicators [1988]	Yes	N.A.	N.A.

Minnesota *(continued)*

	Vital Statistic	State Value	State Rank	National Average
28	School INCENTIVES [1988]	Yes	N.A.	N.A.
29	Alternate CERTIFICATION [1989]	Yes	N.A.	N.A.
30	Teacher INCENTIVES [1988]	Yes	N.A.	N.A.
31	Teacher MENTORS [1988]	Yes	N.A.	N.A.
32	High school COMPETENCY TESTS [1989]	Yes	N.A.	N.A.
33	PRESCHOOL programs [1989]	No	N.A.	N.A.

Mississippi

	Vital Statistic	State Value	State Rank	National Average
1	POPULATION CHANGE [1980–88]	4.2%	33	8.5%
2	Resident POPULATION in METROPOLITAN AREAS [1987]	30.3%	46	76.9%
3	TAXES per $1,000 personal income [1986]	$100	31	$106
4	POVERTY rate [1984–86]	25.6%	50	14.0%
5	Change in EMPLOYMENT [1979–89]	87.1%	39	18.6%
6	Short-term EMPLOYMENT GROWTH [1986–87]	1.4%	35	N.A.
7	UNEMPLOYMENT RATE [November 1989]	6.9%	47	5.2%
8	UNEMPLOYED more than 27 weeks [1987]	20.7%	46	N.A.
9	UNIONIZATION rate [1984]	16%	37	23%
10	Average annual PAY [1987]	$15,938	50	$20,855
11	Change in PERSONAL INCOME [1979–89]	94.1%	31	112.1%
12	Per capita INCOME [1988]	$10,997	51	$16,444
13	JOB GENERATION SCORE [2/84–2/88]	17.92	27	18.38

Mississippi *(continued)*

	Vital Statistic	State Value	State Rank	National Average
14	NEW BUSINESSES SCORE [1/84–1/88]	14.70	19	15.17
15	YOUNG-COMPANY GROWTH SCORE [1/84–1/88]	8.90	40	15.34
16	ECONOMIC SUCCESS TOTAL SCORE [1984–88]	41.52	34	54.26
17	Child POVERTY [1983–87 average]	34.3%	51	20.9%
18	MINORITY school enrollment [1987]	56.0%	4	30.0%
19	HANDICAPPED school enrollment [1989]	11.8%	20	11.3%
20	PUPIL-TEACHER RATIO [1989]	18.4	39	17.4
21	EXPENDITURES PER PUPIL [1988]	$2,548	50	$4,243
22	TEACHER SALARY [1989]	$22,036	47	$29,567
23	GRADUATION RATE [1988]	66.9%	40	71.2%
24	SAT SCORES [1990] (rank, out of 21 states + DC)	N.A.		900
25	ACT SCORES [1989] (rank, out of 28 states)	15.9	28	18.6
26	GRADUATES TAKING 1989 SAT(S) or ACT(A) tests	63.6%	A	N.A.
	Education System Measures			
27	PERFORMANCE indicators [1988]	Yes	N.A.	N.A.
28	School INCENTIVES [1988]	No	N.A.	N.A.
29	Alternate CERTIFICATION [1989]	Yes	N.A.	N.A.
30	Teacher INCENTIVES [1988]	Yes	N.A.	N.A.
31	Teacher MENTORS [1988]	Yes	N.A.	N.A.
32	High school COMPETENCY TESTS [1989]	No	N.A.	N.A.
33	PRESCHOOL programs [1989]	Yes	N.A.	N.A.

Missouri

	Vital Statistic	State Value	State Rank	National Average
1	POPULATION CHANGE [1980–88]	4.5%	31	8.5%
2	Resident POPULATION in METROPOLITAN AREAS [1987]	66.0%	29	76.9%
3	TAXES per $1,000 personal income [1986]	$83	50	$106
4	POVERTY rate [1984–86]	14.3%	29	14.0%
5	Change in EMPLOYMENT [1979–89]	12.6%	30	18.6%
6	Short-term EMPLOYMENT GROWTH [1986–87]	1.6%	31	N.A.
7	UNEMPLOYMENT RATE [November 1989]	5.3%	35	5.2%
8	UNEMPLOYED more than 27 weeks [1987]	9.5%	10	N.A.
9	UNIONIZATION rate [1984]	28%	12	23%
10	Average annual PAY [1987]	$19,601	22	$20,855
11	Change in PERSONAL INCOME [1979–89]	99.5%	30	112.1%
12	Per capita INCOME [1988]	$15,492	23	$16,444
13	JOB GENERATION SCORE [2/84–2/88]	17.91	28	18.38
14	NEW BUSINESSES SCORE [1/84–1/88]	11.01	36	15.17
15	YOUNG-COMPANY GROWTH SCORE [1/84–1/88]	12.01	33	15.34
16	ECONOMIC SUCCESS TOTAL SCORE [1984–88]	40.93	35	54.26
17	Child POVERTY [1983–87 average]	20.5%	29	20.9%
18	MINORITY school enrollment [1987]	17.0%	28	30.0%
19	HANDICAPPED school enrollment [1989]	12.5%	14	11.3%
20	PUPIL-TEACHER RATIO [1989]	15.9	18	17.4
21	EXPENDITURES PER PUPIL [1988]	$3,786	33	$4,243

Missouri *(continued)*

	Vital Statistic	State Value	State Rank	National Average
22	TEACHER SALARY [1989]	$25,981	32	$29,567
23	GRADUATION RATE [1988]	74.0%	29	71.2%
24	SAT SCORES [1990] (rank, out of 21 states + DC)	N.A.		900
25	ACT SCORES [1989] (rank, out of 28 states)	19.0	12	18.6
26	GRADUATES TAKING 1989 SAT(S) or ACT(A) tests	59.8%	A	N.A.
	Education System Measures			
27	PERFORMANCE indicators [1988]	No	N.A.	N.A.
28	School INCENTIVES [1988]	No	N.A.	N.A.
29	Alternate CERTIFICATION [1989]	Yes	N.A.	N.A.
30	Teacher INCENTIVES [1988]	No	N.A.	N.A.
31	Teacher MENTORS [1988]	No	N.A.	N.A.
32	High school COMPETENCY TESTS [1989]	No	N.A.	N.A.
33	PRESCHOOL programs [1989]	No	N.A.	N.A.

Montana

	Vital Statistic	State Value	State Rank	National Average
1	POPULATION CHANGE [1980–88]	2.2%	38	8.5%
2	Resident POPULATION in METROPOLITAN AREAS [1987]	24.2%	49	76.9%
3	TAXES per $1,000 personal income [1986]	$117	7	$106
4	POVERTY rate [1984–86]	16.3%	39	14.0%
5	Change in EMPLOYMENT [1979–89]	−0.7%	49	18.6%
6	Short-term EMPLOYMENT GROWTH [1986–87]	−0.3%	46	N.A.

Montana *(continued)*

	Vital Statistic	State Value	State Rank	National Average
7	UNEMPLOYMENT RATE [November 1989]	6.0%	42	5.2%
8	UNEMPLOYED more than 27 weeks [1987]	18.8%	44	N.A.
9	UNIONIZATION rate [1984]	29%	10	23%
10	Average annual PAY [1987]	$16,438	48	$20,855
11	Change in PERSONAL INCOME [1979–89]	67.6%	49	112.1%
12	Per capita INCOME [1988]	$12,670	42	$16,444
13	JOB GENERATION SCORE [2/84–2/88]	10.93	46	18.38
14	NEW BUSINESSES SCORE [1/84–1/88]	3.00	48	15.17
15	YOUNG-COMPANY GROWTH SCORE [1/84–1/88]	3.31	47	15.34
16	ECONOMIC SUCCESS TOTAL SCORE [1984–88]	17.24	48	54.26
17	Child POVERTY [1983–87 average]	20.1%	27	20.9%
18	MINORITY school enrollment [1987]	7.0%	43	30.0%
19	HANDICAPPED school enrollment [1989]	10.4%	35	11.3%
20	PUPIL-TEACHER RATIO [1989]	15.8	16	17.4
21	EXPENDITURES PER PUPIL [1988]	$4,246	21	$4,243
22	TEACHER SALARY [1989]	$24,414	41	$29,567
23	GRADUATION RATE [1988]	87.3%	4	71.2%
24	SAT SCORES [1990] (rank, out of 21 states + DC)	N.A.		900
25	ACT SCORES [1989] (rank, out of 28 states)	19.8	3	18.6
26	GRADUATES TAKING 1989 SAT(S) or ACT(A) tests	53.9%	A	N.A.

Education System Measures

27	PERFORMANCE indicators [1988]	No	N.A.	N.A.

Montana *(continued)*

	Vital Statistic	State Value	State Rank	National Average
28	School INCENTIVES [1988]	No	N.A.	N.A.
29	Alternate CERTIFICATION [1989]	No	N.A.	N.A.
30	Teacher INCENTIVES [1988]	No	N.A.	N.A.
31	Teacher MENTORS [1988]	Yes	N.A.	N.A.
32	High school COMPETENCY TESTS [1989]	Yes	N.A.	N.A.
33	PRESCHOOL programs [1989]	No	N.A.	N.A.

Nebraska

	Vital Statistic	State Value	State Rank	National Average
1	POPULATION CHANGE [1980–88]	2.0%	39	8.5%
2	Resident POPULATION in METROPOLITAN AREAS [1987]	47.2%	38	76.9%
3	TAXES per $1,000 personal income [1986]	$99	34	$106
4	POVERTY rate [1984–86]	14.6%	31	14.0%
5	Change in EMPLOYMENT [1979–89]	12.4%	32	18.6%
6	Short-term EMPLOYMENT GROWTH [1986–87]	−0.1%	43	N.A.
7	UNEMPLOYMENT RATE [November 1989]	2.9%	4	5.2%
8	UNEMPLOYED more than 27 weeks [1987]	11.0%	23	N.A.
9	UNIONIZATION rate [1984]	18%	31	23%
10	Average annual PAY [1987]	$16,526	47	$20,855
11	Change in PERSONAL INCOME [1979–89]	80.4%	44	112.1%
12	Per capita INCOME [1988]	$15,184	27	$16,444
13	JOB GENERATION SCORE [2/84–2/88]	17.57	29	18.38

Nebraska *(continued)*

	Vital Statistic	State Value	State Rank	National Average
14	NEW BUSINESSES SCORE [1/84–1/88]	5.77	45	15.17
15	YOUNG-COMPANY GROWTH SCORE [1/84–1/88]	9.70	39	15.34
16	ECONOMIC SUCCESS TOTAL SCORE [1984–88]	33.04	42	54.26
17	Child POVERTY [1983–87 average]	18.7%	25	20.9%
18	MINORITY school enrollment [1987]	9.0%	39	30.0%
19	HANDICAPPED school enrollment [1989]	11.7%	21	11.3%
20	PUPIL-TEACHER RATIO [1989]	15.0	10	17.4
21	EXPENDITURES PER PUPIL [1988]	$3,943	28	$4,243
22	TEACHER SALARY [1989]	$24,203	42	$29,567
23	GRADUATION RATE [1988]	85.4%	6	71.2%
24	SAT SCORES [1990] (rank, out of 21 states + DC)	N.A.		900
25	ACT SCORES [1989] (rank, out of 28 states)	19.6	5	18.6
26	GRADUATES TAKING 1989 SAT(S) or ACT(A) tests	68.5%	A	N.A.
	Education System Measures			
27	PERFORMANCE indicators [1988]	Yes	N.A.	N.A.
28	School INCENTIVES [1988]	No	N.A.	N.A.
29	Alternate CERTIFICATION [1989]	No	N.A.	N.A.
30	Teacher INCENTIVES [1988]	No	N.A.	N.A.
31	Teacher MENTORS [1988]	No	N.A.	N.A.
32	High school COMPETENCY TESTS [1989]	Yes	N.A.	N.A.
33	PRESCHOOL programs [1989]	Yes	N.A.	N.A.

Nevada

	Vital Statistic	State Value	State Rank	National Average
1	POPULATION CHANGE [1980–88]	32.4%	1	8.5%
2	Resident POPULATION in METROPOLITAN AREAS [1987]	82.6%	11	76.9%
3	TAXES per $1,000 personal income [1986]	$101	29	$106
4	POVERTY rate [1984–86]	12.4%	21	14.0%
5	Change in EMPLOYMENT [1979–89]	47.1%	2	18.6%
6	Short-term EMPLOYMENT GROWTH [1986–87]	4.2%	7	N.A.
7	UNEMPLOYMENT RATE [November 1989]	4.8%	27	5.2%
8	UNEMPLOYED more than 27 weeks [1987]	7.6%	6	N.A.
9	UNIONIZATION rate [1984]	24%	21	23%
10	Average annual PAY [1987]	$19,521	23	$20,855
11	Change in PERSONAL INCOME [1979–89]	150.4%	5	112.1%
12	Per capita INCOME [1988]	$17,440	13	$16,444
13	JOB GENERATION SCORE [2/84–2/88]	33.33	1	18.38
14	NEW BUSINESSES SCORE [1/84–1/88]	33.33	1	15.17
15	YOUNG-COMPANY GROWTH SCORE [1/84–1/88]	20.36	15	15.34
16	ECONOMIC SUCCESS TOTAL SCORE [1984–88]	87.02	1	54.26
17	Child POVERTY [1983–87 average]	15.2%	9	20.9%
18	MINORITY school enrollment [1987]	23.0%	23	30.0%
19	HANDICAPPED school enrollment [1989]	9.1%	46	11.3%
20	PUPIL-TEACHER RATIO [1989]	20.3	46	17.4
21	EXPENDITURES PER PUPIL [1988]	$3,623	36	$4,243

Nevada *(continued)*

	Vital Statistic	State Value	State Rank	National Average
22	TEACHER SALARY [1989]	$28,840	22	$29,567
23	GRADUATION RATE [1988]	75.8%	20	71.2%
24	SAT SCORES [1990] (rank, out of 21 states + DC)	N.A.		900
25	ACT SCORES [1989] (rank, out of 28 states)	19.0	12	18.6
26	GRADUATES TAKING 1989 SAT(S) or ACT(A) tests	41.6%	A	N.A.
	Education System Measures			
27	PERFORMANCE indicators [1988]	No	N.A.	N.A.
28	School INCENTIVES [1988]	No	N.A.	N.A.
29	Alternate CERTIFICATION [1989]	Yes	N.A.	N.A.
30	Teacher INCENTIVES [1988]	No	N.A.	N.A.
31	Teacher MENTORS [1988]	No	N.A.	N.A.
32	High school COMPETENCY TESTS [1989]	No	N.A.	N.A.
33	PRESCHOOL programs [1989]	No	N.A.	N.A.

New Hampshire

	Vital Statistic	State Value	State Rank	National Average
1	POPULATION CHANGE [1980–88]	19.2%	5	8.5%
2	Resident POPULATION in METROPOLITAN AREAS [1987]	56.3%	34	76.9%
3	TAXES per $1,000 personal income [1986]	$74	51	$106
4	POVERTY rate [1984–86]	5.6%	1	14.0%
5	Change in EMPLOYMENT [1979–89]	41.4%	4	18.6%
6	Short-term EMPLOYMENT GROWTH [1986–87]	4.9%	4	N.A.

New Hampshire *(continued)*

	Vital Statistic	State Value	State Rank	National Average
7	UNEMPLOYMENT RATE [November 1989]	4.1%	13	5.2%
8	UNEMPLOYED more than 27 weeks [1987]	5.5%	1	N.A.
9	UNIONIZATION rate [1984]	16%	37	23%
10	Average annual PAY [1987]	$19,414	24	$20,855
11	Change in PERSONAL INCOME [1979–89]	182.5%	1	112.1%
12	Per capita INCOME [1988]	$19,016	8	$16,444
13	JOB GENERATION SCORE [2/84–2/88]	24.96	7	18.38
14	NEW BUSINESSES SCORE [1/84–1/88]	22.86	9	15.17
15	YOUNG-COMPANY GROWTH SCORE [1/84–1/88]	33.33	1	15.34
16	ECONOMIC SUCCESS TOTAL SCORE [1984–88]	81.15	2	54.26
17	Child POVERTY [1983–87 average]	6.2%	1	20.9%
18	MINORITY school enrollment [1987]	2.0%	49	30.0%
19	HANDICAPPED school enrollment [1989]	10.4%	35	11.3%
20	PUPIL-TEACHER RATIO [1989]	16.2	22	17.4
21	EXPENDITURES PER PUPIL [1988]	$4,457	17	$4,243
22	TEACHER SALARY [1989]	$26,703	29	$29,567
23	GRADUATION RATE [1988]	74.1%	27	71.2%
24	SAT SCORES [1990] (rank, out of 21 states + DC)	928	1	900
25	ACT SCORES [1989] (rank, out of 28 states)	N.A.		18.6
26	GRADUATES TAKING 1989 SAT(S) or ACT(A) tests	62.6%	S	N.A.
	Education System Measures			
27	PERFORMANCE indicators [1988]	Yes	N.A.	N.A.

New Hampshire *(continued)*

	Vital Statistic	State Value	State Rank	National Average
28	School INCENTIVES [1988]	Yes	N.A.	N.A.
29	Alternate CERTIFICATION [1989]	Yes	N.A.	N.A.
30	Teacher INCENTIVES [1988]	Yes	N.A.	N.A.
31	Teacher MENTORS [1988]	No	N.A.	N.A.
32	High school COMPETENCY TESTS [1989]	No	N.A.	N.A.
33	PRESCHOOL programs [1989]	Yes	N.A.	N.A.

New Jersey

	Vital Statistic	State Value	State Rank	National Average
1	POPULATION CHANGE [1980–88]	4.8%	30	8.5%
2	Resident POPULATION in METROPOLITAN AREAS [1987]	100.0%	1	76.9%
3	TAXES per $1,000 personal income [1986]	$99	34	$106
4	POVERTY rate [1984–86]	9.5%	5	14.0%
5	Change in EMPLOYMENT [1979–89]	21.6%	18	18.6%
6	Short-term EMPLOYMENT GROWTH [1986–87]	2.5%	19	N.A.
7	UNEMPLOYMENT RATE [November 1989]	4.7%	25	5.2%
8	UNEMPLOYED more than 27 weeks [1987]	10.0%	16	N.A.
9	UNIONIZATION rate [1984]	26%	16	23%
10	Average annual PAY [1987]	$23,842	5	$20,855
11	Change in PERSONAL INCOME [1979–89]	138.1%	9	112.1%
12	Per capita INCOME [1988]	$21,882	2	$16,444
13	JOB GENERATION SCORE [2/84–2/88]	17.18	33	18.38

New Jersey *(continued)*

Vital Statistic	State Value	State Rank	National Average
14 NEW BUSINESSES SCORE [1/84–1/88]	18.55	15	15.17
15 YOUNG-COMPANY GROWTH SCORE [1/84–1/88]	21.96	9	15.34
16 ECONOMIC SUCCESS TOTAL SCORE [1984–88]	57.69	15	54.26
17 Child POVERTY [1983–87 average]	15.5%	11	20.9%
18 MINORITY school enrollment [1987]	31.0%	18	30.0%
19 HANDICAPPED school enrollment [1989]	16.2%	2	11.3%
20 PUPIL-TEACHER RATIO [1989]	13.6	3	17.4
21 EXPENDITURES PER PUPIL [1988]	$6,564	3	$4,243
22 TEACHER SALARY [1989]	$32,923	9	$29,567
23 GRADUATION RATE [1988]	77.4%	15	71.2%
24 SAT SCORES [1990] (rank, out of 21 states + DC)	891	9	900
25 ACT SCORES [1989] (rank, out of 28 states)	N.A.		18.6
26 GRADUATES TAKING 1989 SAT(S) or ACT(A) tests	65.8%	S	N.A.
Education System Measures			
27 PERFORMANCE indicators [1988]	Yes	N.A.	N.A.
28 School INCENTIVES [1988]	Yes	N.A.	N.A.
29 Alternate CERTIFICATION [1989]	Yes	N.A.	N.A.
30 Teacher INCENTIVES [1988]	Yes	N.A.	N.A.
31 Teacher MENTORS [1988]	Yes	N.A.	N.A.
32 High school COMPETENCY TESTS [1989]	Yes	N.A.	N.A.
33 PRESCHOOL programs [1989]	No	N.A.	N.A.

New Mexico

	Vital Statistic	State Value	State Rank	National Average
1	POPULATION CHANGE [1980–88]	15.9%	9	8.5%
2	Resident POPULATION in METROPOLITAN AREAS [1987]	48.4%	37	76.9%
3	TAXES per $1,000 personal income [1986]	$109	16	$106
4	POVERTY rate [1984–86]	20.7%	45	14.0%
5	Change in EMPLOYMENT [1979–89]	19.5%	22	18.6%
6	Short-term EMPLOYMENT GROWTH [1986–87]	1.3%	36	N.A.
7	UNEMPLOYMENT RATE [November 1989]	5.8%	39	5.2%
8	UNEMPLOYED more than 27 weeks [1987]	12.0%	26	N.A.
9	UNIONIZATION rate [1984]	19%	28	23%
10	Average annual PAY [1987]	$17,767	40	$20,855
11	Change in PERSONAL INCOME [1979–89]	107.3%	26	112.1%
12	Per capita INCOME [1988]	$12,481	45	$16,444
13	JOB GENERATION SCORE [2/84–2/88]	15.64	39	18.38
14	NEW BUSINESS SCORE [1/84–1/88]	12.55	31	15.17
15	YOUNG-COMPANY GROWTH SCORE [1/84–1/88]	8.64	42	15.34
16	ECONOMIC SUCCESS TOTAL SCORE [1984–88]	36.82	39	54.26
17	Child POVERTY [1983–87 average]	27.5%	45	20.9%
18	MINORITY school enrollment [1987]	57.0%	3	30.0%
19	HANDICAPPED school enrollment [1989]	10.8%	30	11.3%
20	PUPIL-TEACHER RATIO [1989]	18.5	41	17.4
21	EXPENDITURES PER PUPIL [1988]	$3,691	35	$4,243

New Mexico *(continued)*

	Vital Statistic	State Value	State Rank	National Average
22	TEACHER SALARY [1989]	$25,205	36	$29,567
23	GRADUATION RATE [1988]	71.9%	32	71.2%
24	SAT SCORES [1990] (rank, out of 21 states + DC)	N.A.		900
25	ACT SCORES [1989] (rank, out of 28 states)	17.8	22	18.6
26	GRADUATES TAKING 1989 SAT(S) or ACT(A) tests	54.5%	A	N.A.
	Education System Measures			
27	PERFORMANCE indicators [1988]	Yes	N.A.	N.A.
28	School INCENTIVES [1988]	Yes	N.A.	N.A.
29	Alternate CERTIFICATION [1989]	No	N.A.	N.A.
30	Teacher INCENTIVES [1988]	Yes	N.A.	N.A.
31	Teacher MENTORS [1988]	Yes	N.A.	N.A.
32	High school COMPETENCY TESTS [1989]	Yes	N.A.	N.A.
33	PRESCHOOL programs [1989]	Yes	N.A.	N.A.

New York

	Vital Statistic	State Value	State Rank	National Average
1	POPULATION CHANGE [1980–88]	1.9%	40	8.5%
2	Resident POPULATION in METROPOLITAN AREAS [1987]	90.5%	9	76.9%
3	TAXES per $1,000 personal income [1986]	$151	3	$106
4	POVERTY rate [1984–86]	15.2%	34	14.0%
5	Change in EMPLOYMENT [1979–89]	15.1%	28	18.6%
6	Short-term EMPLOYMENT GROWTH [1986–87]	2.5%	19	N.A.

New York (continued)

	Vital Statistic	State Value	State Rank	National Average
7	UNEMPLOYMENT RATE [November 1989]	5.1%	31	5.2%
8	UNEMPLOYED more than 27 weeks [1987]	14.9%	35	N.A.
9	UNIONIZATION rate [1984]	39%	1	23%
10	Average annual PAY [1987]	$24,634	3	$20,855
11	Change in PERSONAL INCOME [1979–89]	114.2%	20	112.1%
12	Per capita INCOME [1988]	$19,299	17	$16,444
13	JOB GENERATION SCORE [2/84–2/88]	15.84	38	18.38
14	NEW BUSINESSES SCORE [1/84–1/88]	14.24	22	15.17
15	YOUNG-COMPANY GROWTH SCORE [1/84–1/88]	18.14	20	15.34
16	ECONOMIC SUCCESS TOTAL SCORE [1984–88]	48.22	28	54.26
17	Child POVERTY [1983–87 average]	23.6%	41	20.9%
18	MINORITY school enrollment [1987]	32.0%	15	30.0%
19	HANDICAPPED school enrollment [1989]	11.4%	22	11.3%
20	PUPIL-TEACHER RATIO [1989]	14.9	9	17.4
21	EXPENDITURES PER PUPIL [1988]	$7,151	2	$4,243
22	TEACHER SALARY [1989]	$36,500	4	$29,567
23	GRADUATION RATE [1988]	62.3%	46	71.2%
24	SAT SCORES [1990] (rank, out of 21 states + DC)	882	15	900
25	ACT SCORES [1989] (rank, out of 28 states)	N.A.		18.6
26	GRADUATES TAKING 1989 SAT(S) or ACT(A) tests	65.6%	S	N.A.
	Education System Measures			
27	PERFORMANCE indicators [1988]	Yes	N.A.	N.A.

New York *(continued)*

	Vital Statistic	State Value	State Rank	National Average
28	School INCENTIVES [1988]	Yes	N.A.	N.A.
29	Alternate CERTIFICATION [1989]	Yes	N.A.	N.A.
30	Teacher INCENTIVES [1988]	Yes	N.A.	N.A.
31	Teacher MENTORS [1988]	Yes	N.A.	N.A.
32	High school COMPETENCY TESTS [1989]	Yes	N.A.	N.A.
33	PRESCHOOL programs [1989]	No	N.A.	N.A.

North Carolina

	Vital Statistic	State Value	State Rank	National Average
1	POPULATION CHANGE [1980–88]	11.0%	16	8.5%
2	Resident POPULATION in METROPOLITAN AREAS [1987]	55.3%	35	76.9%
3	TAXES per $1,000 personal income [1986]	$98	36	$106
4	POVERTY rate [1984–86]	14.0%	28	14.0%
5	Change in EMPLOYMENT [1979–89]	27.0%	12	18.6%
6	Short-term EMPLOYMENT GROWTH [1986–87]	3.9%	8	N.A.
7	UNEMPLOYMENT RATE [November 1989]	2.8%	1	5.2%
8	UNEMPLOYED more than 27 weeks [1987]	9.1%	8	N.A.
9	UNIONIZATION rate [1984]	10%	49	23%
10	Average annual PAY [1987]	$17,861	39	$20,855
11	Change in PERSONAL INCOME [1979–89]	135.6%	12	112.1%
12	Per capita INCOME [1988]	$14,128	35	$16,444
13	JOB GENERATION SCORE [2/84–2/88]	22.57	13	18.38

North Carolina *(continued)*

	Vital Statistic	State Value	State Rank	National Average
14	NEW BUSINESSES SCORE [1/84–1/88]	22.09	12	15.17
15	YOUNG-COMPANY GROWTH SCORE [1/84–1/88]	23.12	6	15.34
16	ECONOMIC SUCCESS TOTAL SCORE [1984–88]	67.78	8	54.26
17	Child POVERTY [1983–87 average]	19.5%	26	20.9%
18	MINORITY school enrollment [1987]	32.0%	15	30.0%
19	HANDICAPPED school enrollment [1989]	10.5%	34	11.3%
20	PUPIL-TEACHER RATIO [1989]	17.5	32	17.4
21	EXPENDITURES PER PUPIL [1988]	$3,368	41	$4,243
22	TEACHER SALARY [1989]	$25,650	34	$29,567
23	GRADUATION RATE [1988]	66.7%	41	71.2%
24	SAT SCORES [1990] (rank, out of 21 states + DC)	834	21	900
25	ACT SCORES [1989] (rank, out of 28 states)	N.A.		18.6
26	GRADUATES TAKING 1989 SAT(S) or ACT(A) tests	57.8%	S	N.A.
	Education System Measures			
27	PERFORMANCE indicators [1988]	Yes	N.A.	N.A.
28	School INCENTIVES [1988]	No	N.A.	N.A.
29	Alternate CERTIFICATION [1989]	Yes	N.A.	N.A.
30	Teacher INCENTIVES [1988]	No	N.A.	N.A.
31	Teacher MENTORS [1988]	No	N.A.	N.A.
32	High school COMPETENCY TESTS [1989]	Yes	N.A.	N.A.
33	PRESCHOOL programs [1989]	No	N.A.	N.A.

North Dakota

	Vital Statistic	State Value	State Rank	National Average
1	POPULATION CHANGE [1980–88]	1.6%	41	8.5%
2	Resident POPULATION in METROPOLITAN AREAS [1987]	38.0%	43	76.9%
3	TAXES per $1,000 personal income [1986]	$104	24	$106
4	POVERTY rate [1984–86]	14.9%	32	14.0%
5	Change in EMPLOYMENT [1979–89]	6.2%	43	18.6%
6	Short-term EMPLOYMENT GROWTH [1986–87]	0.3%	39	N.A.
7	UNEMPLOYMENT RATE [November 1989]	4.1%	13	5.2%
8	UNEMPLOYED more than 27 weeks [1987]	12.1%	27	N.A.
9	UNIONIZATION rate [1984]	17%	36	23%
10	Average annual PAY [1987]	$16,157	49	$20,855
11	Change in PERSONAL INCOME [1979–89]	71.3%	47	112.1%
12	Per capita INCOME [1988]	$12,720	41	$16,444
13	JOB GENERATION SCORE [2/84–2/88]	12.50	43	18.38
14	NEW BUSINESSES SCORE [1/84–1/88]	3.77	47	15.17
15	YOUNG-COMPANY GROWTH SCORE [1/84–1/88]	2.24	49	15.34
16	ECONOMIC SUCCESS TOTAL SCORE [1984–88]	18.52	47	54.26
17	Child POVERTY [1983–87 average]	16.4%	18	20.9%
18	MINORITY school enrollment [1987]	8.0%	42	30.0%
19	HANDICAPPED school enrollment [1989]	10.7%	32	11.3%
20	PUPIL-TEACHER RATIO [1989]	15.4	13	17.4
21	EXPENDITURES PER PUPIL [1988]	$3,519	38	$4,243

North Dakota *(continued)*

	Vital Statistic	State Value	State Rank	National Average
22	TEACHER SALARY [1989]	$22,249	46	$29,567
23	GRADUATION RATE [1988]	88.3%	2	71.2%
24	SAT SCORES [1990] (rank, out of 21 states + DC)	N.A.		900
25	ACT SCORES [1989] (rank, out of 28 states)	18.7	17	18.6
26	GRADUATES TAKING 1989 SAT(S) or ACT(A) tests	66.0%	A	N.A.
	Education System Measures			
27	PERFORMANCE indicators [1988]	Yes	N.A.	N.A.
28	School INCENTIVES [1988]	Yes	N.A.	N.A.
29	Alternate CERTIFICATION [1989]	Yes	N.A.	N.A.
30	Teacher INCENTIVES [1988]	Yes	N.A.	N.A.
31	Teacher MENTORS [1988]	Yes	N.A.	N.A.
32	High school COMPETENCY TESTS [1989]	Yes	N.A.	N.A.
33	PRESCHOOL programs [1989]	Yes	N.A.	N.A.

Ohio

	Vital Statistic	State Value	State Rank	National Average
1	POPULATION CHANGE [1980–88]	0.7%	46	8.5%
2	Resident POPULATION in METROPOLITAN AREAS [1987]	78.9%	17	76.9%
3	TAXES per $1,000 personal income [1986]	$102	27	$106
4	POVERTY rate [1984–86]	12.4%	21	14.0%
5	Change in EMPLOYMENT [1979–89]	6.4%	40	18.6%
6	Short-term EMPLOYMENT GROWTH [1986–87]	1.5%	32	N.A.

Ohio *(continued)*

	Vital Statistic	State Value	State Rank	National Average
7	UNEMPLOYMENT RATE [November 1989]	5.9%	41	5.2%
8	UNEMPLOYED more than 27 weeks [1987]	20.9%	47	N.A.
9	UNIONIZATION rate [1984]	31%	7	23%
10	Average annual PAY [1987]	$20,568	13	$20,855
11	Change in PERSONAL INCOME [1979–89]	84.5%	41	112.1%
12	Per capita INCOME [1988]	$15,485	24	$16,444
13	JOB GENERATION SCORE [2/84–2/88]	18.20	26	18.38
14	NEW BUSINESSES SCORE [1/84–1/88]	13.93	25	15.17
15	YOUNG-COMPANY GROWTH SCORE [1/84–1/88]	17.17	22	15.34
16	ECONOMIC SUCCESS TOTAL SCORE [1984–88]	49.30	26	54.26
17	Child POVERTY [1983–87 average]	20.2%	28	20.9%
18	MINORITY school enrollment [1987]	17.0%	28	30.0%
19	HANDICAPPED school enrollment [1989]	11.3%	25	11.3%
20	PUPIL-TEACHER RATIO [1989]	17.6	33	17.4
21	EXPENDITURES PER PUPIL [1988]	$3,998	27	$4,243
22	TEACHER SALARY [1989]	$29,152	20	$29,567
23	GRADUATION RATE [1988]	79.6%	10	71.2%
24	SAT SCORES [1990] (rank, out of 21 states + DC)	N.A.		900
25	ACT SCORES [1989] (rank, out of 28 states)	19.1	9	18.6
26	GRADUATES TAKING 1989 SAT(S) or ACT(A) tests	52.2%	A	N.A.
	Education System Measures			
27	PERFORMANCE indicators [1988]	Yes	N.A.	N.A.

Ohio *(continued)*

	Vital Statistic	State Value	State Rank	National Average
28	School INCENTIVES [1988]	Yes	N.A.	N.A.
29	Alternate CERTIFICATION [1989]	Yes	N.A.	N.A.
30	Teacher INCENTIVES [1988]	No	N.A.	N.A.
31	Teacher MENTORS [1988]	Yes	N.A.	N.A.
32	High school COMPETENCY TESTS [1989]	Yes	N.A.	N.A.
33	PRESCHOOL programs [1989]	Yes	N.A.	N.A.

Oklahoma

	Vital Statistic	State Value	State Rank	National Average
1	POPULATION CHANGE [1980–88]	7.9%	20	8.5%
2	Resident POPULATION in METROPOLITAN AREAS [1987]	58.8%	33	76.9%
3	TAXES per $1,000 personal income [1986]	$105	22	$106
4	POVERTY rate [1984–86]	15.5%	35	14.0%
5	Change in EMPLOYMENT [1979–89]	4.7%	47	18.6%
6	Short-term EMPLOYMENT GROWTH [1986–87]	−1.7%	48	N.A.
7	UNEMPLOYMENT RATE [November 1989]	4.6%	24	5.2%
8	UNEMPLOYED more than 27 weeks [1987]	16.2%	39	N.A.
9	UNIONIZATION rate [1984]	15%	42	23%
10	Average annual PAY [1987]	$18,615	33	$20,855
11	Change in PERSONAL INCOME [1979–89]	81.8%	42	112.1%
12	Per capita INCOME [1988]	$13,269	38	$16,444
13	JOB GENERATION SCORE [2/84–2/88]	6.83	47	18.38

Oklahoma *(continued)*

	Vital Statistic	State Value	State Rank	National Average
14	NEW BUSINESSES SCORE [1/84–1/88]	9.62	42	15.17
15	YOUNG-COMPANY GROWTH SCORE [1/84–1/88]	5.80	44	15.34
16	ECONOMIC SUCCESS TOTAL SCORE [1984–88]	22.25	46	54.26
17	Child POVERTY [1983–87 average]	21.0%	30	20.9%
18	MINORITY school enrollment [1987]	21.0%	26	30.0%
19	HANDICAPPED school enrollment [1989]	11.1%	28	11.3%
20	PUPIL-TEACHER RATIO [1989]	16.5	24	17.4
21	EXPENDITURES PER PUPIL [1988]	$3,093	44	$4,243
22	TEACHER SALARY [1989]	$22,000	48	$29,567
23	GRADUATION RATE [1988]	71.7%	33	71.2%
24	SAT SCORES [1990] (rank, out of 21 states + DC)	N.A.		900
25	ACT SCORES [1989] (rank, out of 28 states)	17.7	24	18.6
26	GRADUATES TAKING 1989 SAT(S) or ACT(A) tests	57.2%	A	N.A.
	Education System Measures			
27	PERFORMANCE indicators [1988]	Yes	N.A.	N.A.
28	School INCENTIVES [1988]	No	N.A.	N.A.
29	Alternate CERTIFICATION [1989]	No	N.A.	N.A.
30	Teacher INCENTIVES [1988]	No	N.A.	N.A.
31	Teacher MENTORS [1988]	Yes	N.A.	N.A.
32	High school COMPETENCY TESTS [1989]	Yes	N.A.	N.A.
33	PRESCHOOL programs [1989]	Yes	N.A.	N.A.

Oregon

Vital Statistic	State Value	State Rank	National Average
1 POPULATION CHANGE [1980–88]	4.1%	34	8.5%
2 Resident POPULATION in METROPOLITAN AREAS [1987]	67.6%	24	76.9%
3 TAXES per $1,000 personal income [1986]	$108	18	$106
4 POVERTY rate [1984–86]	12.6%	24	14.0%
5 Change in EMPLOYMENT [1979–89]	12.5%	31	18.6%
6 Short-term EMPLOYMENT GROWTH [1986–87]	4.4%	6	N.A.
7 UNEMPLOYMENT RATE [November 1989]	5.2%	33	5.2%
8 UNEMPLOYED more than 27 weeks [1987]	9.6%	12	N.A.
9 UNIONIZATION rate [1984]	26%	16	23%
10 Average annual PAY [1987]	$18,888	27	$20,855
11 Change in PERSONAL INCOME [1979–89]	85.4%	40	112.1%
12 Per capita INCOME [1988]	$14,982	28	$16,444
13 JOB GENERATION SCORE [2/84–2/88]	23.15	11	18.38
14 NEW BUSINESSES SCORE [1/84–1/88]	12.85	29	15.17
15 YOUNG-COMPANY GROWTH SCORE [1/84–1/88]	14.86	26	15.34
16 ECONOMIC SUCCESS TOTAL SCORE [1984–88]	50.86	23	54.26
17 Child POVERTY [1983–87 average]	17.7%	22	20.9%
18 MINORITY school enrollment [1987]	10.0%	38	30.0%
19 HANDICAPPED school enrollment [1989]	10.6%	33	11.3%
20 PUPIL-TEACHER RATIO [1989]	18.4	39	17.4
21 EXPENDITURES PER PUPIL [1988]	$4,789	13	$4,243

Oregon *(continued)*

	Vital Statistic	State Value	State Rank	National Average
22	TEACHER SALARY [1989]	$29,500	18	$29,567
23	GRADUATION RATE [1988]	73.0%	31	71.2%
24	SAT SCORES [1990] (rank, out of 21 states + DC)	923	2	900
25	ACT SCORES [1989] (rank, out of 28 states)	N.A.		18.6
26	GRADUATES TAKING 1989 SAT(S) or ACT(A) tests	46.6%	S	N.A.
Education System Measures				
27	PERFORMANCE indicators [1988]	Yes	N.A.	N.A.
28	School INCENTIVES [1988]	Yes	N.A.	N.A.
29	Alternate CERTIFICATION [1989]	Yes	N.A.	N.A.
30	Teacher INCENTIVES [1988]	Yes	N.A.	N.A.
31	Teacher MENTORS [1988]	Yes	N.A.	N.A.
32	High school COMPETENCY TESTS [1989]	No	N.A.	N.A.
33	PRESCHOOL programs [1989]	Yes	N.A.	N.A.

Pennsylvania

	Vital Statistic	State Value	State Rank	National Average
1	POPULATION CHANGE [1980–88]	1.4%	44	8.5%
2	Resident POPULATION in METROPOLITAN AREAS [1987]	84.7%	10	76.9%
3	TAXES per $1,000 personal income [1986]	$102	27	$106
4	POVERTY rate [1984–86]	12.4%	21	14.0%
5	Change in EMPLOYMENT [1979–89]	6.0%	44	18.6%
6	Short-term EMPLOYMENT GROWTH [1986–87]	1.5%	32	N.A.

Pennsylvania *(continued)*

	Vital Statistic	State Value	State Rank	National Average
7	UNEMPLOYMENT RATE [November 1989]	5.1%	31	5.2%
8	UNEMPLOYED more than 27 weeks [1987]	15.3%	37	N.A.
9	UNIONIZATION rate [1984]	35%	3	23%
10	Average annual PAY [1987]	$20,408	16	$20,855
11	Change in PERSONAL INCOME [1979–89]	92.2%	32	112.1%
12	Per capita INCOME [1988]	$16,168	21	$16,444
13	JOB GENERATION SCORE [2/84–2/88]	17.01	34	18.38
14	NEW BUSINESSES SCORE [1/84–1/88]	12.55	31	15.17
15	YOUNG-COMPANY GROWTH SCORE [1/84–1/88]	20.90	13	15.34
16	ECONOMIC SUCCESS TOTAL SCORE [1984–88]	50.46	24	54.26
17	Child POVERTY [1983–87 average]	18.4%	23	20.9%
18	MINORITY school enrollment [1987]	16.0%	30	30.0%
19	HANDICAPPED school enrollment [1989]	12.9%	13	11.3%
20	PUPIL-TEACHER RATIO [1989]	15.9	18	17.4
21	EXPENDITURES PER PUPIL [1988]	$4,989	12	$4,243
22	TEACHER SALARY [1989]	$30,720	16	$29,567
23	GRADUATION RATE [1988]	78.4%	14	71.2%
24	SAT SCORES [1990] (rank, out of 21 states + DC)	883	13	900
25	ACT SCORES [1989] (rank, out of 28 states)	N.A.		18.6
26	GRADUATES TAKING 1989 SAT(S) or ACT(A) tests	58.2%	S	N.A.
	Education System Measures			
27	PERFORMANCE indicators [1988]	Yes	N.A.	N.A.

Pennsylvania *(continued)*

	Vital Statistic	State Value	State Rank	National Average
28	School INCENTIVES [1988]	No	N.A.	N.A.
29	Alternate CERTIFICATION [1989]	No	N.A.	N.A.
30	Teacher INCENTIVES [1988]	No	N.A.	N.A.
31	Teacher MENTORS [1988]	No	N.A.	N.A.
32	High school COMPETENCY TESTS [1989]	Yes	N.A.	N.A.
33	PRESCHOOL programs [1989]	Yes	N.A.	N.A.

Rhode Island

	Vital Statistic	State Value	State Rank	National Average
1	POPULATION CHANGE [1980–88]	5.1%	28	8.5%
2	Resident POPULATION in METROPOLITAN AREAS [1987]	92.6%	5	76.9%
3	TAXES per $1,000 personal income [1986]	$105	22	$106
4	POVERTY rate [1984–86]	11.2%	12	14.0%
5	Change in EMPLOYMENT [1979–89]	15.0%	29	18.6%
6	Short-term EMPLOYMENT GROWTH [1986–87]	2.4%	22	N.A.
7	UNEMPLOYMENT RATE [November 1989]	4.1%	13	5.2%
8	UNEMPLOYED more than 27 weeks [1987]	6.2%	2	N.A.
9	UNIONIZATION rate [1984]	28%	12	23%
10	Average annual PAY [1987]	$18,858	28	$20,855
11	Change in PERSONAL INCOME [1979–89]	121.4%	17	112.1%
12	Per capita INCOME [1988]	$16,793	15	$16,444
13	JOB GENERATION SCORE [2/84–2/88]	16.42	37	18.38

Rhode Island *(continued)*

	Vital Statistic	State Value	State Rank	National Average
14	NEW BUSINESSES SCORE [1/84–1/88]	10.08	41	15.17
15	YOUNG-COMPANY GROWTH SCORE [1/84–1/88]	18.32	17	15.34
16	ECONOMIC SUCCESS TOTAL SCORE [1984–88]	44.82	32	54.26
17	Child POVERTY [1983–87 average]	16.7%	19	20.9%
18	MINORITY school enrollment [1987]	12.0%	35	30.0%
19	HANDICAPPED school enrollment [1989]	15.1%	3	11.3%
20	PUPIL-TEACHER RATIO [1989]	14.5	6	17.4
21	EXPENDITURES PER PUPIL [1988]	$5,329	7	$4,243
22	TEACHER SALARY [1989]	$34,233	7	$29,567
23	GRADUATION RATE [1988]	69.8%	36	71.2%
24	SAT SCORES [1990] (rank, out of 21 states + DC)	883	13	900
25	ACT SCORES [1989] (rank, out of 28 states)	N.A.		18.6
26	GRADUATES TAKING 1989 SAT(S) or ACT(A) tests	58.3%	S	N.A.
Education System Measures				
27	PERFORMANCE indicators [1988]	Yes	N.A.	N.A.
28	School INCENTIVES [1988]	Yes	N.A.	N.A.
29	Alternate CERTIFICATION [1989]	No	N.A.	N.A.
30	Teacher INCENTIVES [1988]	Yes	N.A.	N.A.
31	Teacher MENTORS [1988]	Yes	N.A.	N.A.
32	High school COMPETENCY TESTS [1989]	No	N.A.	N.A.
33	PRESCHOOL programs [1989]	Yes	N.A.	N.A.

South Carolina

	Vital Statistic	State Value	State Rank	National Average
1	POPULATION CHANGE [1980–88]	11.9%	14	8.5%
2	Resident POPULATION in METROPOLITAN AREAS [1987]	60.4%	32	76.9%
3	TAXES per $1,000 personal income [1986]	$101	29	$106
4	POVERTY rate [1984–86]	17.6%	42	14.0%
5	Change in EMPLOYMENT [1979–89]	26.8%	14	18.6%
6	Short-term EMPLOYMENT GROWTH [1986–87]	3.1%	15	N.A.
7	UNEMPLOYMENT RATE [November 1989]	4.5%	22	5.2%
8	UNEMPLOYED more than 27 weeks [1987]	14.4%	31	N.A.
9	UNIONIZATION rate [1984]	8%	50	23%
10	Average annual PAY [1987]	$17,279	44	$20,855
11	Change in PERSONAL INCOME [1979–89]	127.7%	16	112.1%
12	Per capita INCOME [1988]	$12,764	40	$16,444
13	JOB GENERATION SCORE [2/84–2/88]	23.28	10	18.38
14	NEW BUSINESSES SCORE [1/84–1/88]	25.48	6	15.17
15	YOUNG-COMPANY GROWTH SCORE [1/84–1/88]	15.57	24	15.34
16	ECONOMIC SUCCESS TOTAL SCORE [1984–88]	64.33	13	54.26
17	Child POVERTY [1983–87 average]	23.5%	40	20.9%
18	MINORITY school enrollment [1987]	45.0%	7	30.0%
19	HANDICAPPED school enrollment [1989]	12.4%	15	11.3%
20	PUPIL-TEACHER RATIO [1989]	17.2	30	17.4
21	EXPENDITURES PER PUPIL [1988]	$3,408	40	$4,243

South Carolina *(continued)*

	Vital Statistic	State Value	State Rank	National Average
22	TEACHER SALARY [1989]	$25,060	38	$29,567
23	GRADUATION RATE [1988]	64.6%	45	71.2%
24	SAT SCORES [1990] (rank, out of 21 states + DC)	834	21	900
25	ACT SCORES [1989] (rank, out of 28 states)	N.A.		18.6
26	GRADUATES TAKING 1989 SAT(S) or ACT(A) tests	54.9%	S	N.A.
	Education System Measures			
27	PERFORMANCE indicators [1988]	No	N.A.	N.A.
28	School INCENTIVES [1988]	No	N.A.	N.A.
29	Alternate CERTIFICATION [1989]	Yes	N.A.	N.A.
30	Teacher INCENTIVES [1988]	No	N.A.	N.A.
31	Teacher MENTORS [1988]	No	N.A.	N.A.
32	High school COMPETENCY TESTS [1990]	Yes	N.A.	N.A.
33	PRESCHOOL programs [1989]	Yes	N.A.	N.A.

South Dakota

	Vital Statistic	State Value	State Rank	National Average
1	POPULATION CHANGE [1980–88]	3.5%	35	8.5%
2	Resident POPULATION in METROPOLITAN AREAS [1987]	28.7%	48	76.9%
3	TAXES per $1,000 personal income [1986]	$96	39	$106
4	POVERTY rate [1984–86]	16.2%	37	14.0%
5	Change in EMPLOYMENT [1979–89]	10.4%	37	18.6%
6	Short-term EMPLOYMENT GROWTH [1986–87]	2.1%	28	N.A.

South Dakota *(continued)*

	Vital Statistic	State Value	State Rank	National Average
7	UNEMPLOYMENT RATE [November 1989]	3.9%	10	5.2%
8	UNEMPLOYED more than 27 weeks [1987]	14.6%	32	N.A.
9	UNIONIZATION rate [1984]	15%	42	23%
10	Average annual PAY [1987]	$14,963	51	$20,855
11	Change in PERSONAL INCOME [1979–89]	78.4%	46	112.1%
12	Per capita INCOME [1988]	$12,475	46	$16,444
13	JOB GENERATION SCORE [2/84–2/88]	15.60	40	18.38
14	NEW BUSINESSES SCORE [1/84–1/88]	3.00	48	15.17
15	YOUNG-COMPANY GROWTH SCORE [1/84–1/88]	4.38	46	15.34
16	ECONOMIC SUCCESS TOTAL SCORE [1984–88]	22.98	45	54.26
17	Child POVERTY [1983–87 average]	21.3%	33	20.9%
18	MINORITY school enrollment [1987]	9.0%	39	30.0%
19	HANDICAPPED school enrollment [1989]	11.4%	22	11.3%
20	PUPIL-TEACHER RATIO [1989]	15.4	13	17.4
21	EXPENDITURES PER PUPIL [1988]	$3,249	42	$4,243
22	TEACHER SALARY [1989]	$20,480	51	$29,567
23	GRADUATION RATE [1988]	79.6%	10	71.2%
24	SAT SCORES [1990] (rank, out of 21 states + DC)	N.A.		900
25	ACT SCORES [1989] (rank, out of 28 states)	19.4	7	18.6
26	GRADUATES TAKING 1989 SAT(S) or ACT(A) tests	66.3%	A	N.A.
	Education System Measures			
27	PERFORMANCE indicators [1988]	No	N.A.	N.A.

South Dakota *(continued)*

	Vital Statistic	State Value	State Rank	National Average
28	School INCENTIVES [1988]	No	N.A.	N.A.
29	Alternate CERTIFICATION [1989]	No	N.A.	N.A.
30	Teacher INCENTIVES [1988]	Yes	N.A.	N.A.
31	Teacher MENTORS [1988]	Yes	N.A.	N.A.
32	High school COMPETENCY TESTS [1989]	Yes	N.A.	N.A.
33	PRESCHOOL programs [1989]	Yes	N.A.	N.A.

Tennessee

	Vital Statistic	State Value	State Rank	National Average
1	POPULATION CHANGE [1980–88]	7.1%	22	8.5%
2	Resident POPULATION in METROPOLITAN AREAS [1987]	67.0%	26	76.9%
3	TAXES per $1,000 personal income [1986]	$90	48	$106
4	POVERTY rate [1984–86]	17.8%	43	14.0%
5	Change in EMPLOYMENT [1979–89]	17.1%	25	18.6%
6	Short-term EMPLOYMENT GROWTH [1986–87]	3.4%	12	N.A.
7	UNEMPLOYMENT RATE [November 1989]	4.5%	22	5.2%
8	UNEMPLOYED more than 27 weeks [1987]	10.3%	18	N.A.
9	UNIONIZATION rate [1984]	19%	28	23%
10	Average annual PAY [1987]	$18,501	34	$20,855
11	Change in PERSONAL INCOME [1979–89]	114.7%	19	112.1%
12	Per capita INCOME [1988]	$13,659	37	$16,444
13	JOB GENERATION SCORE [2/84–2/88]	21.37	17	18.38

Tennessee *(continued)*

	Vital Statistic	State Value	State Rank	National Average
14	NEW BUSINESSES SCORE [1/84–1/88]	25.02	7	15.17
15	YOUNG-COMPANY GROWTH SCORE [1/84–1/88]	20.54	14	15.34
16	ECONOMIC SUCCESS TOTAL SCORE [1984–88]	66.93	9	54.26
17	Child POVERTY [1983–87 average]	25.2%	44	20.9%
18	MINORITY school enrollment [1987]	23.0%	23	30.0%
19	HANDICAPPED school enrollment [1989]	12.4%	15	11.3%
20	PUPIL-TEACHER RATIO [1989]	19.3	44	17.4
21	EXPENDITURES PER PUPIL [1988]	$3,068	45	$4,243
22	TEACHER SALARY [1989]	$25,619	35	$29,567
23	GRADUATION RATE [1988]	69.3%	37	71.2%
24	SAT SCORES [1990] (rank, out of 21 states + DC)	N.A.		900
25	ACT SCORES [1989] (rank, out of 28 states)	17.9	19	18.6
26	GRADUATES TAKING 1989 SAT(S) or ACT(A) tests	61.0%	A	N.A.
Education System Measures				
27	PERFORMANCE indicators [1988]	Yes	N.A.	N.A.
28	School INCENTIVES [1988]	Yes	N.A.	N.A.
29	Alternate CERTIFICATION [1989]	Yes	N.A.	N.A.
30	Teacher INCENTIVES [1988]	Yes	N.A.	N.A.
31	Teacher MENTORS [1988]	No	N.A.	N.A.
32	High school COMPETENCY TESTS [1989]	Yes	N.A.	N.A.
33	PRESCHOOL programs [1989]	Yes	N.A.	N.A.

Texas

	Vital Statistic	State Value	State Rank	National Average
1	POPULATION CHANGE [1980–88]	17.9%	7	8.5%
2	Resident POPULATION in METROPOLITAN AREAS [1987]	81.0%	15	76.9%
3	TAXES per $1,000 personal income [1986]	$96	39	$106
4	POVERTY rate [1984–86]	16.2%	37	14.0%
5	Change in EMPLOYMENT [1979–89]	29.5%	21	18.6%
6	Short-term EMPLOYMENT GROWTH [1986–87]	2.2%	26	N.A.
7	UNEMPLOYMENT RATE [November 1989]	6.9%	47	5.2%
8	UNEMPLOYED more than 27 weeks [1987]	13.2%	29	N.A.
9	UNIONIZATION rate [1984]	11%	48	23%
10	Average annual PAY [1987]	$20,463	14	$20,855
11	Change in PERSONAL INCOME [1979–89]	111.6%	23	112.1%
12	Per capita INCOME [1988]	$14,640	34	$16,444
13	JOB GENERATION SCORE [2/84–2/88]	11.23	44	18.38
14	NEW BUSINESSES SCORE [1/84–1/88]	22.25	11	15.17
15	YOUNG-COMPANY GROWTH SCORE [1/84–1/88]	11.39	34	15.34
16	ECONOMIC SUCCESS TOTAL SCORE [1984–88]	44.87	31	54.26
17	Child POVERTY [1983–87 average]	23.3%	39	20.9%
18	MINORITY school enrollment [1987]	49.0%	5	30.0%
19	HANDICAPPED school enrollment [1989]	9.9%	41	11.3%
20	PUPIL-TEACHER RATIO [1989]	N.A.	31	17.4
21	EXPENDITURES PER PUPIL [1988]	$3,608	37	$4,243

Texas *(continued)*

	Vital Statistic	State Value	State Rank	National Average
22	TEACHER SALARY [1989]	$26,513	31	$29,567
23	GRADUATION RATE [1988]	65.3%*	44	71.2%
24	SAT SCORES [1990] (rank, out of 21 states + DC)	874	16	900
25	ACT SCORES [1989] (rank, out of 28 states)	N.A.		18.6
26	GRADUATES TAKING 1989 SAT(S) or ACT(A) tests	45.7%	S	N.A.
	Education System Measures			
27	PERFORMANCE indicators [1988]	Yes	N.A.	N.A.
28	School INCENTIVES [1988]	No	N.A.	N.A.
29	Alternate CERTIFICATION [1989]	No	N.A.	N.A.
30	Teacher INCENTIVES [1988]	Yes	N.A.	N.A.
31	Teacher MENTORS [1988]	Yes	N.A.	N.A.
32	High school COMPETENCY TESTS [1989]	No	N.A.	N.A.
33	PRESCHOOL programs [1989]	Yes	N.A.	N.A.

*The number of Texas' teachers for 1989 was not available. However, 1988 data were used in the calculation of the rankings to maintain comparability among the states.

Utah

	Vital Statistic	State Value	State Rank	National Average
1	POPULATION CHANGE [1980–88]	15.7%	10	8.5%
2	Resident POPULATION in METROPOLITAN AREAS [1987]	77.2%	18	76.9%
3	TAXES per $1,000 personal income [1986]	$117	7	$106
4	POVERTY rate [1984–86]	11.9%	18	14.0%

Utah *(continued)*

	Vital Statistic	State Value	State Rank	National Average
5	Change in EMPLOYMENT [1979–89]	23.9%	17	18.6%
6	Short-term EMPLOYMENT GROWTH [1986–87]	−0.1%	43	N.A.
7	UNEMPLOYMENT RATE [November 1989]	3.5%	6	5.2%
8	UNEMPLOYED more than 27 weeks [1987]	10.2%	17	N.A.
9	UNIONIZATION rate [1984]	18%	31	23%
10	Average annual PAY [1987]	$18,303	37	$20,855
11	Change in PERSONAL INCOME [1979–89]	107.7%	25	112.1%
12	Per capita INCOME [1988]	$12,013	49	$16,444
13	JOB GENERATION SCORE [2/84–2/88]	17.49	30	18.38
14	NEW BUSINESSES SCORE [1/84–1/88]	18.70	14	15.17
15	YOUNG-COMPANY GROWTH SCORE [1/84–1/88]	14.86	26	15.34
16	ECONOMIC SUCCESS TOTAL SCORE [1984–88]	51.05	22	54.26
17	Child POVERTY [1983–87 average]	13.2%	5	20.9%
18	MINORITY school enrollment [1987]	6.0%	45	30.0%
19	HANDICAPPED school enrollment [1989]	10.2%	39	11.3%
20	PUPIL-TEACHER RATIO [1989]	24.5	51	17.4
21	EXPENDITURES PER PUPIL [1988]	$2,454	51	$4,243
22	TEACHER SALARY [1989]	$23,023	43	$29,567
23	GRADUATION RATE [1988]	79.4%	12	71.2%
24	SAT SCORES [1990] (rank, out of 21 states + DC)	N.A.		900
25	ACT SCORES [1989] (rank, out of 28 states)	18.9	15	18.6
26	GRADUATES TAKING 1989 SAT(S) or ACT(A) tests	67.1%	A	N.A.

Utah *(continued)*

	Vital Statistic	State Value	State Rank	National Average
	Education System Measures			
27	PERFORMANCE indicators [1988]	Yes	N.A.	N.A.
28	School INCENTIVES [1988]	No	N.A.	N.A.
29	Alternate CERTIFICATION [1989]	Yes	N.A.	N.A.
30	Teacher INCENTIVES [1988]	No	N.A.	N.A.
31	Teacher MENTORS [1988]	No	N.A.	N.A.
32	High school COMPETENCY TESTS [1989]	Yes	N.A.	N.A.
33	PRESCHOOL programs [1989]	Yes	N.A.	N.A.

Vermont

	Vital Statistic	State Value	State Rank	National Average
1	POPULATION CHANGE [1980–88]	8.7%	19	8.5%
2	Resident POPULATION in METROPOLITAN AREAS [1987]	23.1%	50	76.9%
3	TAXES per $1,000 personal income [1986]	$112	12	$106
4	POVERTY rate [1984–86]	10.2%	7	14.0%
5	Change in EMPLOYMENT [1979–89]	31.3%	8	18.6%
6	Short-term EMPLOYMENT GROWTH [1986–87]	2.5%	19	N.A.
7	UNEMPLOYMENT RATE [November 1989]	3.7%	9	5.2%
8	UNEMPLOYED more than 27 weeks [1987]	6.5%	5	N.A.
9	UNIONIZATION rate [1984]	18%	31	23%
10	Average annual PAY [1987]	$17,703	41	$20,885
11	Change in PERSONAL INCOME [1979–89]	133.8%	13	112.1%

Vermont *(continued)*

	Vital Statistic	State Value	State Rank	National Average
12	Per capita INCOME [1988]	$15,382	26	$16,444
13	JOB GENERATION SCORE [2/84–2/88]	25.53	4	18.38
14	NEW BUSINESSES SCORE [1/84–1/88]	14.24	22	15.17
15	YOUNG-COMPANY GROWTH SCORE [1/84–1/88]	20.18	16	15.34
16	ECONOMIC SUCCESS TOTAL SCORE [1984–88]	59.96	14	54.26
17	Child POVERTY [1983–87 average]	16.1%	15	20.9%
18	MINORITY school enrollment [1987]	2.0%	49	30.0%
19	HANDICAPPED school enrollment [1989]	13.9%	•6	11.3%
20	PUPIL-TEACHER RATIO [1989]	13.6	3	17.4
21	EXPENDITURES PER PUPIL [1988]	$5,207	8	$4,243
22	TEACHER SALARY [1989]	$26,861	28	$29,567
23	GRADUATION RATE [1988]	78.7%	13	71.2%
24	SAT SCORES [1990] (rank, out of 21 states + DC)	897	7	900
25	ACT SCORES [1989] (rank, out of 28 states)	N.A.		18.6
26	GRADUATES TAKING 1989 SAT(S) or ACT(A) tests	62.2%	S	N.A.
	Education System Measures			
27	PERFORMANCE indicators [1988]	No	N.A.	N.A.
28	School INCENTIVES [1988]	Yes	N.A.	N.A.
29	Alternate CERTIFICATION [1989]	Yes	N.A.	N.A.
30	Teacher INCENTIVES [1988]	No	N.A.	N.A.
31	Teacher MENTORS [1988]	Yes	N.A.	N.A.
32	High school COMPETENCY TESTS [1989]	Yes	N.A.	N.A.
33	PRESCHOOL programs [1989]	Yes	N.A.	N.A.

Virginia

	Vital Statistic	State Value	State Rank	National Average
1	POPULATION CHANGE [1980–88]	12.1%	13	8.5%
2	Resident POPULATION in METROPOLITAN AREAS [1987]	71.7%	21	76.9%
3	TAXES per $1,000 personal income [1986]	$91	46	$106
4	POVERTY rate [1984–86]	10.6%	9	14.0%
5	Change in EMPLOYMENT [1979–89]	36.5%	6	18.6%
6	Short-term EMPLOYMENT GROWTH [1986–87]	3.9%	8	N.A.
7	UNEMPLOYMENT RATE [November 1989]	4.1%	13	5.2%
8	UNEMPLOYED more than 27 weeks [1987]	10.3%	18	N.A.
9	UNIONIZATION rate [1984]	15%	42	23%
10	Average annual PAY [1987]	$19,963	18	$20,855
11	Change in PERSONAL INCOME [1979–89]	150.9%	4	112.1%
12	Per capita INCOME [1988]	$17,640	11	$16,444
13	JOB GENERATION SCORE [2/84–2/88]	25.68	3	18.38
14	NEW BUSINESSES SCORE [1/84–1/88]	27.94	4	15.17
15	YOUNG-COMPANY GROWTH SCORE [1/84–1/88]	26.22	4	15.34
16	ECONOMIC SUCCESS TOTAL SCORE [1984–88]	79.84	3	54.26
17	Child POVERTY [1983–87 average]	14.9%	8	20.9%
18	MINORITY school enrollment [1987]	27.0%	20	30.0%
19	HANDICAPPED school enrollment [1989]	10.8%	30	11.3%
20	PUPIL-TEACHER RATIO [1989]	16.1	21	17.4
21	EXPENDITURES PER PUPIL [1988]	$4,149	23	$4,243

Virginia *(continued)*

	Vital Statistic	State Value	State Rank	National Average
22	TEACHER SALARY [1989]	$29,056	21	$29,567
23	GRADUATION RATE [1988]	71.6%	35	71.2%
24	SAT SCORES [1990] (rank, out of 21 states + DC)	895	8	900
25	ACT SCORES [1989] (rank, out of 28 states)	N.A.		18.6
26	GRADUATES TAKING 1989 SAT(S) or ACT(A) tests	60.2%	S	N.A.
	Education System Measures			
27	PERFORMANCE indicators [1988]	Yes	N.A.	N.A.
28	School INCENTIVES [1988]	Yes	N.A.	N.A.
29	Alternate CERTIFICATION [1989]	No	N.A.	N.A.
30	Teacher INCENTIVES [1988]	Yes	N.A.	N.A.
31	Teacher MENTORS [1988]	Yes	N.A.	N.A.
32	High school COMPETENCY TESTS [1989]	No	N.A.	N.A.
33	PRESCHOOL programs [1989]	Yes	N.A.	N.A.

Washington

	Vital Statistic	State Value	State Rank	National Average
1	POPULATION CHANGE [1980–88]	11.8%	15	8.5%
2	Resident POPULATION in METROPOLITAN AREAS [1987]	81.2%	14	76.9%
3	TAXES per $1,000 personal income [1986]	$107	19	$106
4	POVERTY rate [1984–86]	11.7%	16	14.0%
5	Change in EMPLOYMENT [1979–89]	27.3%	11	18.6%
6	Short-term EMPLOYMENT GROWTH [1986–87]	3.1%	15	N.A.

Washington *(continued)*

	Vital Statistic	State Value	State Rank	National Average
7	UNEMPLOYMENT RATE [November 1989]	5.5%	36	5.2%
8	UNEMPLOYED more than 27 weeks [1987]	14.1%	30	N.A.
9	UNIONIZATION rate [1984]	34%	4	23%
10	Average annual PAY [1987]	$20,110	17	$20,855
11	Change in PERSONAL INCOME [1979–89]	108.6%	24	112.1%
12	Per capita INCOME [1988]	$16,569	17	$16,444
13	JOB GENERATION SCORE [2/84–2/88]	25.22	6	18.38
14	NEW BUSINESSES SCORE [1/84–1/88]	13.47	28	15.17
15	YOUNG-COMPANY GROWTH SCORE [1/84–1/88]	14.23	32	15.34
16	ECONOMIC SUCCESS TOTAL SCORE [1984–88]	52.92	19	54.26
17	Child POVERTY [1983–87 average]	16.9%	21	20.9%
18	MINORITY school enrollment [1987]	15.0%	32	30.0%
19	HANDICAPPED school enrollment [1989]	9.7%	42	11.3%
20	PUPIL-TEACHER RATIO [1989]	20.4	47	17.4
21	EXPENDITURES PER PUPIL [1988]	$4,164	22	$4,243
22	TEACHER SALARY [1989]	$29,176	19	$29,567
23	GRADUATION RATE [1988]	77.1%	18	71.2%
24	SAT SCORES [1990] (rank, out of 21 states + DC)	N.A.*		900
25	ACT SCORES [1989] (rank, out of 28 states)	N.A.*		18.6
26	GRADUATES TAKING 1989 SAT(S) or ACT(A) tests	N.A.*		N.A.

Education System Measures

27	PERFORMANCE indicators [1988]	Yes	N.A.	N.A.

Washington *(continued)*

	Vital Statistic	State Value	State Rank	National Average
28	School INCENTIVES [1988]	No	N.A.	N.A.
29	Alternate CERTIFICATION [1989]	Yes	N.A.	N.A.
30	Teacher INCENTIVES [1988]	No	N.A.	N.A.
31	Teacher MENTORS [1988]	No	N.A.	N.A.
32	High school COMPETENCY TESTS [1989]	No	N.A.	N.A.
33	PRESCHOOL programs [1989]	No	N.A.	N.A.

*Washington State administers its own college entrance examination tests.

West Virginia

	Vital Statistic	State Value	State Rank	National Average
1	POPULATION CHANGE [1980–88]	−3.4%	51	8.5%
2	Resident POPULATION in METROPOLITAN AREAS [1987]	36.3%	44	76.9%
3	TAXES per $1,000 personal income [1986]	$115	9	$106
4	POVERTY rate [1984–86]	22.8%	49	14.0%
5	Change in EMPLOYMENT [1979–89]	−6.7%	51	18.6%
6	Short-term EMPLOYMENT GROWTH [1986–87]	1.9%	29	N.A.
7	UNEMPLOYMENT RATE [November 1989]	8.1%	51	5.2%
8	UNEMPLOYED more than 27 weeks [1987]	31.8%	50	N.A.
9	UNIONIZATION rate [1984]	34%	4	23%
10	Average annual PAY [1987]	$18,820	29	$20,855
11	Change in PERSONAL INCOME [1979–89]	67.4%	50	112.1%
12	Per capita INCOME [1988]	$11,658	50	$16,444

West Virginia *(continued)*

	Vital Statistic	State Value	State Rank	National Average
13	JOB GENERATION SCORE [2/84–2/88]	13.26	42	18.38
14	NEW BUSINESSES SCORE [1/84–1/88]	14.39	21	15.17
15	YOUNG-COMPANY GROWTH SCORE [1/84–1/88]	10.41	37	15.34
16	ECONOMIC SUCCESS TOTAL SCORE [1984–88]	38.07	38	54.26
17	Child POVERTY [1983–87 average]	30.4%	47	20.9%
18	MINORITY school enrollment [1987]	4.0%	48	30.0%
19	HANDICAPPED school enrollment [1989]	13.4%	10	11.3%
20	PUPIL-TEACHER RATIO [1989]	15.1	11	17.4
21	EXPENDITURES PER PUPIL [1988]	$3,858	30	$4,243
22	TEACHER SALARY [1989]	$21,904	49	$29,567
23	GRADUATION RATE [1988]	77.3%	16	71.2%
24	SAT SCORES [1990] (rank, out of 21 states + DC)	N.A.		900
25	ACT SCORES [1989] (rank, out of 28 states)	17.4	26	18.6
26	GRADUATES TAKING 1989 SAT(S) or ACT(A) tests	52.1%	A	N.A.
	Education System Measures			
27	PERFORMANCE indicators [1988]	Yes	N.A.	N.A.
28	School INCENTIVES [1988]	No	N.A.	N.A.
29	Alternate CERTIFICATION [1989]	No	N.A.	N.A.
30	Teacher INCENTIVES [1988]	No	N.A.	N.A.
31	Teacher MENTORS [1988]	No	N.A.	N.A.
32	High school COMPETENCY TESTS [1989]	No	N.A.	N.A.
33	PRESCHOOL programs [1989]	Yes	N.A.	N.A.

Wisconsin

	Vital Statistic	State Value	State Rank	National Average
1	POPULATION CHANGE [1980–88]	3.2%	36	8.5%
2	Resident POPULATION in METROPOLITAN AREAS [1987]	66.5%	27	76.9%
3	TAXES per $1,000 personal income [1986]	$124	5	$106
4	POVERTY rate [1984–86]	11.8%	17	14.0%
5	Change in EMPLOYMENT [1979–89]	12.0%	34	18.6%
6	Short-term EMPLOYMENT GROWTH [1986–87]	4.5%	5	N.A.
7	UNEMPLOYMENT RATE [November 1989]	4.1%	13	5.2%
8	UNEMPLOYED more than 27 weeks [1987]	19.3%	45	N.A.
9	UNIONIZATION rate [1984]	29%	10	23%
10	Average annual PAY [1987]	$18,890	26	$20,855
11	Change in PERSONAL INCOME [1979–89]	90.2%	33	112.1%
12	Per capita INCOME [1988]	$15,444	25	$16,444
13	JOB GENERATION SCORE [2/84–2/88]	19.80	20	18.38
14	NEW BUSINESSES SCORE [1/84–1/88]	10.85	37	15.17
15	YOUNG-COMPANY GROWTH SCORE [1/84–1/88]	14.41	30	15.34
16	ECONOMIC SUCCESS TOTAL SCORE [1984–88]	45.06	29	54.26
17	Child POVERTY [1983–87 average]	15.8%	13	20.9%
18	MINORITY school enrollment [1987]	13.0%	34	30.0%
19	HANDICAPPED school enrollment [1989]	10.3%	37	11.3%
20	PUPIL-TEACHER RATIO [1989]	16.0	20	17.4
21	EXPENDITURES PER PUPIL [1988]	$4,747	14	$4,243

Wisconsin *(continued)*

	Vital Statistic	State Value	State Rank	National Average
22	TEACHER SALARY [1989]	$31,046	14	$29,567
23	GRADUATION RATE [1988]	84.9%	7	71.2%
24	SAT SCORES [1990] (rank, out of 21 states + DC)	N.A.		900
25	ACT SCORES [1989] (rank, out of 28 states)	20.1	1	18.6
26	GRADUATES TAKING 1989 SAT(S) or ACT(A) tests	53.5%	A	N.A.
	Education System Measures			
27	PERFORMANCE indicators [1988]	No	N.A.	N.A.
28	School INCENTIVES [1988]	No	N.A.	N.A.
29	Alternate CERTIFICATION [1989]	No	N.A.	N.A.
30	Teacher INCENTIVES [1988]	No	N.A.	N.A.
31	Teacher MENTORS [1988]	No	N.A.	N.A.
32	High school COMPETENCY TESTS [1989]	No	N.A.	N.A.
33	PRESCHOOL programs [1989]	No	N.A.	N.A.

Wyoming

	Vital Statistic	State Value	State Rank	National Average
1	POPULATION CHANGE [1980–88]	0.3%	48	8.5%
2	Resident POPULATION in METROPOLITAN AREAS [1987]	29.0%	47	76.9%
3	TAXES per $1,000 personal income [1986]	$205	2	$106
4	POVERTY rate [1984–86]	12.3%	20	14.0%
5	Change in EMPLOYMENT [1979–89]	−5.5%	50	18.6%
6	Short-term EMPLOYMENT GROWTH [1986–87]	−4.6%	50	N.A.

Wyoming *(continued)*

	Vital Statistic	State Value	State Rank	National Average
7	UNEMPLOYMENT RATE [November 1989]	5.8%	39	5.2%
8	UNEMPLOYED more than 27 weeks [1987]	17.1%	41	N.A.
9	UNIONIZATION rate [1984]	19%	28	23%
10	Average annual PAY [1987]	$18,817	30	$20,855
11	Change in PERSONAL INCOME [1979–89]	46.3%	51	112.1%
12	Per capita INCOME [1988]	$13,718	36	$16,444
13	JOB GENERATION SCORE [2/84–2/88]	1.00	50	18.38
14	NEW BUSINESSES SCORE [1/84–1/88]	1.00	50	15.17
15	YOUNG-COMPANY GROWTH SCORE [1/84–1/88]	1.00	50	15.34
16	ECONOMIC SUCCESS TOTAL SCORE [1984–88]	3.00	50	54.26
17	Child POVERTY [1983–87 average]	15.5%	11	20.9%
18	MINORITY school enrollment [1987]	9.0%	39	30.0%
19	HANDICAPPED school enrollment [1989]	11.2%	26	11.3%
20	PUPIL-TEACHER RATIO [1989]	14.6	7	17.4
21	EXPENDITURES PER PUPIL [1988]	$5,051	10	$4,243
22	TEACHER SALARY [1989]	$27,685	26	$29,567
23	GRADUATION RATE [1988]	88.3%	2	71.2%
24	SAT SCORES [1990] (rank, out of 21 states + DC)	N.A.		900
25	ACT SCORES [1989] (rank, out of 28 states)	19.4	7	18.6
26	GRADUATES TAKING 1989 SAT(S) or ACT(A) tests	59.8%	A	N.A.
Education System Measures				
27	PERFORMANCE indicators [1988]	No	N.A.	N.A.

Wyoming *(continued)*

	Vital Statistic	State Value	State Rank	National Average
28	School INCENTIVES [1988]	No	N.A.	N.A.
29	Alternate CERTIFICATION [1989]	No	N.A.	N.A.
30	Teacher INCENTIVES [1988]	No	N.A.	N.A.
31	Teacher MENTORS [1988]	No	N.A.	N.A.
32	High school COMPETENCY TESTS [1989]	No	N.A.	N.A.
33	PRESCHOOL programs [1989]	No	N.A.	N.A.

Sources of Vital Statistics

1. Department of Commerce, Bureau of the Census, in *Statistical Abstracts of the United States 1989,* p. xv.

2. Department of Commerce, Bureau of the Census, in *Statistical Abstracts of the United States 1989,* p. xvi.

3. Department of Commerce, Bureau of the Census, in *Statistical Abstracts of the United States 1989,* Tables 457, 700.

4. Plotnick, Robert D., and Danziger, Sheldon, "Poverty Rates by State in the Mid-1980's: An Update," *Focus,* Fall 1988.

5. Data Resources Institute, Inc., Department of Labor, Bureau of Labor Statistics, in *NEA Today,* March 1990, p. 8.

6. Department of Labor, Bureau of Labor Statistics, *Local Area Unemployment Statistics,* unpublished data, 1988.

7. Data Resources Institute, Inc., Department of Labor, Bureau of Labor Statistics, in *NEA Today,* March 1990, p. 8.

8. Department of Commerce, *Geographic Profile of Employment and Unemployment* (Washington, D.C.: Government Printing Office, 1988).

9. Department of Commerce, Bureau of Labor Statistics, in "Report on the States," *INC.,* October 1985, p. 92.

10. Department of Commerce, Bureau of the Census, in *Statistical Abstracts of the United States 1989,* Table 664.

11. Data Resources Institute, Inc., Department of Labor, Bureau of Labor Statistics, in *NEA Today,* March 1990, p. 8.

12. Department of Commerce, Bureau of Labor Statistics, in *The Washington Post,* April 21, 1989, p. F1.

13–16. Brown, Paul B., "Report on the States," *INC.,* October 1989, p. 85.

17. Children's Defense Fund, *Children 1990,* "Key Numbers on Children in the States," pp. 37–45, Washington, D.C., 1990.

18–26. Department of Education, Office of Planning, Budget and Evaluation, Planning and Evaluation Service, *State Education Statistics,* May 1990.

27–33. The Corporation for Enterprise Development, *The 1990 Development Report Card for the States,* Washington, D.C., April 1990.

27, 28. U.S. Department of Education, Office of Educational Research and Improvement, *Creating Responsible and Responsive Accountability Systems,* September 1988.

29. Council of Chief State School Officers, *Education in the States: State Education Indicators 1988,* Washington, D.C., 1988.

30. Southern Regional Education Board, "Incentive Programs— 1988," unpublished table, Atlanta, Georgia, 1988.

31. American Association of Colleges for Teacher Education, *Teacher Education Policy in the States,* Washington, D.C., 1988.

32, 33. National Governors Association, *Results in Education, 1988,* Washington, D.C., 1988.

Vital Statistics Footnotes

2. Based on metropolitan areas as defined by the Census Bureau, June 30, 1988.

3. Includes state income, property, and other taxes.

4. Persons in household units with incomes below the poverty line.

6. Employment of workers on nonagricultural payrolls.

13. Relative rating based on the number of new jobs and percent growth in jobs (BLS data), standardized on a 1–to–33.33 scale.

14. Relative rating based on the number of new companies (with at least 10 employees) and the proportion of business new establishments in the state, standardized on a 1–to–33.33 scale.

15. Relative rating based on both absolute and percentage growth in employment, standardized on a 1-to-33.33 scale.

16. Sum of standardized scores for Factors 13–15; highest possible score is 100.00.

19. The percentage of handicapped students includes all handicapped students counted under EHA and Chapter 1 of ESEA, as amended (SOP).

20. The number of Texas' teachers for 1989 was not available. However, 1988 data were used in the calculation of the rankings to maintain comparability among the states.

22. Washington State administers its own college entrance examination tests. Consequently, the percentages of ACT or SAT test takers are too low to classify Washington as either an ACT or SAT State.

23. Graduation rates for public schools only because recent data on private high school graduates were not available by State. The adjusted graduation rate was calculated by dividing the number of public high school graduates by the public ninth grade enrollment four years earlier. Ninth grade enrollments include a prorated portion of the secondary school students who were unclassified by grade. Graduation rates were also corrected for interstate population migration. Information on the number of persons of graduating age receiving GEDs is not currently available. The figure for Florida differs from the official graduation rate developed by the Florida State Department of Education, which applies a different formula.

26. The 1989 estimated percentage of high school graduates taking the ACT or SAT was calculated by dividing the number of 1989 ACT or SAT test takers by the number of 1988 public and 1980 private high school graduates. The number of 1989 high school graduates was not available, nor were later data on private school graduates.

27. States that have a comprehensive system of performance indicators for schools.

28. States in which school performance triggers rewards, sanctions, or other consequences.

29. States that offer alternative routes to teacher certification.

30. States that have fully implemented statewide teacher incentive programs such as career ladders, teacher mentors, and incentive pay.

31. States that sponsor activity that offers evaluation and/or support for employed beginning teachers.

32. States that require a competency test for high school graduation.

33. States with early childhood (pre-kindergarten) education programs, not including those for handicapped or Chapter 1 youngsters.

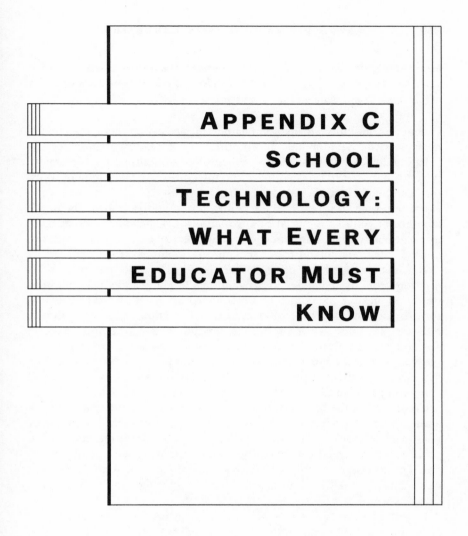

APPENDIX C
SCHOOL
TECHNOLOGY:
WHAT EVERY
EDUCATOR MUST
KNOW

The Chinese pictograph for crisis *combines the symbols for* opportunity *and* **danger**. *By that definition, the coming of computers is one more crisis for America's schools. Of all the innovations that now promise to restore the quality of public education, none offers greater opportunities than computer-based teaching and management methods. The danger is that educators may be unable to take advantage of them unless they receive considerably more training in the use of new technology.*

The accreditation committee of the International Society for Technology in Education recently asked the experts in education and technology both what technology can do for our schools and what educators must know in order to use this new opportu-

nity. In the report below, Dr. Lajeane G. Thomas, of Louisiana Tech University, and Don Knezek, of the Education Service Center in San Antonio's Region 20, tell us about the promise and the problems.

Computers, and the information technologies based on them, may be the most versatile development in education since schools themselves. As teaching devices, they can feed information to students with efficiency far beyond that of textbooks and classroom lectures. As management tools, they can help to monitor students' progress, ensure that those who need extra help receive it before their grades suffer, and ease virtually all the administrative tasks required of any complex organization. And as communications systems, computers can give educators access to the latest in educational research and foster their professional growth.

But making good use of computers requires a wide variety of skills different from those needed in conventional teaching and school administration. Educators today may be called on to work with word processing, spreadsheet, and data-base software; evaluate computer-based programs; plan new facilities; select appropriate computer hardware and software; and apply for grants to pay for it. Only the youngest and luckiest have had the chance to work with computers during their professional training. The rest have a great deal of learning to do before the success of educational computing is assured.

Complicating the picture further is the restructuring movement, which aims to change the way schools are organized and governed. One major goal of restructuring is to give teachers a greater say in the educational process, but this trend is also modifying both curricula and teaching methods. The schools that emerge from this transformation will surely demand new managerial skills of educators, and may require greater technological savvy as well.

In order to clarify the role of technology in restructured schools, the Accreditation Committee of the International Society for Technology in Education recently sought advice from seventy-four professionals in education and instructional technology. The poll offered a summary of the goals of school restructuring in five areas of reform: learning experiences, teachers, curriculum, organizational leadership and structure, and governance and funding. Then it asked how technology might promote those goals, and what skills educational professionals would need in such an environment.

The survey's most encouraging results came as no surprise. Marvin Cetron and Margaret Gayle have already provided a good introduction to the educational uses of information technology. Our poll largely confirmed their optimistic view of these new tools. The educators we contacted found countless opportunities to apply technology in every area of reform. By a large majority, they believe that computers and their off-spring can repair much of the damage wrought by overcrowding, tight budgets, bureaucratic inefficiency, and the other problems that have un-dermined our schools. So far, so good.

But some other findings, if not exactly unexpected, are both new and troubling. A recurring theme among the experts' answers was the impor-tance of technical training for school administrators. In many cases, they cited varieties of training that few have received.

We did our best to make sure that the survey covered as broad a range of skills and personnel as possible. It examined thirty-three distinct areas of technological skill that might be useful in restructuring education. Some were relatively general, such as familiarity with the administrative applica-tions of computers. Others were specific end-user skills, such as desktop publishing, electronic mail, and the use of spreadsheet programs for nu-meric modeling. And some were high-level abilities, such as the evalua-tion and selection of appropriate hardware and software. The study included four job categories—upper-level administrators, principals, con-tent supervisors, and computer coordinators—and rated four levels of skill, from simple awareness of the item to complete mastery. Though some skills may have been overlooked and some job categories omitted, we think the list gives a good overview of the knowledge required in today's changing schools.

The results were startling. In the entire list, only one skill, for one group of administrators, rated at the bottom level. Content supervisors, the experts believed, can get by if they are aware of the use of technology in transportation management, but need not have practical knowledge or experience in the field. Every skill on the list was considered important enough that some administrators should have practical experience in it, and nearly all should be mastered by at least some school personnel. This is a far higher level of technological sophistication than the vast majority of school administrators now bring to their jobs.

Several skills were rated crucial for all: Before entering any program that leads to certification or a degree, candidates should have mastered word processing, the use of computerized data bases, and the use of telecommunications for access to information. To date, few if any pro-grams have such a prerequisite.

No fewer than sixteen skills were rated nearly as important. All adminis-trators, our advisers said, should at least have hands-on experience in these areas:

- Project management
- Program/campus/district evaluation
- Public relations to promote technology

- Seeking grants and funding sources
- Application of research findings
- Use of spreadsheets for numeric modeling
- Time management
- Electronic mail
- Presentation applications
- Networking and communications
- Planning computer implementation
- Facilitation and design of appropriate staff training
- Supporting instruction with technology
- Student assessment
- School record-keeping

At least some administrators should have mastered all of these skills, in varying combinations. In addition, they should be familiar with emerging technologies.

That adds up to nineteen "foundation competencies," skills of such general importance that virtually everyone needs them to some degree. We also identified two smaller groups of skills, one related to instruction, the other to administration, either within the school building or at the district level. Principals and content supervisors should have mastered some of the instructional skills and have had at least some practical experience in the others, while administrators and principals require the administrative skills. Computer coordinators need most of the skills in both categories.

The instruction-related skills include desktop publishing, evaluation and selection of appropriate hardware and software, computer management of instruction, classroom record-keeping, and distance learning (a lesser concern for principals than for content supervisors and computer coordinators.)

The most important administrative skills were familiarity with administrative software, facilities planning and management, financial management planning and reporting, inventory control, and scheduling of students, teachers, and classrooms. Three other skills, less important for computer coordinators than for the others, were personnel management, forecasting enrollments and demographics, and transportation management.

What is both important and disturbing here is not so much the individual skills themselves as that so many of them seem so necessary for so many school administrators. Mastering just one of these skills can take months, as anyone who has worked with a complex word processor or spreadsheet program can testify. Many school administrators still carry out their duties with traditional pencil-and-paper methods, and very few have fully integrated computers into their work. Even today, few training programs give school administrators-to-be the technological skills that, as we have seen, are becoming crucial to their jobs. Bringing administrators "up to speed" in this area is a bottleneck that could slow the restructuring movement and delay school reforms that are badly needed. It is one more problem that educators must solve, and quickly.

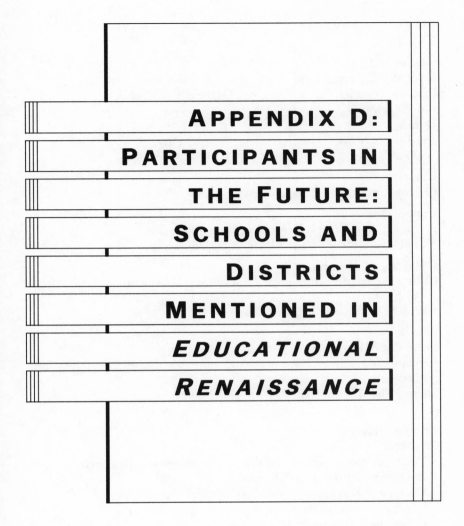

APPENDIX D: PARTICIPANTS IN THE FUTURE: SCHOOLS AND DISTRICTS MENTIONED IN *EDUCATIONAL RENAISSANCE*

Alabama
Lowndes County

Alaska
Mount Edgecumbe High School

Arizona
Dr. David C. Berliner, Arizona State University

Arkansas
HIPPY (Home Instruction Program for Preschool Youngsters)

California
Bakersfield, Kern Union High School District
East Los Angeles, Jaime Escalante, Garfield High School
Los Angeles
Oakland
San Diego, School Superintendent Thomas Payzant
Walnut Creek

Colorado
Cherry Creek, School Superintendent Robert Tschirki

Connecticut
Hartford, Aetna Institute for Corporate Education
New Haven, Dr. Edward Ziglar, Yale University

District of Columbia
Christa McAuliffe Institute for Educational Pioneering
Head Start
Secretary of Education Lauro Cavazos

Florida
Dade County
Lakeland and Winter Haven, Polk County School Superintendent John
   Stewart
Miami, The Academy of Tourism and Travel

Illinois
Arlington Heights
Chicago
   Dr. Mortimer J. Adler, Institute for Philosophical Research
   Beethoven Elementary School
   Center for Successful Child Development
   Chicago Schoolwatch
   Corporate Community School
   Mihaly Csikszentmihalyi, University of Chicago
   Substance teachers' cooperative
   Zenos Colman School

Indiana
Indianapolis, Key School
Mishawaka, Nyloncraft, Inc., preschool program

Iowa
Council Bluffs, Iowa Western Community College
Dr. William L. Lepley, Director of Education

Kansas
Kansas City

Kentucky
Anchorage school district
Elliot County
Lexington
Louisville
　Fairdale High School
　Jefferson County School Superintendent Donald Ingwerson
　Lassiter Middle School

Maine
Dexter Regional High School

Maryland
Baltimore, Walbrook High School
Prince Georges County, School Superintendent John Murphy
Suitland High School

Massachusetts
Boston
　Boston University, Chelsea project
　Lesley College
　Technical Education Research Center
Cambridge
　Harvard University
　Howard Gardner, Harvard University
Chelsea
Fall River
Lawrence, Grieco Brothers, Inc., preschool program
Wellesley Middle School

Michigan
Grand Rapids, Anoka-Hennepin School District
Mount Clemens, School Superintendent Blanche Fraser
Rochester
Ypsilanti, Perry Preschool

Minnesota
Minneapolis, "Chicken Soup," a corporate day-care center

Missouri
Independence County
Platte County

Nebraska
Fremont, School Superintendent James Buchanan

New Hampshire
Hancock Preschool

New Jersey
Jersey City
Montclair
Newark, People United for Better Schools
Princeton, Wendy Kopp, Teach for America

New York
Brighton High School
Mamaroneck High School
New York City
  Academy of Finance
  Academy of Tourism and Travel
  Bronx High School of Science
  Central Park East Secondary School
  Chalkdust teachers' cooperative
  Chancellor Joseph A. Fernandez
  District 4, East Harlem
  Eugene Lang, the I Have A Dream Foundation
  Hudson Elementary School
  Manhattan Center for Science and Mathematics
  New York Prep School
Ossining Middle School
Pleasantville
Rochester

North Carolina
Chapel Hill, National Center for the Paideia Program, at the
    University of North Carolina
East Lincoln
Huntersville, J. M. Alexander Junior High School
Lincolnton, Lincoln County School of Technology
West Lincoln

Ohio
Cincinnati
  Bloom Middle Schools
  Cincinnati Youth Collaborative
  Great Oaks Joint Vocational School
  McKinley Elementary School
  Porter Middle School
  Taft High School
Dayton, School Superintendent Franklin Smith

Oklahoma
Oklahoma City, Francis Tuttle Vo Tech Center
Stillwater, The Midlands Consortium, Oklahoma State University

Oregon
Medford, South Medford High School
Portland, Financial Service Technology Academy

Pennsylvania
Hempfield Area School District, School Superintendent Margaret
    Smith
Philadelphia
    Academy of Applied Electrical Science
    Academy of Automotive and Mechanical Science
    Philadelphia Business Academy
    Philadelphia Health Academy
Pittsburgh
    Business and Finance Academy
    Schenley High School
    Westinghouse High School

Rhode Island
Providence, Hope Essential High School

South Carolina
Orangeburg

Tennessee
Clay County
Former Governor Lamar Alexander

Texas
Houston
    McCullough High School
    Microprocessor-Based Equipment Technology Academy
Laureles
Red Lick
Santa Gertrude School District
West San Antonio, Edgewood Independent School District

Virginia
Arlington, School Superintendent Arthur Gosling
Fairfax County
    Mantua Elementary School
    School Superintendent Robert Spillane
Norfolk Technical Vocational Center
Tidewater Basin area, New Horizons Center

Washington
Seattle
    Citizens Education Center
    Dr. Pamela Grossman, University of Washington

Wisconsin
Milwaukee, Rethinking Schools teachers' cooperative
Pardeeville, School Superintendent Gerald Skaar

INDEX